# Crossings in Realitas

Published by The Lakehouse Publications,
Lake Macquarie City, Australia, 2015.
Second edition, 2019.
Copyright © Jan Mitchell, 2019.
Cover design by Helen Marshall.

All rights reserved. No part of this publication may be reproduced, stored in a retrieval system, or transmitted in any form or by any means, electronic, mechanical, photocopying or recording or otherwise, without the prior written permission of the author and publisher.

ISBN-13: 9781466385887

A catalogue record for this book is available from the National Library of Australia

Printed in Australia

Author's contact: janmitchell2021@gmail.com

Titles by this author available from the publisher: 10 Rosemary Row, Rathmines, NSW 2283.
Also available from amazon.com.au, ingramspark.com and other online sources.

# Crossings in Realitas

Part two of

a cruising memoir

Jan Mitchell

The Lakehouse Publications

# By the same Author

*tinker, tailor, soldier, sailor…the life of Colin Kerby, OAM*
*Two in a Top Hat – Part one of a cruising memoir*
*Hear the Ocean Sing – Part three of a cruising memoir*

# Dedication

To my sons, James and David Mitchell.
I give you our family cruising story from my
viewpoint. Your stories will be your own to tell.

# Frontispiece

*Realitas* on Sydney Harbour

# Table of Contents

Table of Illustrations — i
Acknowledgements — iv
About the author — v
Boats we have owned — x
Glossary — xv

| Chapter | | Page |
|---|---|---|
| 1 | The End of a Voyage | 1 |
| 2 | New Way of Life Begins | 9 |
| 3 | The Reality of a Phantom | 29 |
| 4 | A Summer Holiday Afloat | 39 |
| 5 | Christmas in Tasmania | 51 |
| 6 | Cruising in Local Waters | 73 |
| 7 | Lord Howe Island at Last | 85 |
| 8 | Voyage across the Tasman | 99 |
| 9 | New Zealand and Home Again | 113 |
| 10 | A Second Visit to Lord Howe Island | 117 |
| 11 | Big Changes | 125 |
| 12 | Fun on the South Coast | 145 |
| 13 | Coastal Cruising North | 159 |
| 14 | Cruising to the Lord Howe Rise | 169 |
| 15 | Summer Holiday in Broken Bay | 183 |
| 16 | South in Company with Jamie | 199 |
| 17 | Queensland - Mecca of Winter Cruising | 213 |
| 18 | The Tropics at Last | 237 |
| 19 | Far North Queensland | 251 |
| 20 | Homeward Bound | 267 |

# Table of Illustrations

| | | |
|---|---|---|
| 1 | Frontispiece: *Realitas* on Sydney Harbour | |
| 2 | Jan and Ian Mitchell | v |
| 3 | *Fig.1* Phantom 32 lines, dimensions & layout | ix |
| 4 | *Fig.2.* The Queensland coast | xi |
| 6 | Jamie on deck wearing his life jacket | 3 |
| 7 | Ian using a sextant | 4 |
| 8 | Caprice at CYCA after circumnavigation | 7 |
| 9 | Jamie: front cover of Women's Day | 9 |
| 10 | Jan with David and Jamie in mid-1978 | 11 |
| 11 | The rudder before Ian's modifications | 38 |
| | The rudder after Ian's modifications | 38 |
| 12 | David in the cockpit with his kitten | 48 |
| 13 | Seven year-old David rows the dinghy | 50 |
| 14 | Jamie photographing the *Greenpeace* | 54 |
| 15 | Jan keeps watch | 56 |
| 16 | *Realitas* in the River Tamar | 56 |
| 17 | Ian strips and rinses the generator | 61 |
| 18 | *Fig. 4.* Bass Strait Islands – Deal Island and Furneaux Group | 62 |
| 19 | Fig. 5 Kent Group | 65 |
| 20 | The lighthouse on Deal Island | 67 |
| 21 | Jan gets warm at Jervis Bay | 69 |
| 22 | Jamie with the rosellas at Jervis Bay | 70 |
| 23 | *Realitas* on the Gladesville Marina slipway | 75 |
| 24 | Realitas rafted up with other CCC boats | 77 |
| 25 | Ian tries out spinnaker flying | 79 |
| 26 | Looking south from Mt Eliza towards Mts Lidgbird and Gower | 86 |
| 27 | White tern and chick on a bare branch | 87 |
| 28 | David swinging on the banyan vines | 88 |
| 29 | *Aragunnu* leaves Lord Howe Island | 89 |
| 30. | David descending Mt. Gower | 91 |

| | | |
|---|---|---|
| 31 | *Realitas* at anchor in Esmerelda Cove | 93 |
| 32 | Tall ship outside Sydney Heads, Australia Day 1988 | 97 |
| 33 | Jamie reading in his bunk | 104 |
| 34 | Jamie, tethered to *Realitas*, floats on his back mid-ocean | 106 |
| 35 | *Fig. 5* Cook Strait and the Marlborough Sounds | 110 |
| 36 | *Realitas* at the wharf in Picton | 111 |
| 37 | View from train on Kaikoura coast | 115 |
| 38 | *Realitas* anchored, stern to tree ashore, Marlborough Sound | 118 |
| 39 | Looking back at French Pass | 121 |
| 40 | *Realitas* heads across Golden Bay, Ian and Jamie in cockpit | 123 |
| 41 | Ian and the boys cooling off in the cockpit | 128 |
| 43 | Clive Wilson leads *Realitas* into the lagoon | 129 |
| 44 | New Year's Day diners on *Wine Dark* | 131 |
| 45 | Jan, Jamie and David in wetsuits | 133 |
| 46 | Barry Gow and Janet White (*Scotch Mist*) | 134 |
| 47 | Ian searches for source of water in engine oil | 144 |
| 48 | At sea south of Jervis Bay | 148 |
| 49 | On board *Realitas*: L to R: Mike & Judy Handlinger, Jan Mitchell, | 148 |
| 50 | The Seahorse Inn, Boydtown | 150 |
| 51 | Boyd's Tower, lookout for right whales | 150 |
| 52 | Handlinger and Mitchell families at east coast lookout | 152 |
| 53 | Small dolphin swimming in our bow wave | 153 |
| 54 | Jamie on the sailboard | 154 |
| 55 | *Realitas* aground at Bittangabee | 151 |
| 56 | Nelligen Bridge over the Clyde River | 156 |
| 57 | David 'skiing' on his boogie board | 156 |
| 58 | *Fig.6* Northern Coast of NSW | 163 |
| 59 | *Fig.7* The Lord Howe Rise | 172 |

| | | |
|---|---|---|
| 60 | Tropic bird in a rocky nest on Mt. Lidgbird's Goat House Cave | 174 |
| 62 | Balls Pyramid | 176 |
| 63 | Met Officer launching weather balloon | 177 |
| 64 | *Realitas at* anchor in Middleton Reef lagoon | 179 |
| 65 | *Realitas* under spinnaker | 182 |
| 66 | Jamie on his 18th birthday | 185 |
| 67 | Jamie in the cockpit on *Possibilities* | 199 |
| 68 | David with his first multihull | 200 |
| 69 | Ian and our boys, Christmas 1998 | 204 |
| 70 | *Possibilities* at anchor in Batemans Bay | 207 |
| 71 | *Possibilities* departs Eden | 208 |
| 72 | *Fig.8* The Broadwater | 221 |
| 73 | *Fig.9* Moreton Bay | 223 |
| 74 | *Fig.10* The Great Sandy Straits | 228 |
| 75 | *Fig. 11* Hervey Bay | 229 |
| 76 | Jan with dinghy at Grahams Creek | 234 |
| 77 | Jan snorkelling on the reed | 248 |
| 78 | Reef fish in the pass to the Coral Sea | 265 |
| 79 | Ian, wearing waterproofs, steps into cockpit | 270 |
| 80 | Two bearded sailors: Jamie & Ian, 2000 | 273 |

# Acknowledgements

My husband, Ian, gives me unstinting support for my writing. Without his understanding and technical assistance with my computer, my books wouldn't get written.

I also thank my husband and sons for allowing me to reveal so much personal information about our family, for being wonderfully supportive and making helpful comments about the text.

Most important too, is the comradeship and support I gain from my writers group, the Lake Macquarie branch of the Fellowship for Australian Writers (LMFAW). They inspire me, give me moral courage and critique my writing.

Helen Marshall created the first version of this cover. She has also modified my photos and created maps and charts for me. Thank you, Helen. Thanks also to Ken Robinson for fixing errors in two maps when Helen had computer problems. Frances Robertson refined the cover for this revised edition of the book.

When I attended the Sydney Writers Festival in 2014 I heard a lecture by Gillian Rubinstein (aka Liane Hearn), which gave me inspiration for my title and a better focus so that I could complete this book.

Allan Herring read an early draft, and Dirk Visman read another draft. Their comments helped lead me to the final version of the manuscript. Dirk also most helpfully edited my glossary of sailing terms. My daughter in law, Lisa Herring did a superb job of proof reading for me. Thank you all.

Only now that I have finished the second book about the voyages Ian and I have made, do I see my way towards a third book, making this work part two of a trilogy. The first book was *Two in a Top Hat* and the third is *Hear the Ocean Sing*.

# About the Author

Jan and Ian Mitchell, 2010

Jan Mitchell and her husband, Ian, bought their first yacht in 1972, a steel Temptress design called *Jenny II*. She provided a steep learning experience, but was never going to fulfil Ian's dream of sailing around the world.

*Caprice*, a twenty-five foot (7.6m) fibreglass sloop (Top Hat design) was a more realistic choice for inexperienced sailors with a limited budget. Jan wrote the story of the Mitchell's world circumnavigation in *Caprice*, originally publishing it in installments in several magazines. In 2012, Jan collated these articles into a book, *Two in a Top Hat*.

The Mitchells returned from around the world with Jamie, two years old, and Jan pregnant with David, who was born the following March.

To educate their boys and afford another ocean cruising yacht, they lived and worked in Sydney for many years. Jan took on full time work as a high school English teacher when David was four, her earnings going into 'the boat fund.'

*Realitas*, a thirty-two foot Phantom yacht, became their holiday reality in 1984, ten years after they had originally set out to sail the world. In *Realitas,* the Mitchell family sailed up and down the NSW coast, out to Lord Howe Island, which became a favourite destination, to Tasmania and to New Zealand. These holiday voyages developed in the two boys a love of sailing and the sea.

As soon as they had earned enough money, Jamie and David both bought their own yachts – Jamie a sister ship to *Caprice*, while David has concentrated on multihulls.

This left Jan and Ian free in the new millennium to further their own cruising plans and they made a voyage to Far North Queensland in *Realitas*.

# Boats we have owned

Ian and I have owned a total of six yachts, all mono-hulls. Ian had dreamed of boats and sailing since late childhood. He inspired me and sailing became a shared goal. We married towards the end of 1971 and early the next year, bought our first yacht. Each of our boats has provided a learning experience, but perhaps none more than the first.

| | | |
|---|---|---|
| *Jenny II* | Steel Temptress 33 (33') | 1972 – 1973 |
| *Caprice* | Fibreglass Top Hat (25') | 1973 – 1978 |
| *Taria* | Fibreglass Hood 23 (23') | 1981 – 1983 |
| *Realitas* | Fibreglass Phantom 32(32') | 1984 – 2000 |
| *Libelle* | Steel Alan Payne P400 (40') | 2000 – 2001 |
| *Osprey-A* | Fibreglass Brolga 33 (33') | 2004 – |

*Jenny II* taught us that we couldn't hold down two full time jobs and make a steel yacht ready for a long voyage.

In *Caprice*, we learned to sail, and to trust her seaworthy design. We took her on a shakedown cruise to Lord Howe Island (400 nautical miles north-east of Sydney), when she proved her worth many times over, keeping us safe through equinoctial gales and bringing us home again.

Once Ian had full-time work following our four year world circumnavigation in *Caprice*, and we'd bought a house near Hornsby, *Taria* became a stop-gap vessel until we could afford another sea-going yacht. *Taria*, Maori for 'at last', allowed us to go day sailing or even stay out overnight on a weekend. Despite the fact that several Hood 23s participated in Junior Offshore Group (JOG) racing, we found *Taria* was very lightly built compared with *Caprice*, and we were not particularly happy taking her out to sea except in very favourable conditions.

*Realitas* was the ocean-going yacht we bought in 1983. She became our family floating holiday home for eighteen years. On *Realitas*, our boys learned to love ocean sailing.

When the boys were independent and had their own yachts, Ian and I wished to continue cruising again. We were confident we could cope with a big steel boat for world cruising. Optimistically, we bought *Libelle*, only to discover our age and health were not up to maintaining this beautifully designed yacht.

*Osprey A* turned out to be the closest to our ideal yacht – fibreglass for easy maintenance, well designed by Australian engineer, Joubert, and an excellent sea boat. At thirty-three feet, she is large enough to be comfortable, yet small enough for short-handed sailing. She is the subject of my next book.

# Phantom 32 lines, dimensions and layout

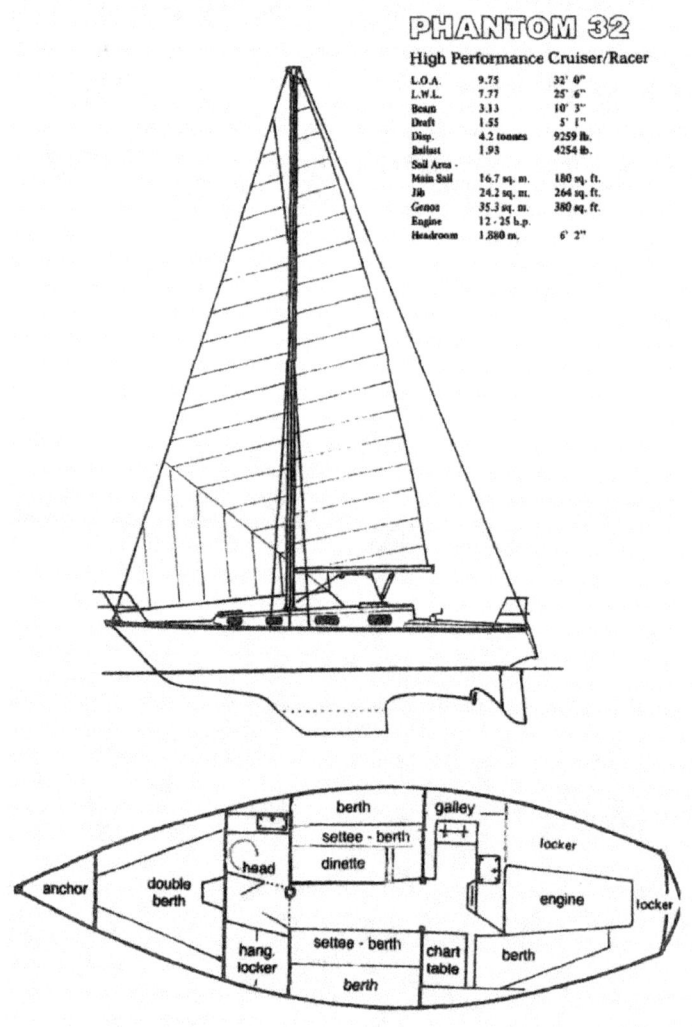

Figure 1.

# The Queensland Coast

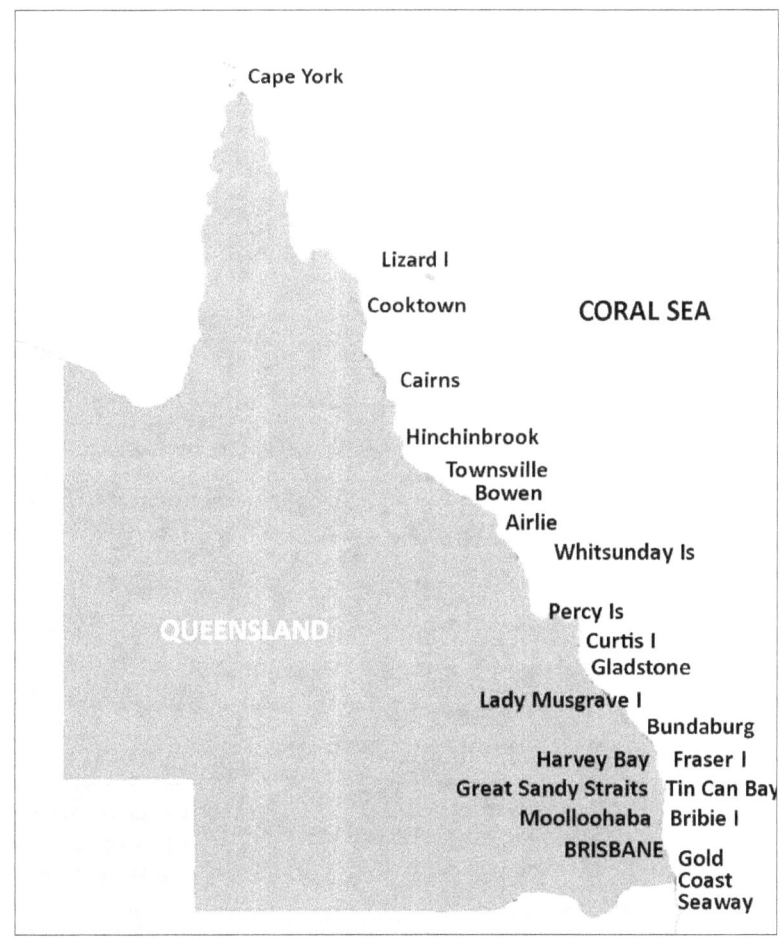

Figure 2.

# The NSW Coast

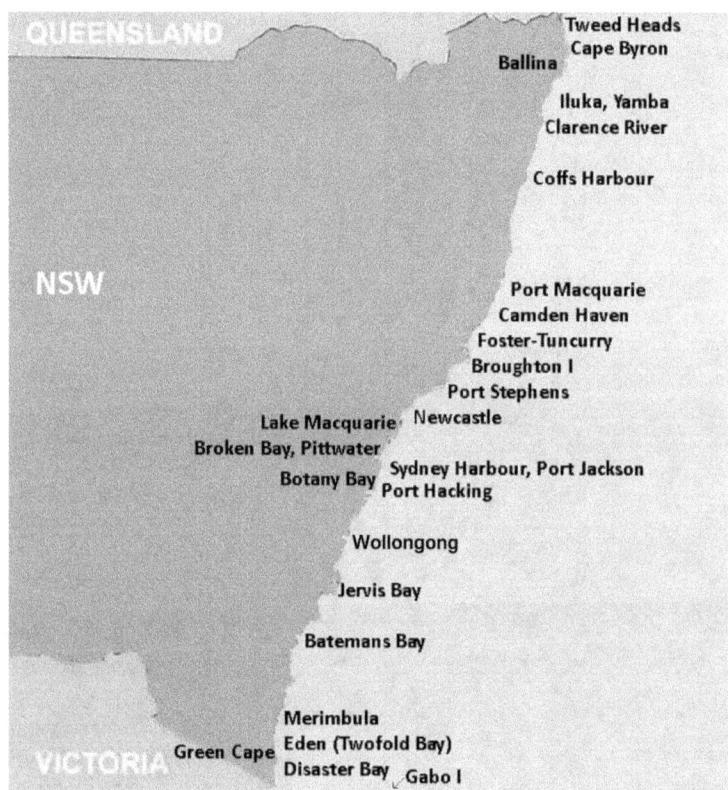

Figure 3.

# Glossary

| | |
|---|---|
| Aft | Towards the back of the boat. |
| Anti-foul | Paint to reduce marine growth on the hull. |
| Astern | Moving backwards. |
| Beam | The width of the boat at its widest. |
| Berth | 1. Bunk or bed. 2. Space alongside a wharf or in a marina. |
| Bilge | The lowest space inside the boat, where any liquids may gather. |
| Block | A single or multiple pulley with one or more sheaves enclosed between cheeks. |
| Bosun's Chair | Small temporary seat which is used to haul a person up the mast, e.g. to make repairs. |
| Bow | Front end of the boat. |
| Centre of gravity | Location where the total weight of the boat is said to act through, and where all motion pivots, so is the area with the least motion. |
| Coaming | The raised edge along the outer side of the deck, which restricts water entering the cockpit and prevents items from rolling overboard. |
| Cockpit | The recessed section at the back of the boat from which it is steered. |
| Companionway | The entrance from the cockpit to the interior. |
| Dan Buoy | Floating marker pole carried on-board and used to throw into the water to mark location of man or object fallen overboard. |
| Forepeak | Inside the boat at the bow, or front portion of the boat. |
| Furler | Device used to vertically roll-up the headsail to reduce (i.e. 'reef') sail area, or roll sail up. |
| Galley | Area for cooking and food preparation. |

| | |
|---|---|
| Genoa | Large headsail used for sailing in light to moderate winds. Larger than a 'Jib' headsail. |
| GPS | The Global Positioning System by which the navigator uses satellites to determine the position of the boat. |
| Gybe | To direct a boat so that a stern wind swings the sails from one side to the other side of the boat. |
| Gunwale | The outer edge of the deck, which is pronounced and occasionally spelt 'gunnel'. |
| Halyard | A rope used for hauling a sail up the mast. |
| Hard on the wind | The bow is pointed as closely into the wind as possible so that the boat sails forward. (NB: a sailboat cannot sail directly into the wind.) |
| Harness | Webbing worn by a crew member which secures him/her by a lanyard to a strong part of the boat, preventing a person falling overboard. |
| Heave to | To slow or stop the boat by backing the headsail. Past tense – hove to. |
| Heel (of a vessel) | To lean to one side. |
| Jib | Triangular-shaped headsail. A working sail for average conditions. |
| Keel | Heavy section of the boat under the hull that that works to keep the boat upright. |
| Knots | A knot is one nautical mile per hour. Boat speed is measured in knots. |
| Lanyard | Rope used to secure (e.g. a person) to a strong point. |
| Lee shore | The shore (land) downwind of the boat. |
| Limber holes | Holes used to drain water from one area to another. |
| Lines | Ropes on a boat have different names according to their purpose. |
| Log | Mechanical or electronic device for measuring boat speed through the water. |

| | |
|---|---|
| Nautical mile (nm) | Distance as measured over the surface of water. One nautical mile equals 1.852 km or 1.151 statute (land) miles. |
| Navigation station | Area where the navigator works their calculations to determine their position, marks their maps and keeps official records of the voyage, and uses the radios to communicate with other boats and shore stations. |
| Navigator | The person who calculates the position of the boat and records its progress. |
| Osmosis | Defect which arises when water penetrates between the fibreglass layers of the boat, causing delamination of the layers and weakening the boat. |
| Outboard | Small self-contained motor used to propel a dinghy or other vessel. |
| Painter | A rope attached to the bow of a dinghy which is used to tie it up. |
| Port | The left hand side of the boat, when facing forward. |
| POB | Abbreviation for 'Persons on board'. |
| Pratique | Process of going through customs and immigration when a boat enters a foreign country. |
| Quarantine | All crew on a boat must remain aboard until cleared by a health officer. A 'Q' flag is flown from the mast to indicate a health clearance is required. |
| Quarter berth | Bunk (bed) located to one side and partly under the cockpit. |
| Radio Channels | Dedicated radio frequencies for specific communication purposes, such as universal calling and emergency channels. |
| Reefing | Reducing the sail area by tying up or furling part of the sail. |

| | |
|---|---|
| Self-steering | An electronic or mechanical system capable of automatically steering the boat in a set direction. |
| Sheave | A grooved wheel which directs or changes the direction of a rope or line. |
| Sheets | Ropes connected to the bottom back corner of a sail (the clew). Using them to tighten or loosen the sail controls the amount of power generated by the sail. |
| Spinnaker | Very large, powerful and often colourful downwind sail flown from the front of the boat. |
| Spinnaker Pole | Pole used to hold the spinnaker in position. |
| Starboard | The right hand side of the boat, when facing forward. |
| Stays & Shrouds | Strong wire or rope rigging used to support a mast (e.g. the 'forestay' runs from the top of the mast to the bow). |
| Stern | Back of the boat. |
| Stringer | Longitudinal timber which reinforces the hull. |
| Sumlog | The brand name for an electronic instrument used to measure distance covered through the water. |
| Tack | To turn the boat across the oncoming wind so that the wind now comes into the sails from the opposite side of the boat. (A sailboat must sail a zig-zag course to make way into the wind.) |
| Turning block | A device containing a grooved sheave or pulley which is used to change the direction of force on a line (rope). |
| VHF and HF radio | Two-way radios for communicating ship to ship or ship to shore. They have multiple communication channels as well as dedicated calling channels for different purposes. VHF signals travel by line of sight and HF has a much greater range of signal. |

| | |
|---|---|
| Wind vane | Literally the vane attached to the self-steering system, which is moved by the wind, and controls the mechanism. The term is commonly used to mean the entire mechanical self-steering system. |
| Wing out | To position one sail either side of the boat, like wings, for running downwind. Past tense - wung out. |

'Like a beautiful and unscrupulous woman, the sea … was glorious in its smiles, irresistible in its anger, capricious, enticing, illogical, irresponsible; a thing to love, a thing to fear. It cast a spell, it gave joy, it lulled boundless faith; then with quick and causeless anger it killed. But its cruelty was redeemed by the charm of its inscrutable mystery, by the immensity of its promise, by the supreme witchery of its possible favour.'

Joseph Conrad, *An Outcast of the Islands* (1896), Part I, Chapter 2.

# 1  The End of a Voyage

Ian undid the buckle holding him against the chart table and brought the folded chart to the companionway. Leaning out to me, he pointed to the most recent neat pencil cross.

'That's our position at noon,' he said. 'We'll be into the southerly current soon, so I'm setting our course towards Port Stephens.'

'Mmmm, I suppose that's best.' I didn't like it. I didn't like the unknown currents; I didn't like being so close to land and in the shipping channels. Since leaving New Zealand's Cape Reinga two weeks earlier, we had seen nothing but wide expanses of open ocean and some swirling sea birds. Now the east coast of Australia was beckoning. We were returning to Sydney and our four year voyage around the world was almost over. On our shakedown cruise in 1973, the currents had toyed with us mercilessly. Now that nightmare was dictating our caution See *Two in a Top Hat*).

Part of me wanted to be safe on land for my babies. I looked at our beautiful blond two year old son, playing beside me on the cockpit floor and felt our growing child flex its muscles in my belly. Another part of me wanted our idyllic existence to continue. Yet, all the way across the Pacific, I had dreamed of gardening, of growing vegetables and getting my hands into my own plot of dirt.

Ian and I swapped places. 'Time we had some lunch,' I said, going below. Our little family was fast outgrowing *Caprice's* small cabin. We had very little money left. It was time to go home, not least for the birth of our second child.

After lunch, Ian stayed on watch while Jamie and I napped. When I awoke, I stepped outside, sweeping the horizon with my eyes.

'No sign of land yet?' I asked.

'Not sure,' said Ian. 'That smudge of grey just over the starboard bow – that could be land or a cloud.'

'Or land behind a cloud,' I said.

Now I was excited. I was ready to finish the voyage and be back on land. I was fed up with the pregnancy nausea that had continued right through the second trimester.

'I'll be glad to be able to stop taking *Debendox*,' I said. *Debendox* was the anti-nausea drug I had been prescribed in Rarotonga, Cook Islands.

I hated taking any medication during pregnancy, but the vomiting had been so bad, I'd had to have something. My weight was falling instead of increasing, but abandoning Ian and the voyage was so unthinkable, we hadn't even considered it.

'Hey, you'd better get some rest,' I said, kissing my husband. 'You're likely to be up most of the night.'

'Keep an eye on the wind direction. It'll probably change a few degrees as the wind eases,' he said.

'I'll call you if I need you.'

When Ian was in his bunk, I took a long, careful scan of the horizon, then went below to sweep the cabin floor before Jamie pattered salty wet footprints over it. This might be our last day at sea – the last day of our circumnavigation. Jamie poked his head against the netting that held him securely in his bunk.

'Hello my angel, did you have a good sleep?'

'Out, Mummy. Want out.'

Opening the netting, I said, 'Let's take off your nappy first,' and I blew a raspberry on his soft, warm tummy.

I dropped his wet nappy into the bucket at the back of the cockpit. Jamie had followed me outside. He crawled into my lap.

I savoured a cuddle with my son who frequently pushed me aside. It was typically brief.

'Water, want play with water,' he demanded, sliding to the cockpit floor. There was a wisp of smoke in the distance – a ship moving south, far enough away not to bother us. Each time *Caprice* rose on a wave, I searched for it, occasionally glimpsing its progress.

When Jamie was asleep for the night, Ian used the radio direction finder to establish our position off the coast. We strained to make out the Morse code radio beacons for Mascot and Williamtown, the airports for Sydney and Newcastle.

When we were sure of each signal, I read off the compass

bearing. Ian went to the chart table to triangulate the angles.

'Good news,' he said. 'The current is not sweeping us off course.'

We changed direction to follow the coast south towards Sydney Heads. After dark, the loom of lights on shore became visible. Ships, too, were easier to spot. The north-easterly wind was easing.

*Jamie on deck wearing his life jacket*

Awakening to the sound of the motor running, I could see Ian's shape in the cockpit, steering us south. It was a very slow passage down the coast with only very light breezes. Ian started the engine occasionally but we had a dirty fuel line and soon we'd be back to sailing. He preferred to clean the line in daylight.

Keeping a check on our position was paramount. Our navigation had to be 'spot on'. In 1977, we had no GPS; the US system was first developed in 1973 and became fully operational for civilian boaties only in 1995. For coastal navigation, we used a sextant, hand-bearing compass and radio direction finder to measure angles from known points.

Distance through the water was recorded by a knot meter. I had to record an accurate time-reading when Ian took the sextant sight and take a note of how far we had travelled.

While Ian did the arithmetic and looked up tables to work the 'sight', I took Jamie out on deck with me, keeping watch for ships.

Perhaps it was as well our approach to Sydney was slow. We were being given time to prepare ourselves mentally for the momentous changes that were about to occur in our lives. Night watches, while Jamie slept, had been a great time for thinking about all sorts of serious things and examining our emotions, but I didn't have that luxury on those final nights at sea. We followed the coast all night and all the next day, dodging ships as we angled in closer to the land.

*Ian uses a sextant to measure the angle of the sun to the horizon*

During the warmth of the day, we bathed. The sea water was no longer warm enough for us to stand on the side-deck and pour buckets of water over ourselves. Instead, I heated a kettle of salt water to warm what was in the bucket and we stripped and washed in the cockpit. By towelling off thoroughly, we removed most of the salt. Unless the weather was unfavourable, we always made sure we were clean and in clean clothes before coming into port and facing officials. Likewise, I cleaned the cabin.

The next night, the light from Barrenjoey lighthouse on the headland at the northern end of Palm Beach beckoned strongly soon after sundown. In the early hours of the morning, I checked off the suburbs as we drifted past: Newport, Collaroy, Dee Why, Harbord, Manly. Out to the east, the sky began to grow lighter, the stars starting to fade. The planets remained visible longer. Soon, only Venus and a pale sickle moon were hanging in the deep blue vault, while away to the east, the orange and pink glow on the horizon grew steadily. Soon deep blue made way for egg shell blue, then violet and pink, before the sun burst over the horizon, its fiery brilliance wiping the red rime from the distant clouds. To the west, the city lights were flicking off and Macquarie lighthouse ceased to send out its comforting signal.

Ian brought the boat on course to enter Sydney Heads. A few aluminium dinghies and small runabouts were dodging about under North Head, their owners fishing.

As we angled across the heads, we could see small surf breaking on the reef marked by Hornby Lighthouse. A large green and yellow ferry turned in towards Manly wharf.

It was Sunday morning and Sydney Harbour was waking up. Land odours tickled our noses – seaweed, dust, smoke, car smells. Just as well it was a holiday, or we'd have received the full assault from traffic and coal-fired power station pollution.

Ian edged *Caprice* into Watsons Bay, close to the Pilot Station and the Customs office. While he dropped the sails and readied the anchor, I manned the tiller in a well-practised routine. The anchor down, we hugged each other. It was 8.30 am on November 20th 1977.

'We've done it!' I said. 'Remember when I told your mother we'd come back safely?'

Ian grunted. He was struggling with the knowledge that it could be a very long time before he was able to sail at sea again.

'Would you find the "Q" flag please?' he said.

The "Q" flag is for "quarantine" and we needed to haul it up the signal halyard to let the officials at the shore station know we required practique – clearance to enter the country. Until then, we were not permitted to go ashore or contact anyone.

We had no radio anyway and mobile telephones had not yet been invented. We weren't sure whether we would be cleared in on a Sunday, or have to wait until Monday.

I handed the "Q" flag out to Ian and put Jamie's harness on so he could go into the cockpit. Ian came back inside and stowed the charts we'd been using, bringing out the one for Sydney Harbour. Then he began to put our passports, ship's papers and other documents the officials would need onto the chart table.

I tidied away our bedding and made the cabin presentable for visitors. Looking at the flags, I had an idea.

'Why don't we dress ship for sailing up the harbour?'

I felt proud of our achievement in sailing around the world in such a small boat and wanted to tell the world.

'That's a good idea. Let's do it,' said Ian.

I started linking the flags together. There were twenty-four different national flags from the countries we had visited and I added in all the signal flags we had too.

We did obtain our entry clearance that day. After the customs, immigration and agriculture officials had completed their paper-work Ian took down the "Q" flag and hauled the string of multi-coloured flags up the halyard, where they fluttered from the spreaders to the safety rail.

'I think we should go to The CYCA at Rushcutters Bay,' said Ian, 'until we sort out where we can moor *Caprice*.'

The harbour was crowded with Sunday racers and all sorts of vessels. We brought *Caprice* in alongside the CYC floating dock and, leaving me with Jamie, Ian went off to the club office to see where we could tie up.

To my great disappointment, no one seemed to take any notice of us. I had expected the flags to say, 'This vessel has just returned from a long ocean voyage.' Maybe *Caprice* looked too small for people to believe what we had done. At the very least, I expected that the club would call a newspaper, which would send a reporter. I felt crushed and deflated.

We rang a couple of friends and they came down to the club to visit us, but even the champagne, cheese and bickies they'd brought seemed something of an anticlimax.

Another friend visited and I offered him a cup of coffee. He looked at me strangely. 'Have you got coffee?' he asked.

What did he think we drank on board? This was our home, after all. During the past four years, we had sailed about thirty five in a thousand nautical miles twenty-five foot yacht, returning with a two year old and with me six months pregnant. I thought we'd done something remarkable and no one seemed to care.

Caprice *at CYCA on our return to Sydney*

Someone had noticed our return though. The next day, Mike Garrett turned up to talk to us. Mike was the salesman for Formit Fibreglass, the builders of Top Hat yachts.

'We want to use your voyage for publicity,' he said. 'I'm here to offer you a deal.'

The deal was he would provide us with a mooring for a year if I wrote articles for *Australian Seaspray* magazine, edited by his mate, Peter Dabbs. Our story would provide his company with good publicity.

We were delighted to accept. We were broke and a free mooring for our boat was something we hadn't dreamt of. There was even a promise of payment for my articles. Those articles, originally published it in 1978, became *Two in a Top Hat,* the first volume of my cruising memoir.

# 2  A New Way of Life Begins

It took years for us to realise how those articles affected people. The exclamation, 'You're the Mitchells!' said with a degree of awe, gave me a strange, shivery feeling, along with the thought in my head, "We are really very ordinary!" It also brought to mind the reverence with which we had held Eric and Susan Hiscock, authors of *Cruising under Sail* and *Voyaging under Sail,* and gurus of cruising sailors since the late 1960s.

I hated being a suburban mum. My parents lived in New Zealand, so I couldn't call on them for help.

*Jamie's picture on the front cover of* Woman's Day *August 14th, 1978*

Our only close friends in Sydney were Judy and Mike, who were at work all day. They babysat for us one night, allowing us to travel into Sydney to see a film, *Star Wars*, which they had recommended. It was culture shock. Not just the film, but the people too. 'How different Sydney-siders are from the Pacific Islanders and yachting fraternity,' I said to Ian. 'Those people smiled, chatted, helped each other.'

Folk in a big city are different. That night, I recollect seeing a fellow with a purple Mohawk. He wore piercings and chains. The memory of the chain from his ear lobe to his nipple still gives me the horrors. I have an image of the chain catching on a door handle as he walks through. Ooooh, the ensuing pain!

The streets were hot and smelled of tar and exhaust fumes, to us, odours so unaccustomed at sea and in the islands or even in Sydney's outer suburbs.

At the time, I was still pregnant with David. Ian and I had never been separated from Jamie. We both felt uneasy about him.

'I feel as though an elastic band attaching me to Jamie has been stretched so tightly it's pinging,' I said to Ian.

'Me too. It's really weird to have both of us away from him.'

In early March, David was born. I was booked to have his birth induced. When it came to the day, I couldn't face a repeat of Jamie's birth when I'd been talked into an induction. I phoned the hospital.

'I'm not coming in this morning. I don't want my labour to be induced.'

'But what will the doctor say?'

'I don't care what the doctor says.' I put down the phone.

David had a different idea. Late that morning, I went into labour. I rang Ian, whose workplace was forty minutes away.

'I think you had better come home soon,' I told him, as I had another contraction.

Fortunately, Ian left straight away. We arrived at the hospital just in time and David was born half an hour later. After his birth in March, at weekends my breaks from writing articles were whenever the baby required breastfeeding.

Jamie had difficulty coping with all these dramatic changes in his life. When Mummy disappeared for a few days and returned with a squalling, red-faced baby he was puzzled, disappointed and frustrated. One day I found Jamie had tipped David out of his crib and was poking at him to get up and play. I had promised him a playmate.

Having babies in their house obviously affected our friends, because despite their best intentions not to have family until Judy had completed her PhD, she fell pregnant.

It was time for us to find our own nest. We tried to find a boat big enough for us to live on, but no one would give us a mortgage for a boat, not without the collateral of a land based property that couldn't be sailed away. The reality was that we needed to buy a house.

'I don't want to pay rent, Ian. That way we'll never get ahead financially, nor be able to buy another boat,' I said.

'I suppose we'll have to sell *Caprice* for a deposit on a house.'

'It looks like it. I know how much you'll miss your boat. I'll miss her too. I'll get a job as soon as the kids are old enough, then we'll be able to save for another boat.'

*Jan with David and Jamie in mid-1978(Photo by Fairfax Press)*

David cried a lot with colic and woke easily, frequently disrupting our sleep. Suburbia and work were crushing Ian. We were going to lose our boat and Ian began to despair of ever going to sea again.

Life in the suburbs seemed pretty grim, and Ian developed deep depression. The psychiatrist Ian consulted said, 'You'll need to take antidepressants for the rest of your life. We will have to try a few drugs before we find the one that's right for you.'

The first two drugs did nothing to relieve Ian's depression, but gave him really acute hearing. The next one made him very dozy. He phoned me from work one morning.

'I got to work a bit late this morning. I came off the motorcycle.'

'Bloody hell! Were you hurt? What about the bike?'

'I'm fine and the bike's still rideable. I was on the Pacific Highway, nearing Pymble, in the left-hand lane. I checked the middle lane before moving over. A car in the middle lane rammed into the back of me. I had completely misjudged time and distance. I hit the road and slid straight down the middle of the lane with the bike sliding behind me.'

'Crikey!'

'I think I was limp like a drunk. I did a perfect landing onto the outside of my left thigh and on my left forearm.'

'Did you lose much skin?'

'No. I had on my waterproofs. They protected me. Surprising though, where they were in contact with the road, the fabric really heated up. I was a bit surprised to see that I wasn't burnt.'

'Phew, that's a relief. What about the bike?'

'Only a broken indicator light, fortunately. The accident was utterly my fault.'

'Why do you think you misjudged the distance?'

'The medication, I think.'

'I don't like you taking that stuff.'

'I know. I don't like it either. I got an attack of the shakes while talking to the cops. Bloody embarrassing.'

'Are they going to charge you?'

'I don't think so.'

When Ian saw the psychiatrist again, the doctor prescribed a fourth drug - one that would send his blood pressure through the roof if he ate certain common foods. Ian wasn't sure whether or not to take these pills. He put them in a drawer. I was terrified he would make a dietary mistake and die. I took the drugs and flushed them down the toilet. Ian has never resorted to psychotherapeutic drugs since that time. After some months of searching, he found a psychiatrist with whom he felt comfortable and began the long process of a talking cure.

Seven months after our return to Sydney, I wrote the following about how we were coping (or not) with shore life. I sent it to *Australian Seaspray*:

> For all of us, Ian, me and our 2 1/2 year old son, Jamie, these months have been a very confused period of our lives. That confusion has been compounded by David's birth in March. To start with, Ian needed to visit the boat regularly. He also begged anyone who showed interest to accompany him day-sailing at weekends.
>
> I went once, but I hated it so much, I refused to go again. Day-sailing to me means a lot of hassle for small rewards. As well as the effort of getting to the boat and taking her off her mooring, there is the problem of wind eddies due to the proximity of land. We never seemed to have up the right amount of sail. Ocean sailing has to be of at least a week's duration to make it worthwhile for the difficult aspects such as seasickness and the worry of entering port again. I haven't day-sailed again yet, but Ian has taken Caprice out twice as often as he did in the seven months we owned her prior to our departure from Sydney.
>
> About a week ago, in a now rare half hour of quiet conversation with Ian, I had an overwhelming desire to be at sea again with him. The reason: I have become lonely for his company.
>
> So many times, we have been asked how our relationship survived when we were confined together in a small space for such long periods of time. In my turn, I am asking how other people's relationships survive when they see so little of their mates.
>
> Now that we are a family with two small children, I find our time alone together limited to an hour or so in the evenings when the children are both in bed. After that, if it's not David needing a feed, it's Jamie ousting Ian from our bed. Many days I've had to phone Ian at work to say, "Good morning"!

At the time of the completion of the voyage, our arrival was a tremendous relief to me. Pregnancy at sea had been a very difficult experience. It was neither comfortable nor enjoyable coping with a toddler while heavily pregnant in a boat that heeled with the wind. I hated taking drugs to prevent nausea, which was aggravated by the boat's motion. Also, Jamie, then two, had an overwhelming desire for space. His chief refrain had become, "Wanna go. wanna run!" To be ashore for a time was important not only for his physical development, but also for his socialization with other children.

We thought we might somehow solve our accommodation problems by buying our next cruising boat now and living aboard. It took many weeks for the unreality of that notion to sink in. Apart from the fact that it is against regulations to live aboard for an extended period of time in Sydney waters, banks just don't give home loans for boats!

Now, we are faced with painting and varnishing Caprice so that she can be sold. She represents our savings and deposit for a house. Sadly, we have realized that the suburban home mortgage game has caught us up. How else will we ever be able to save enough money to cruise extensively again? Will we survive sufficiently long to put our roots aboard another cruising yacht — the 38 footer we have dreamed about ever since we decided to be a cruising family?

For Ian, ocean cruising is the only way of life. I hope that the lifestyle has infected me sufficiently that I feel the same way five years from now when we plan to voyage again.

⚓

For both of us, it already felt as though our circumnavigation had been someone else's voyage. I struggled with my new role and Ian disliked the restrictions of being confined indoors most working days. I suppose riding a motor- cycle helped a little. At first he rode my Honda 90 step through to and from work. We'd stored that little motor bike at Ian's mother's house while we were overseas. Later Ian bought a second hand Honda 250.

Who knows how Ian would have coped if he'd had to travel by train into the city to an office every day. He rode from Thornleigh to Manly Vale, on a route that included bush land. His job involved designing and testing models in the hydraulics laboratory and the lab was situated beside a small dam, which supplied the water for three different laboratories. Bush and a public recreation area surrounded the dam.

We also bought a car as soon as possible, taking a loan to do so. I found coping with public transport and two babies impossible.

In spring 1978, we sold *Caprice,* signed a mortgage and bought our first house. Sad as we were to see our little boat go to another owner, there was no way four of us could live aboard a twenty-five foot Top Hat yacht and Ian go to work.

It seemed crazy to us that no one would give us a mortgage on a boat big enough for our family, but we were able to secure one for a house. Even the latter was not easy. The bankers regarded us as a footloose, irresponsible couple to have spent four years wandering the world and spending our savings. Or maybe they were just jealous. I saw them as fat, pompous and wholly unimaginative tyrants, sitting securely behind their big desks.

'What will you do about white goods?' one banker asked.

'What are white goods?' I asked. Truly, I didn't know.

He looked shocked. 'Washing machines and refrigerators,' he said.

'I've done without for the past four years,' I replied. 'I can wash nappies by hand for a bit longer if I have to.'

He seemed totally disbelieving. We'd had our adventure, and now society seemed bent on squeezing us into conformity.

Eventually, we found an old brick cottage with two bedrooms and a sunroom on a flat block of land, close to shops schools and the train station at Waitara.

It was fully fenced and had gates to keep potentially wandering children in the yard. Although part of the ceiling had to be replaced in the second bedroom and the walls needed repainting throughout, the water and electricity worked, the floors were solid and the roof didn't leak. Most importantly, we could afford it.

And I did wash nappies by hand until someone gave us an old washing machine. In fact, we furnished the whole house with cast offs, gradually buying better quality second-hand when we could afford to. A mortgage and city work became our reality.

Neither of us had ever lived in the suburbs before, and here we were with two small children and no family nearby for support. After the freedom of sailing around the world in our own yacht, we felt thoroughly trapped, stuck without a boat.

Finding a babysitting group brought new opportunities and new friendships. I found the group through attending the local playgroup which met once a week. A babysitting group is a brilliant concept for hard-up young couples to be able to afford a night out, or even a trip to the obstetrician without having a toddler along too.

We babysat for each other, using plastic tokens as payment to keep track of hours owed. It had another advantage – our kids already knew the mum who came to their home, having met her and her children socially. Many of the members were newcomers to Sydney and, in the group, I found new friends. Flexi-time was a welcome innovation new to us. Ian could leave for work quite early in the morning and return home in time to prevent me from injuring the children during that late afternoon time dreaded by all frazzled mothers, when small children are tired and grumpy and mothers at their wits end.

Ian would ring about 3.00 pm 'How are you coping today? Do you need me home early?'

'Please,' I would reply desperately.

He could be home an hour later.

Ian would take Jamie to the local playground, where he could give one-on-one attention to a little boy who was no longer getting much of that from his mother.

David was plagued by tummy aches, which later we found were caused by cow's milk intolerance. He was ingesting the proteins through my breast milk. He cried a lot, had frequent ear infections and trips to the doctor.

'I'll write you a script for antibiotics.'

'I don't want to give him antibiotics again.'

'Do you want him to burst an eardrum? He could become deaf.'

I felt pressured into those antibiotics. Gradually, we found solutions to all these problems and we adjusted. The storm was abating.

The only boat we had left was our *Avon* dinghy. My memory is that I insisted we keep that dinghy, while Ian would have let it go with the yacht. I knew that we needed some way to get out on the water even if it was no more than taking a dinghy ride on the local Berowra River.

Soon, Ian decided to buy a Seagull outboard motor. That motor was unreliable and very smelly, emitting clouds of oily smoke. How we laughed later when we read Julia Hazel's description of the clouds of smoke emitted by the Seagull motor she'd purchased in the 1980s to propel her yacht in the French canals. She aptly named her outboard *Little Stinky*.

We explored Berowra River many times, both in the dinghy and by walking the tracks along its banks. Crosslands Park became a favourite spot while we were without a yacht. Those days were pleasant enough, especially during the summer when we could roll out of the boat into the river for a swim if we felt too cramped, but our souls itched to be on the ocean. How could we pay off a mortgage and obtain another sailing boat?

A year after our return to shore life, Richard, a long time engineering friend of Ian's, contacted him. Richard regularly sailed to Hobart for the Boxing Day Sydney to Hobart yacht race. He was the navigator on a thirty-one foot racing yacht.

'Mate, how would you like to help bring *Shenandoah* back from Hobart in January?'

'That sounds good. What crew position would I be?'

'You'd replace me. Dagmar's coming down to Hobart and we're staying there for a holiday after the race. The crew needs a navigator to bring them back.'

'That sounds okay. I'll have to square it with Jan first though. I'll get back to you.' Ian put down the phone and turned to me. 'What do you think? Should I go?'

'Of course you should go. I'll miss you, but it won't be for long. Tell Richard you'll go.'

Ian eagerly accepted the job of navigator. Soon after New Year, 1979, he flew to Hobart, joined the crew at Constitution Dock and they set sail the following day to return to Sydney Harbour. On the third night they anchored at Wine Glass Bay. Being a racing boat, *Shenandoah* carried no dinghy. Ian wanted to go for a walk along the beach, so he decided to swim the hundred metres to shore. He dived in and half way to the beach, became so cold, he began to wonder if he would succumb to hypothermia before he reached shore. After a run on the sand, he warmed up enough to swim back out to the boat and climb on board.

From Wine Glass bay, Eden was the next stop, then Bermagui, Jervis Bay and Wollongong before arriving home. On one of those long overnight legs, Ian recounted to me how in the middle of the night, he was so tired he hallucinated. He had nodded off in the cockpit while on watch and when he awoke, Joshua Slocum was sitting in the cockpit with him.

For a time, Slocum steered the boat, giving Ian a rest. (Slocum was famously the first yachtsman to cruise around the world via Cape Horn.)

That voyage satisfied Ian's itch for cruising for a few months. It also gave him some respite from the constant friction between the children. He certainly seemed happier when he returned home and found it easier to return to work.

It was difficult to save on only one income; I needed work too. When David was a year old, I registered with the NSW Department of Education for casual teaching work. My sister was staying with us at the time. She came into the city with me to help with the children and watched David take his first independent step while I was being interviewed. I felt this had to be a portent of some kind for David, but puzzled about what it meant.

It was a first step for me too, back into paid work, and that work was a relief for me too when I could find baby sitters. It gave me a break from the incessant demands of two small children as well as giving me time to collect my own thoughts.

By 1980, our savings from my casual teaching income was growing. Soon we'd have enough to buy another boat. Ian's income paid the loans and our living expenses.

After a year, my income helped us to buy a small day-sailer, a Hood 23, which we called *Taria*. That boat saved Ian's sanity – perhaps mine too. She was perfect for a day out or a weekend in Pittwater or Broken Bay, which is where we moored her.

While Jamie was happy on the boat, David was not so keen. From early babyhood, every time we took him on board, his shrieks would become higher and higher pitched the further the boat heeled. Today, David loves the water and sailing, but he still wants to avoid heeling and multihulls are his preference.

One day, Ian said, 'Let's go for a sail out to sea. It's a beautiful day and I'd like to sail east for several hours, then turn round and come back to Broken Bay.'
He wanted to get away from the land.

'I still think *Taria* is too small and light for ocean sailing, but I suppose we'll come along. It *is* a very nice day.'

People sailed the Hood 23 for JOG racing (Junior Offshore Group), so I thought we'd be safe enough in those light conditions.

Ian used the experience to try to instill in the children the idea that on the boat at sea, they had to do exactly as he instructed because he was the captain and our safety might rely on everyone's obedience. David, at two, was more amenable, but Jamie was never easy to convince about any rules.

Seasickness has plagued me for our entire ocean sailing lives, always worse when I have been living shore-side or moored in very protected waters. Ian wanted me to test out a new seasickness remedy during that short trip out to sea in *Taria*. It was one used by some of the Sydney-Hobart racing sailors.

Ian had found the combination of Phenergan and Ephedrine hydrochloride effective for him and told me about it excitedly on his return from Hobart.

'You've got to try this Jan. It's what the astronauts use. It really works. This could be the end of your sea-sickness!'

'Okay. I'll give it a go. Anything to alleviate 'mal de mer'. My reaction to the drugs was somewhat different to Ian's. The *Phenergan* (or its blue colouring) sent me high, laughing wildly and, if Ian had asked, I would have happily jumped over-board.

After half an hour I became dozy and dropped into a deep sleep for a couple of hours. I certainly was not seasick, but obviously, the adult dose was way too high for my chemically sensitive system.

When Ian told his GP brother about the remedy, Lindsay was horrified. 'You can't use Ephedrine hydrochloride. That's dangerous. You have to use the synthetic version – pseudo-ephedrine hydrochloride.' That, we discovered was *Sudafed*.

'Maybe it was the Ephedrine that caused you to hallucinate when you were coming back from Hobart,' I ventured.

'Perhaps.' Ian didn't seem convinced.

Later on, I tried the child's level of 5mg Phenergan and a quarter of a tablet of Sudafed. That treatment worked for me for about a year, before my body rejected the antihistamine drug. It puzzles me why an antihistamine should work against seasickness, but that is a question for pharmacists.

Another weekend, we sailed from Pittwater down to Sydney Harbour and back. I wasn't happy with *Taria's* performance. She didn't have the solidity of the Top Hat at sea, her displacement being very much lighter.

'If you go below, have a look at the way the hull is flexing, even in these light seas,' Ian said.

We both began to feel uncertain of the boat for sailing off shore. 'I don't want to go out to sea in this boat again,' I said to Ian when we were back on our mooring and working together to pack away sails and any other gear.'

I wasn't so absolutely clear about this until the day we tried to anchor in the bay inshore from Palm Beach. We had intended to go ashore and climb up to Barrenjoey lighthouse. A savage wind gust swept across the water and lay *Taria* over, touching her mast in the water.

'*Caprice* wouldn't have reacted like that in calm water,' I said. 'As far as I'm concerned, the sooner we get a strong sea-going vessel the better.'

The final straw was when a fellow Hood 23, *Montego Bay* sank one evening while racing off Sydney heads. I had to do something towards buying a more solid ocean-going yacht.

I was still teaching high school on a casual relief basis while continuing to look for permanent work, applying for every job other than teaching that I thought I could possibly perform.

Six times I was short listed. Each time they asked questions about family and when they discovered I had two young children, they lost interest in me.

In 1982, when David was four, we arrived home from a holiday at a Water Resources Commission dam, to find a telegram pushed under the front door.

'I wonder what that is?' Ian said.

The envelope was addressed to me, so I opened it and looked up at my husband.

'The Department of Education has offered me a job teaching English at Cheltenham Girls High School. Where's Cheltenham?'

'I don't know'

I soon found that Cheltenham G.H. was a school with high academic and behavioural standards, drawing its students from the well-educated, mostly professional families in the Beecroft-Epping area just north of Macquarie University.

Reluctantly, I accepted the position on the condition I could find day care for David, and at Beecroft, I found a pre-school which could offer full-day care for him. The pressure was on me to accept what I had been offered.

Teaching kids who could read and write and, mostly enjoyed doing so, became a pleasure at first, although very demanding in terms of preparation and marking. Jamie went to before and after school care close to home. Even in peak hour during the 1980s, Cheltenham was only a twenty minute drive from Normanhurst - although it took twice that long to get to work when I had to deliver the children en route.

My mother had been right all those years ago when she encouraged me to train as a high school teacher. She had emphasised the importance of the job being family friendly, with hours and holidays coinciding fairly closely with those of primary schools.

However, whilst non-teaching work would have involved a 5.00 pm knock-off time, teaching meant that after seeing to the boys' needs, I was working until midnight most of the term.

It was a very demanding life but, for me, better than my

being a stay at home mother. That would have driven me crazy with boredom. Besides, to fulfil our dreams of having both a house and a cruising yacht, we needed the two incomes. I convinced Ian we should delay buying a bigger yacht for a short while.

Almost a year after starting teaching at Cheltenham, I felt the urge to move to a quieter, more pleasant residential area. We had lived in the little old railway workers' cottage near Waitara station for four years, and it seemed like a good time to capitalise on that house and move on.

Ian is never very interested in houses – houses don't sail – so he has always left house buying to me, reserving the right to a final inspection and the possibility of veto in the event of structural problems.

The decision to move might have also had something to do with the following event. My much younger sister was staying with us.

'Shelley, I need to go shopping in Hornsby for fruit and vegies. Would you mind the kids please?'

'Okay.'

'It's raining so I'll take the car. You boys stay here with Shelley. I should be back in under an hour.'

As I exited the shopping centre I saw a strange sight across the street. Two small boys were hidden under a broken umbrella and a traffic warden was trying to stop them from crossing the street. Horror struck, I realised who those kids were. I dropped the box of fruit and vegetables just as my best friend appeared on the scene.

'Take care of the shopping,' I called back to her as I hurried across the street.

'Thank you so much,' I said to the traffic warden. 'I'll deal with these kids now.'

Because those two little boys were mine! Where was my sister? My car was parked only a few metres away, so I put the children into their car seats. By then, Judy had worked out the situation and brought the shopping over. I thanked her too and then questioned Jamie.

'Where's Shelley?' I was hopeful she had accompanied them somehow.

'At home.'

'How did you get up here?' I asked unnecessarily.

'We walked,' Jamie said. 'I found the umbrella in the gutter and we carried that so we didn't get too wet.'

I could tell he thought he'd done well by helping to shelter himself and his little brother from the rain. However, I was angry they'd followed me in the first place. We drove the three blocks home in silence.

I reported my story to Ian at the end of the day.

'We need to move somewhere further away from the shopping centre,' I said. 'As the boys get older, they'll want to spend more and more time at the shops. Better to just remove the temptation than have to fight it.'

'I suppose so,' said Ian with resignation. He was probably wondering how much longer before he could go to sea again.

I put the house on the market during early summer. Weeks later, I was full of frustration. One day when Ian came home from work, I poured it out to him.

'The real estate agent brought more business people to inspect the house today. They don't get it that those people won't buy until rezoning of the area is much closer.'

'What are you going to do about it?' asked my practical man.

'I think I can sell it myself.'

'How?'

'I'll advertise in the Sydney Morning Herald,' I said as the idea firmed up in my head.

My faith in real estate agents and their ability to hear what I told them was very strained. They wanted to sell the property for high-rise and semi-commercial purposes, it being so close to the centre of Hornsby. In fact, the rezoning change they talked of as though it would happen inside of a few months, did not occur for another ten years. By advertising in the Sydney Morning Herald, I sold the house within two weeks to a newly graduated architect and his wife.

'They fell in love with the old bull-nosed verandah, ' I told Ian. 'As far as I'm concerned, they can have the bull nosed verandah, so long as they pay us a good price.'

I had all of January to search for another house. I had already been looking and before long, found a house in a dead-end, tree-lined street, with a big tree in the back yard. Jamie wanted a tree-house and to me, that seemed a reasonable request for a small boy.

The house I had selected was in Normanhurst, close to a bush valley located only a couple of hundred metres away. The house wasn't brick, which I had insisted on during my first house hunt. Instead, it was built of the dreaded fibre-asbestos board commonly known as 'fibro'. By that time, I understood brick retained the heat during summer and was slow to warm up in winter. Fibro changed temperature more easily. While that characteristic had some disadvantages, it was actually cheaper on power usage. So long as we didn't break any of the fibre-board we were safe from the asbestos dust.

I knocked on the door, and within minutes made friends with the owners. Barbara and Michael were keen to sell privately too. We negotiated a price, Ian made a building inspection and the deal was done within a week.

One of my babysitters lived in the same street, and I knew that the kind of people who lived in her street were 'my kind of people'. At the time, I thought I was being a snob, but the difference was that most of our new neighbours were educated and our former neighbours were not. We simply had different interests.

I wondered how long the architect and his wife would remain in the house we had sold them.

By keeping the estate agents out of the transactions, I managed both deals with the total cost to us of only about two and a half thousand dollars – mainly the state stamp duty tax.

To my mind, that put us closer to our goal of another yacht bigger than the Hood 23.

Ian had bought a large shed about a year after we'd bought the first house. For this, he'd built substantial foundations and a floor from timber. The new owners of our house were not prepared to buy the shed too, so we were taking it with us.

'I'll pack up the house,' I told Ian, 'but you need to do the shed.'

I was unaware of how stressed Ian was about moving until he came down with shingles across his back and down his right arm.

The day we went to the solicitor to sign the contracts for the house sale, Ian had to take his sling off so he could sign his name. He didn't pack up the shed. We ended up paying a neighbour to put everything on the back of his big truck, dismantled shed included, and move it with us about five kilometres to our 'new' house. From there, we sold the shed and bought one that fitted into our yard.

Everyone was happy except Ian. He didn't know when he might be able to have his dreamed of boat. To him, moving house seemed to delay everything, but I felt very satisfied with myself.

I had settled the deal on both houses by the end of January and we were able to exchange contracts and move only a couple of weeks into the new school year. There seemed little point for the boys to change schools though, as they still went to the same before and after school care.

Our next goal was to save enough for that ocean-going yacht we were both dreaming of.

# 3 The Reality of a Phantom

The next summer holidays, we started in earnest to look for a larger boat. The boys were growing bigger and six year old David was slowly becoming accustomed to being on a heeling yacht. We felt we had well out-grown *Taria*.

'Now that I'm in a full-time job,' I said to Ian, 'and my earnings are growing in the "boat fund", could we afford a bigger boat now, albeit with a loan? Can we get one with the house for collateral?'

'You're right. It is time we started looking more seriously.'

We scanned all the newspapers for sailing boat advertisements and inspected a few steel yachts. To me, these were still very depressing, just like the dark smelly racing yachts we'd looked at some years earlier. One weekend, Ian was sprawled on the lounge room floor with Saturday's *Sydney Morning Herald*. I was searching the ads in *The Trading Post*.

'What do you reckon a Phantom 32 is?' he asked me.

'I don't know. I've never heard of it. What's it built of?'

'Fibreglass. And the price is affordable.'

'Give them a call and ask,' I suggested.

We didn't have any idea about the design, so we decided to spend the next day, Sunday, having a look. Ian made an appointment with the broker.

'It's out on a mooring, so I'll only take you out if you are a serious buyer,' warned the yacht broker when we arrived.

We felt we weren't, but smiled and nodded anyway.

'Oh yes,' Ian assured him. 'We are seriously looking for a boat in that size and price range.' My husband could never lie outright.

The boys loved the speed boat ride a couple of miles up the Parramatta River to Five Dock Bay and we went on board *Rosina II*.

Very soon, David said, 'I need to go to the toilet.' If we were going to buy a boat, he wanted to make sure he could cope with the marine toilet.

I liked the interior spaciousness of *Rosina II*: a big double berth forward and beside that, an enclosed toilet with a hand basin, but no shower.

There were two good sized pilot bunks, and two settees in the main cabin, plus a quarter-berth under the port side of the cockpit.

A large table and a navigation station gave a look of solidity to the interior. The galley was equipped with a gimballed two burner, pressure kerosene stove and a large icebox. To me, she seemed to be a safe, family boat.

'Look Ian, she's even got lee cloths,' I said, pulling the cloths out from under the mattresses and clipping them in place, 'and lots of strong handholds too. You boys could have a berth each, with these lockers alongside for your books and toys and Dad and I would sleep up here in the forepeak.'

'I bags this bunk,' said Jamie.

Ian removed the engine cover. 'Look Jan. A 28 hp Bukh diesel.'

There was no way either of us wanted another petrol inboard engine. Petrol fumes are heavy and do not disperse easily from the bilge of a boat. They are very easily ignited and boat explosions are frequently deadly. A pressure kerosene stove was also a safe option we liked.

Over a picnic lunch in the park near the brokers, we discussed the yacht we'd just seen. She didn't quite conform to Ian's desire for a sleek hulled, long-keeled steel yacht, but...

'She's a practical boat for ocean passages and there's plenty of room for the two boys,' I said. 'I'm keen. Besides, remember all the hard labour we did on *Jenny II's* steel hull. Our leisure time is more precious now we both work full-time as well as looking after Jamie and David.'

'I suppose you're right,' said Ian.

*Jenny II*, a 33' steel Temptress, was the very first yacht we'd bought. We'd spent hundreds of hours learning to maintain her steel hull. I remembered that experience all too vividly, my fingertips rubbed raw, almost eliminating my identifying patterns of whorls.

We no longer had the time or energy to look after steel.

After school, I took the children to swimming, music, soccer and gymnastics. Cooking dinner and supervising homework meant I frequently did not attend to marking and lesson preparation until after the children were asleep.

Fortunately, Ian did his share of chores. He washed the dishes, made the next day's lunches and read to the boys, as well as the usual male tasks of car, lawn and house maintenance at weekends.

Saturday mornings often involved travelling to sporting venues. Sundays were our only opportunity to get out on the water or into the bush.

'She'll probably make a good family boat. The design looks similar to a Sparkman and Stephens 34, but fatter,' Ian said. 'Although her beam is nearly eleven feet, she looks as though she will sail, though perhaps not quite as well as the S&S yachts that seem to have inspired her design.'

'You know, she has in place nearly all those items we have listed as being essential for our "next boat". ' I paused while Ian looked thoughtful and then I listed the items: 'Gimballed kerosene stove, icebox, diesel engine, big water tank, big enough fuel tank, lee cloths, hand holds, accessible tool locker, plenty of stowage, and more.'

The thought of Ian pushing to fulfil his long held dream of a steel yacht filled me with dread. I liked the pleasant décor and homeliness of this boat. 'Do you want to make an offer on her?' I asked.

'Yes, I think so,' he said at last. 'She comes with the mooring too. That would be a big advantage. It's so difficult to get a mooring in the harbour. Remember how much trouble we had renting one for *Taria,* even in Broken Bay.'

We went back to the broker and made an offer. The owners were not easy to contact, we learned. They were in the USA and their older son had been left in charge of selling their yacht. This gave us time to find out all we could about Phantom Yachts.

The following weekend, we visited the factory at Riverstone in the western suburbs where Phantom Yachts were built. We were pleased to find a solid factory at the address. This was no ghostly business.

After seeing the production method, I asked, 'Is there anyone who already has one, whom we can talk to?'

The factory owner described an address where he had delivered a boat to be completed. To our amazement, the description he gave sounded just like our street. It turned out that neighbours about ten doors away were in fact the owners of a sister-ship! What's more, they were friends with the family which owned *Rosina II*.

Our neighbour, John, showed us his photograph albums, documenting how he had completed his boat and fitted it out at the same time as his friends had been fitting out *Rosina II*. He had a fibreglass plug, cut out from the hull when he made the exhaust exit, which reassured us about the thickness of the fibreglass and the quality of its construction.

Only a couple of years after completing their boat, John's friends had moved to work in the USA, hence the need to sell. Finally, we received word from the broker that they had accepted our offer.

During our test sail we had noticed that unless conditions were very calm, the tiller was quite hard work. Nevertheless, we paid our deposit and went ahead with the pre-purchase out-of-the-water inspection.

'I'm fairly sure we're going to buy her Jan,' said Ian.' 'She hasn't been antifouled for over a year and I think we should take the opportunity to antifoul the hull. Cleaning off the marine growth will let us carefully inspect the hull for osmosis and any other damage.'

'Good idea,' I said, 'No point in paying for two lots of slipping. And it will also give you plenty of time to inspect and photograph the rudder.'

'I feel confident I can alter the rudder balance and ease the pressure on the tiller,' said Ian.

Once we'd given the hull and rudder a thorough inspection, we were very reassured that she didn't have osmosis and that Ian could adjust the rudder. We decided to continue with the purchase. On the ninth of March 1984, a loan organised, *Rosina II* became ours, along with her Parramatta River mooring at Five Dock Bay in Drummoyne.

The same broker through whom we bought *Rosina II* sold *Taria* for us. She had been a purely utilitarian purchase, and unlike the affection we had held for *Caprice*, we gave *Taria* no emotion at all. We didn't even take a photograph of her.'

'I can't call a boat with lots of dark green trim, *Rosina,*' I said. 'Do you think that might be the name of the former owner's wife?'

'I don't like her name either,' said Ian. 'Let's change it.'

We know of the superstition about changing boat names, but we were not superstitious and had changed the name of our Top Hat, *Capri*, to *Caprice*, the Hood 23 which had been *Valeel*a we changed to *Taria* (Maori for 'At Last'), and now *Rosina II* became *Realitas*, Latin for reality. Despite her design being a 'phantom', she was very tangible. Moreover, Ian's reality was sailing on the ocean.

A couple of weeks after we had taken ownership of *Realitas,* our neighbours, John and Joan came by Five Dock Bay to visit us in their Phantom, *Spinner*. They anchored close by and invited us on board to inspect the way they had fitted out their vessel, compared with how ours had been done.

John was obviously the better craftsman and I admired how he had finished the interior of *Spinner*. However, *Realitas* was ours. She was new and roomy to us, safe for undertaking ocean passages and we each had enough space on board. We all loved her. John's wife, Joan, told us that Rosina wasn't her friend's name, but I still didn't like the name and our boat already had a new identity by then.

'It will be Easter soon,' said Ian over dinner one evening. 'I'd like to sail up to Port Stephens. What do you think, Jan?'

Before I could even answer, Jamie piped up. 'Goody! I'd like that Dad.'

'Me too,' echoed David.

'Hold on,' I said. 'Dad was asking me. Yes Ian, I think that would be possible, but I want an outboard motor before we go.'

'Of course,' said Ian. 'I find rowing the *Avon* dinghy out to our mooring too heavy with four on board and luggage too. It was so easy by comparison with two up and a baby.' I nodded in agreement.

'I saw a chart comparing features of outboard motors recently.' I found the magazine. 'Look at this Ian,' I pointed to the chart. 'The Suzuki 2hp seems like it will do the job we want. At 9kg, I can lift it too.'

The new Japanese outboards were affordable by the early 1980s and were so much more reliable than the smelly old Seagull outboard we still owned.

'Yes, that does look like a good option. I've seen one of those at the boat ramp. It started easily and I've heard they have a good reputation.'

'It's important to me to be able to lift it in and out of the car boot. If I can't, it means I can never go to the boat on my own to sand and varnish or clean,' I said.

'I agree that's worth considering. Something else we need to think about is not having a motor that's too big when the boys want to drive the dinghy. And they will before too long,' said Ian. 'It's just as well the *Avon* has a transom for attaching a motor. Thank you for not letting me leave the inflatable with *Caprice* when we sold her.'

On my way to and from work, I drove past the Suzuki outboard motor dealership. One afternoon, I went in and purchased a new motor ready for our voyage up the coast to Port Stephens. Once we had our new Suzuki, we advertised and sold the Seagull motor. No more *stinky!*

During that Easter holiday, we revelled in having a diesel engine and an outboard that were both clean and reliable. When we wished to explore the nooks and crannies of the Port Stephens area, we could choose to sail if there was wind, or motor if not. There was a good breeze from the south-east on the way up and we shared steering, enjoying being out at sea again at last. Apart from the short trips with *Taria*, it had been five years since I'd been to sea.

After a stop-over at Nelson Bay, Ian said, 'Let's go further up.'

'Further up' took us to Salamander Bay, where we found a large bay with moorings and plenty of space to anchor. More importantly, on the beach were a cold water shower and toilet block. There were no public toilets or showers at the marina in Nelson Bay.

Someone on the beach pointed out to us the route to the Salamander shopping precinct. After a one kilometre walk, we found the mall with a large supermarket, pharmacies, butchers, fruit and vegetables, bakeries and hardware. Alongside is a moderate sized industrial shopping area with hardware and other services. Added to that, there is the bus stop for transport back to Newcastle and thence to the train lines.

'This area has everything a cruising yachtie could want!' I said, and Ian agreed.

Fame Cove is a hideaway delight of the area, being shaped like a keyhole. After you come in through the narrow entrance, you can see the cove open out into an almost circular anchorage. This secluded spot is perfect for shelter from adverse winds or storms. The only downside is the mozzies (mosquitoes) at sundown – they are voracious biters.

Beach front walks were popular with us all, as was exploring up creeks in our inflatable – an ideal craft for such exploits because it draws only a couple of inches when the outboard is not in use.

One day during Easter, we met Horst and Tilly, a couple we'd known from 1975 during our time on *Caprice* in Durban, South Africa. Like us, they had been on an extensive world cruise. Horst had built *Myuna*, which he and Tilly had sailed around the world.

They had returned home to Australia, had two children, bought a boat and found a way to live on board near Mona Vale. Horst had slogged for a time in the aluminium smelter at Gove, in far North Queensland to be able to afford his bigger boat, which they named *Jandu*.

Trained as an electrical engineer, Horst was a practical man who loved to improve his boats. Horst bought *Jandu*, a forty-two foot Swanson, cheaply from an old gentleman who had become too ill to complete his project. Horst and Tilly were busy turning it into a comfortable home for themselves and their two young children, just as they could afford to do so. They lived on her in a secluded area of lower Pittwater locally known as "The Puddle."

'How would you like to come onto our boat for a while?' Horst asked Jamie.

Jamie grinned and nodded.

As we sailed alongside *Jandu*, we watched Horst show Jamie how to steer with the wheel. I could see in Jamie's stance as he steered that he was very proud to be given control of this big boat. Horst appeared to be paying no attention to him.

'I'll bet you anything that Horst is aware of exactly what Jamie is doing,' said Ian.

'Of course he is. He'd know if Jamie deviated off course just by the motion of the boat.' I said.

During our voyage home from Port Stephens, we found the electronic *Autohelm* on *Realitas* was very noisy as it struggled to control the boat at sea.

Very soon it had depleted the battery. To our disgust we were forced to hand steer, which, in our family, is not what cruising is about. Even on *Caprice* we'd installed a simple QME steering system which we'd imported from England. We determined to buy an *Aires* wind vane before any more trips.

One weekend, instead of going on board *Realitas*, we visited Don and Margie McIntyre's small marine importing business in Cremorne, where we ordered an *Aries* wind vane. I was impressed a week or so later when Don McIntyre himself delivered this wonder machine to our door. This was not quite yachting royalty dropping in, but to us, it seemed close to it. And the *Aires* was the Rolls Royce of yacht steering systems in the 1980s.

Don was already becoming well known in adventure sailing circles, but a few years later, he was to become very famous for his 1995 BOC Challenge solo voyage round the world in *Buttercup*. Since then, he has made many voyages into Antarctic waters and with his love of adventure, he is always well prepared with a well-found boat. His best known adventure was in 1995 when he and his wife, Margie, spent the winter in Antarctica.

With a reliable inboard motor on *Realitas*, an outboard motor for our *Avon* dinghy, and a high quality mechanical self- steering,

We were now into a different kind of cruising to that we'd experienced on *Caprice*.

During 1984, we spent all our spare time on *Realitas*. We'd go out after the boys' Saturday morning soccer matches were over and stay until Sunday afternoon. While we were sailing on the harbour, we visited all the waterways and islands, exploring everywhere from Quarantine Bay near South Head to travelling up the Parramatta River as far as we could reach.

Nearly every weekend, we took people sailing with us, unless we were attending to maintenance, and there was a lot of maintenance to do. *Realitas* had sat unattended on her mooring for nearly a year before we bought her. Ian wanted everything on board to work properly, and he was prepared to work hard to make it so.

'I am puzzled about that noise when we are under engine,' Ian said while we were motoring along one windless day. 'What do you think it could be?'

I listened hard. 'I can tell that the engine noise is irregular, but I have no idea what might be the cause,' I said.

'I think the propeller shaft could be bent,' said Ian. 'Possibly we bent it when we hit that rock at the corner of Bottle and Glass Bay the day we took your father there. There was no hull damage, but perhaps we bumped the prop.'

In between helping Ian by being a sounding board, and then passing tools while he was working, I spent hours cleaning out lockers and the water tanks, and polishing the fibreglass to protect it. I made and installed a 'weather curtain' to shelter the open companionway from flying spray or rain, made mozzie nets for the hatches and generally kept the interior of the boat clean and maintained. I was also the person who frequently drove across the city to pick up parts for the engine or the pressure kerosene stove.

At the end of August, we planned to slip *Realitas* again. It was only six months since we'd antifouled her during our pre-purchase inspection, but now Ian wanted to install the modification he'd designed and made for the rudder.

'Before we go out to sea again, I want to be able to use the electronic self-steering unit,' said Ian. 'I also want to check the propeller shaft alignment.'

'Okay. Shall I book the Gladesville slipway?'

'Thanks Jan. Five days should do it. I'll take a flex day on Friday and there's bank holiday on Monday. I've checked the tides and we can put her up on Thursday afternoon. I'm going to take the paint back to the bare fibreglass on the underwater hull.'

'Why?' I asked. 'We checked the hull for osmosis back in February.'

'I know,' said Ian, 'but I intend to paint the underwater area of the hull with a couple of coats of epoxy before we put on the antifoul this time.'

'Will that lower the risk of osmosis in future?'

'That's the plan,' said Ian. 'I'll sand off all those tiny bubbles we found and the epoxy will seal them, preventing them growing any further. The main thing is to install the rudder modification though. The tiller will become easier to handle then. Look, I'll show you how the modification will work.' Ian quickly sketched out his design. He tried to explain the technical details to me of his plans for the rudder because he always wanted me to feel involved with all aspects of our boats. I liked that, but I didn't always follow those technical details.

As soon as *Realitas* was secured into her cradle on the slipway rails that Thursday afternoon, we started scraping off barnacles and slime. Once she had been pressure hosed as clean as she could be without wet sanding, Ian began removing the rudder and the prop shaft. He also took out the toilet valve and the galley water inlet valve. They were both made of nylon and Ian replaced them with safer bronze fittings. If the plastic cracked out at sea, our boat would go down, probably taking our little family with it.

'How long will it take to get the prop shaft out?' I asked.

'Only a couple of hours, I hope,' said Ian.

That was at eight o'clock on Friday morning. I soon became used to multiplying Ian's time estimates by three. At 2.30 pm, we loaded the bent prop shaft into the car for me to take to Porters, the propeller and shaft experts in Sydney. They had a special machine to make sure the shaft was true.

When I returned from Porters, Ian beckoned me over.

'Has the bilge stopped dripping?' I asked.

'Mostly, but I want you to take a look at this,' he said. 'Do you see the discolouration?' He pointed to an area of the hull.

'It looks damp,' I said.

'It does, but it's not bad.'

'No. There's no bubbling at the surface of the glass,' I noted.

'Would you find the hairdryer please and a double adaptor? I want you to heat that area for half an hour or so to see if it will dry out.'

A hairdryer was always a standard tool for our boats. I rarely used one on my hair. While I applied heat with the hairdryer, Ian finished sanding the hull and then wiped down the surface.

After a break, he stirred the epoxy primer, ready to apply the first coat to the hull and I went back to look at the area I'd been drying. It covered only about fifteen square centimetres, but once the fibreglass had cooled down, I could tell there was still moisture in there. I turned the hairdryer back on it while Ian started painting the other side of the hull. After several periods of drying and cooling, I stopped. I wasn't totally happy with it, but I had succeeded in removing most of the water.

When the patch was cool, Ian painted it. The test would be how it looked the next morning. When we arrived early in the morning, I ran down to look at the paint.

'It must have dried out enough Ian,' I said. 'The epoxy would have bubbled over the fibreglass if it had been too wet.'

'I think you're right,' he said. 'Okay, let's get the next coat of epoxy on.'

This time, we both painted, one each side, but painting with a brush was slow work.

'Why don't we use rollers, Ian? See. Those guys are painting antifoul on with rollers,' I said. 'I'm going to ask them about the finish.'

When I had talked to the people on the other slipway, and looked at their paintwork, I knew we were going about this job the hard way. A five inch brush is very tough on the wrists.

'I'm buying rollers next time we do this,' I said.

'A shame it's Sunday and we can't buy any today,' said Ian.

'It will have to be brushes this weekend.'

*The rudder before Ian's modifications*

*The rudder after Ian's modifications*

When Porters re-opened on Monday, I zoomed off in the car to pick up the shaft. Now they had corrected the alignment, I had to handle the shaft very carefully not to bend it getting it back to

the yard. Porters had also made a bronze tiller head fitting to Ian's specification. Manhandling the long shaft out of the car and lining it up in the engine was a tricky business involving Ian using string and magic, or so it seemed to me. There was certainly
string.

'What's the string for?' I asked.

'To check I've got a straight line. Couldn't you figure that out for yourself?'

'No.' My lack of a sense of mechanics, maths and physics still takes Ian by surprise.

Eventually, Ian was satisfied that engine and shaft were lined up as well as he could make them. He fixed new rubbers onto the flexible coupling and tightened everything up, including the engine bearers.

The prop went back on and the rudder too. Last of all, he connected the tiller and the new tiller head to the top of the rudderstock. However, he didn't have the tools to create a keyway right then, and promised himself to do it later.

But what a different looking rudder! While I had been away driving, Ian had been fixing to the old rudder the new parts he had designed, making it almost balanced. We applied a last coat of antifouling paint and removed the masking tape. How smart *Realitas* looked with her smooth black underwater parts. Ian also applied several coats of racing antifoul to the propeller. Barnacles always seemed to attach themselves to the prop first. The racing antifoul was harder and smoother, not ablative like the one we used on the hull.

While waiting for the tide to rise, we polished the topsides and washed down the deck. It didn't matter now should the antifouling paint get wet.

When *Realitas* returned to the water and floated freely again, Ian turned on her engine and motored round the corner into Five Dock Bay, while I drove the car back to the boat ramp, ready to pick up Ian when he had moored the boat and came ashore.

'You can hear that the engine is much smoother now,' said Ian, grinning happily. 'I must have got it right.'

I grinned too. We were tired but satisfied with our efforts.

Over the next few weeks, we made inspection hatches for both water tanks and installed an elbow in the toilet hose, making it difficult for water to siphon into the boat and overflow the toilet bowl.

How good it was to own a well-found yacht and be able to go to sea again.

*Realitas* wasn't a fast boat – five knots being her maximum speed in comfort, but she sailed relatively well and did what we asked of her. In strong gusts, she was inclined to heel more than I liked, and especially when she needed a sail change she could put her gunwale down and increase speed to eight knots. At those times, I had to duck quickly when cold seawater whipped across the deck and tried to shower me. I didn't like that scenario. Then, only Ian could control the tiller. He loved it, grinning from ear to ear as the wind gusted the hood of his jacket off his head and the salt spray flew into his face. Even the annoyance of salt spray on his glasses didn't knock his enthusiasm.

# 4  A Summer Holiday Afloat

Summer was fast approaching and we prepared *Realitas* for our first Christmas holiday season afloat. We planned to have Christmas and Boxing Day at home, before leaving on the twenty-seventh of December.

Each weekend, I brought more things on board with us – canned food, extra sheets and towels, pots and pans, a new stainless steel whistling kettle, an ample first aid kit, and a litre of sunscreen. Ian had spares for the engine – water pump impellers, engine hoses, copper washers, nuts and bolts, spark plugs for the outboard and spare burners and wicks for the stove – the list seemed endless and it was my job to find plastic boxes for these items, label them and stow them where they could be found again. We also bought a second hand storm jib which was almost unused, and ordered a new trysail (heavy weather mainsail replacement) from a sailmaker.

With a southerly change due, we left our mooring at the planned time, ready to sail to Pittwater. However, there was a hitch as we were sailing down the harbour. After slipping in August, Ian had forgotten to install a keyway into the shaft to lock the rudder in line with the keel. The wind was strong and the tiller began to slip on its shaft, making it almost impossible to turn the tiller and steer the boat under sail.

'I'll have to take the sails down,' said Ian. 'The rudder will be easier under motor. We can pick up a mooring in Bottle and Glass Bay. Jan, get the boat hook ready please.'

Ian had enough strength to manoeuvre *Realitas* up to a mooring and I picked it up. While I kept the kids out of the way, Ian drilled a hole between the tiller-head and the rudder shaft, tapped it and screwed in a bolt to keep it all in position. (He called this a "scotch-key".) Finally, we were ready to leave the harbour and able to turn north.

Outside the heads a southerly wind blew a steady twenty-five to thirty knots, gusting to thirty-five. With both wind and the inshore current behind us, we swept the fifteen nautical miles up the coast to Barrenjoey in a couple of hours.

There, Ian tried to lower the foresail before we turned into the wind to sail up Pittwater, but the halyard was jammed at the masthead.

The tension rose while we edged our way into the lee of the headland, but once we were protected from the worst of the wind, Ian managed to bring the sail in and we both relaxed again.

'I hope that is the end of mishaps for this holiday,' I said as we motored south down Pittwater to Lovett Bay.

We spent a few days visiting friends who lived in that area – Nick and Anne Reeve and their two boys at Little Lovett Bay and the family we'd met on *Makaretu* in French Polynesia, who lived on the south side of Lovett Bay. Their youngest had turned one in Tahiti during 1977, and Jamie had attended her birthday party when he was eighteen months old. Horst and Tilly and their two children lived close by on *Jandu* too. From there, it was a short passage around to America Bay in the Hawkesbury River for New Year's Eve fireworks and the letting off of old flares.

After New Year, we sailed home to our mooring again, but didn't stay long. The next day, Ian spent a few hours properly fixing the tiller on the rudder shaft. (It had been slightly off centre), He also fitted a cleat to take a third reef in the mainsail.

'The tiller should stay firm now, and with that cleat on the boom, we can reef right down out at sea,' said Ian happily. 'We need to do that to balance the storm jib in heavy sailing conditions.'

'You're gradually adapting *Realitas* to take the kind of sailing you prefer, aren't you?' I commented and Ian nodded.

That night, we sailed back down harbour and anchored at Store Beach near Manly, where we fell asleep about midnight. Following a leisurely breakfast, we progressed out of the heads and turned south with the northerly behind us, but that wind was short-lived.

'Ah, the joys of coastal sailing,' I muttered. 'There's nothing like the wide open spaces of the ocean with no land around to mess up the wind.'

Soon, the wind turned westerly and dropped off prior to a southerly change. We had to motor the last couple of miles into

Gunnamatta Bay at Port Hacking, where we anchored overnight to await a favourable wind change.

On Sunday morning, Ian replaced the shackles for the backstay and forestay with larger ones. He wanted stronger fastenings. That evening when the wind returned to the north we set off again, well rested. While the children were still too young to help with watch keeping we preferred to sail at night when they were asleep. Ian's log book entry for 0345 on January 7th, 1985 reads as follows:

*Have been maintaining about 5kts at 190° (T).*
*Raised full main as wind slowly moving W.*

'If you look out Jan, you should be able to see Beecroft Head,' said Ian mid-morning. The head marks the northern entrance to Jervis Bay.

Jamie raced into the cockpit. 'I can see it,' he shouted.

When the wind died we motored, passing Point Perpendicular and its lighthouse on the headland by noon. At 1330, we dropped anchor off a beach in the northern part of Jervis Bay. It was time to let the kids out to play on a beach and for us to rest. They needed to release their pent up energy.

'I want to visit Huskisson tomorrow morning,' said Ian. When we arrived, he chose not to enter the river. 'I don't know the tides for the river mouth, Jan,' he said. 'I think it's safer to leave *Realitas* out here and go in by dinghy.'

'That's okay. I'll stay on board to keep watch. You take the boys with you.'

'Thanks. I don't want *Realitas* to be stuck in there for days waiting for a tide high enough to bring her out again.'

When they returned, a brisk north-easterly was blowing, creating lots of chop. As Ian motored over the bar, I could see the boys sitting in the front of the dinghy, being soaked every time a wave lopped over the bow. They stripped off and changed into dry clothes while Ian began pulling in the anchor chain and I started the engine.

'In this chop, we couldn't have brought *Realitas* out over the bar without thumping her keel,' I said to Jamie. 'Just as well Dad decided to leave her outside.'

The bow was plunging wildly in the shallow water and we had no effective winch, so each time the bow dropped, Ian pulled in more chain and looped it around the anchor cleat. Just as the anchor broke free from the mud and the boat was suddenly free, I put the engine into gear and quickly steered us clear of the shore. Now the anchor was swinging wildly from the bow and banging into the hull.

As we eased into deeper water, I slowed the revs a little, allowing Ian to bring in the rest of the anchor chain. Soon, he had the anchor tamed on its roller and tied down.

'Why are you so pale?' I asked when he returned to the cockpit. Ian held up a bloodied finger. 'In my hurry to break the anchor free, the chain caught my finger,' he said.

I hadn't realised he'd injured himself and felt sick at the thought the chain might have amputated his finger.

I left him at the tiller and went to find a *Bandaid* for the bruised and bleeding finger.

'I think we need to buy a decent anchor winch,' I said, as I put the sticking plaster over the wound. 'This is too dangerous. You need all your digits.' The *Bandaid* was barely adequate and soon the blood oozed through. I made a mental note that we needed to improve our first aid kit

We returned to the beach where we'd been anchored before. It was relatively sheltered there from the strong northerly and we relaxed. At a quarter to two in the morning, when we were sleeping soundly, Ian awoke when the boat's motion changed. The wind had turned southerly, putting us on a lee shore.

He woke me and we dressed hastily pulling on wet weather coats and pants over our jeans and jumpers. While Ian went out to pull in the anchor, I started the engine and prepared to take the boat clear of the beach. Fortunately, this time, there were no jammed fingers.

Ian came back to the cockpit and took the tiller from me. 'Could you go below and bring out the storm jib please,'

I went down and fossicked under our double bunk, pulling up the bed-base boards until I found the right sail bag. Now, our bed was a mess, but I couldn't be concerned about that. We had to take ourselves the whole length of Jervis Bay (eight nautical miles) to anchor securely out of the strong wind.

'What about the dinghy?' I said.

'I'll get the reefed main up first and then pull the dinghy tight up under the stern. It should be all right there. Just steer straight into the wind.'

Repeatedly, the spray broke across the deck, soaked our faces and trickled down our necks under our waterproofs. Clouds obscured the stars and moon. It was truly 'a dark and stormy night.' As we toiled on into the wind and rain, we began to catch glimpses of the lights at Vincentia on the still distant southern shore. We couldn't anchor right off Vincentia, because that is the naval base, but it was the only visible landmark to head for.

About two and a half hours later, we were close enough to Vincentia to anchor outside the restricted area. By checking with the depth sounder, Ian estimated where he wanted to anchor. I maneuvered *Realitas* into position, while he dropped the sails and then the anchor. I passed some ties out to Ian and he lashed the sails down.

The drama over, we felt our exhaustion – we were ready to plonk back into our bunks for some sleep before the kids woke up. But the night had more in store for us yet. We were just finishing a hot drink when Ian looked serious again. He was listening.

'I think we're dragging anchor,' he said.

He put his head out of the companionway. 'Yes. The wind has swung from south-west to south-east,' he said. 'We'll have to try re-anchoring.'

I swore and did my coat up, ready to go outside again into the rain. The second anchoring effort worked, the anchor held, and we were able to return to bed for what little of the night remained. As I dropped off to sleep, I recognised that we had returned to our old habits on board. In tense situations we worked together as a team with little speaking, both recognising what had to be done and, mostly, we just did it.

'Goodnight,' I murmured, and fell asleep almost immediately.

The wind stayed in the south-east for a couple of days, during which time we relaxed at the beach near the rocks known as 'Hole in the Wall'. When the barometer began to climb again, the wind moved further north and we were ready to continue our voyage south.

'Isn't this a contrast?' I said to Ian, when he had the spinnaker up and the northerly wind was filling it, taking us comfortably towards Eden, near the border with Victoria.

Late at night on Sunday 13th January, we crawled into Snug Cove, Twofold Bay, looking for a place to stop. In the morning, we admitted to ourselves that we'd done rather well in the dark, anchoring well clear of any obstructions.

'We'll head over to Eden's fishing boat wharves after breakfast, Jan. While I wash down the boat and top up the water tanks, you might like to go into the town to top up our fresh provisions.'

'Okay. It'll be nice to have some fresh bread and meat. 'I said. 'How far is it?' I'd never been to Eden before.

When we were tied up alongside a fishing boat, Ian gave me directions to the town centre about a kilometre away, but up a steep hill. It was an energetic walk.

Before the fishing boats started coming in from sea for the night, we moved back off the wharf and anchored in the bay.

We spent two more days exploring Eden and visited the local museum – a highlight, though Ian nitpicked about a technical error. He was sure the information on the sign about the

quadrant, a navigational instrument that preceded the sextant, was wrong.

'What does it matter?' I said, for once impatient with Ian's perfectionism. I was too fascinated by the information about whaling which had been the reason the town had been established.

Eden had been a whaling centre from the 1800s until whaling was prohibited. Other forms of fishing provided the town with prosperity in the 1970s and 80s – a tuna cannery and a fish freezing plant in the town, dairy farming, cheese making and tourism in the locality. These businesses provided good livings, but the most obvious industry was the wood chip mill on the southern shore of Twofold Bay.

Wood chipping of local timber was supposed to be sustainable, but it didn't look like that to me. We walked through areas of native forest that had been clear-felled, and then replanted with pine, which was just starting to grow. A mountain of wood chips lay next to the dock, ready for loading on a ship. The wood chipping continues to this day, the chips still being exported to Japan.

We turned our bow north on Thursday 17th January 1985, taking a day to sail to Bermagui.

We went on again the next day, motoring out to sea with no wind and raised the sails when a light easterly came in. However, it stayed very light all day and we eventually drifted into Ulladulla for the night.

'Can't we stop here for a bit?' asked David

'I've got to get home,' said Ian. 'You might have nearly ten more days, but my holiday is finished. I have to go back to work on Monday.'

On Saturday, the wind blew from the north-west. After lunch, we set off with the sails winched tightly in – a close-reach – for six hours to arrive back in Jervis Bay. We loved Jervis Bay, but it was time to keep on heading north while the wind was favourable, and we made it back to Sydney Harbour in one overnight hop.

By the time we picked up our mooring in Five Dock Bay on this summer voyage, we'd covered four hundred and twenty nautical miles over twenty days. *Realitas* seemed truly ours now, and we no longer felt we were sailing someone else's boat.

We decided to sail to Broken Bay and Pittwater for Easter, 1985. David had received a kitten for his birthday in March and he wanted to take it with us.

'I don't see why not,' I said. 'It's probably safer than leaving her unattended at home.'

'I'm not so keen,' said Ian. 'I don't want animals on the boat.'

'It's just a little kitten,' I countered. 'It will spend most of its time curled up with David.'

As usual, I won the day. We packed up the car, including the cat and her water and food dishes. The fact that Sascha was car sick after fifteen minutes was not a good sign. Ian was very grumpy.

*David and his kitten, Sascha*

'I told you I didn't want that damned cat with us.'

I cleaned up the cat's vomit from the floor of the car as best I could, and we drove on in silence with the car windows wide open. David was worried Sascha would leap out the open window, so we closed his side again. It was not a happy Easter that year. Sascha, we found, also got seasick!

I had tried to keep the kitten's bowls out of Ian's way by tucking them under the table, but the dish of food must have slid across the floor as *Realitas* heeled. Ian stepped in it. Inevitably, there was more shouting.

We sailed down Pittwater to visit Horst, Tilly and kids on *Jandu* at 'The Puddle' near Mona Vale. Horst and Tilly welcomed us and we rafted our boat alongside theirs.

'Would you like to come on board *Realitas* for coffee and cake?' I invited. 'I'm sure it's my turn to be hostess.'

Having eaten his cake, David asked, 'May I take Anja for a ride in the dinghy Dad?'

He was seven now and starting to feel confident he could manage the dinghy and outboard by himself. There was very little distance the children could go. 'The Puddle' was a fairly confined area, and so long as they didn't head out the short channel into deeper water, we thought they would be fairly safe. Tilly and I helped the children put on their life jackets and they climbed into our inflatable.

Ian started the motor for David who, grinning widely, set off very slowly.

After he had circled *Jandu,* David tried to stop the boat by coming alongside *Realitas* and catching hold of the gunwale. With no gears, the running motor was too strong for him to hold on, and the dinghy went forward, leaving David dangling.

Four year old Anja was in the dinghy by herself, not knowing what to do. The dinghy circled away from the boats and she burst into tears accompanied by loud howls. The dinghy finally circled back and jammed itself between the two yachts.

Horst leapt out of the cockpit and into our dinghy to rescue his daughter. He turned off the outboard and secured the painter to *Realitas*.

*Seven year-old David rows the dinghy*

Meanwhile, David was still hanging from the gunwale. The scene struck Ian and me as so ludicrous, we were laughing too much to help him. But eventually, Ian, still spluttering, leaned over and pulled David aboard.

David's face expressed horror. How could his attempt to impress Anja have gone so horribly wrong? I was still laughing so much, I couldn't speak. Our German/Australian friends didn't seem to see the funny side. They hadn't watched David's changing expressions as he worked out what was happening and it dawned on him that he had got things terribly wrong.

We didn't see ourselves as irresponsible parents. Both our families spent large amounts of time on our boats. Our kids needed to learn how to handle dinghies and keep themselves safe around water.

No one was hurt in this incident, but David never again had the chance to take Anja for a dinghy ride.

# 5  Christmas in Tasmania

Ian and I were used to sailing long distances at sea without modern communications but most of our sailing during 1984 and 1985 had been day sailing while we got used to having the children on board and we all became familiar with the boat and how to handle her. We'd done a couple of overnighters on the trip to Eden in January, but now we were ready to travel further afield.

As summer approached, I said to Ian, 'We could sail down to Tasmania and have Christmas with Judy and Mike?'

Judy and Mike Handlinger are like family to us and our children loved being together. We'd shared their house upon our return to Sydney after the world circumnavigation in *Caprice*. With Judy's parents and siblings in Tasmania and mine in New Zealand, in Sydney our two families had spent Christmas together most years. The Handlingers had recently moved to Launceston and their children were four and seven, while Jamie had just turned ten and David was nearly eight. Christmas together in Tasmania seemed a good idea.

'I'd like that,' said Ian. 'Do you think we can manage the timing?'

I checked the calendar for December. '

'There are eight days between high school ending and Christmas day,' I said. 'I think I can have everything on board ready to leave as soon as school breaks up. Don't forget, Cheltenham breaks up a few days earlier than the boys' school does.'

'Okay, we'll give it a go, so long as you realise we might not make it to Launceston for Christmas day.'

'I'll sort some decorations and things for Christmas at sea in case the weather delays us.'

I contacted Judy and she was thrilled with the idea. Her sister, Pat, whom we knew well, had also moved from Sydney back to Tassie. We would see her again too. After the decision was made, there were few weekend sails. Ian made a long list of tasks he wanted to complete before departure, and we worked long and hard to ensure they were completed.

Most important was to have all the mast lights working for at night, because we'd be sailing non-stop to reach Launceston in time. Fixing the lights entailed my winching Ian up to the top of the mast in the boatswain's chair, its pockets holding tools and spares. I pulled him up on the spinnaker halyard and we used the main halyard as a safety rope, so I had two lines to handle. Because I found it difficult to haul his entire weight, Ian would half pull himself up and then I would keep the ropes taut and cleated, so that if he lost his grip, he wouldn't fall more than a few centimetres.

There was a deck light fixed under the spreader supposedly to shine onto the deck for changing sails at night. We had tried before to get it working, and failed. Some of the wire was corroded and we took hours to find the fault and fix it. A deck light made a huge difference to work at night. We also installed extra navigation lights on deck. We had found that crew on vessels close to us didn't look up and see the masthead lights, so that deck level lights were also necessary, especially in harbour when the city lights blocked out our masthead lights.

The boys spent a lot of time out in Five Dock Bay, jumping the dinghy over their own wake or just exploring while we worked. Ian limited them to one tank of petrol in the outboard – enough time for us to get down to work for a couple of uninterrupted hours.

Apart from the masthead lights, Ian attended to maintenance of the winches, diesel tank and engine. We installed a new compass and electric wires for its night light, put up a radar reflector, bought and installed a Dan buoy (man overboard position marker) and refurbished the spinnaker pole ends.

We had thought the boat bow-heavy with a water tank under the forward bunk, so we opened up that space for stowage, closing off the water lines there and instead, against the hull, installed a small fifty litre flexible tank for the bathroom leaving the main water tank to feed the galley pump. The flexible tank sat as far aft as the space under our bunk allowed and so was closer to the boat's centre of gravity. The bow became more buoyant as a result. We cleaned out the main water tank, rinsing it with strong chlorine bleach.

When school finished for the year, we were ready to go on board that evening after Ian finished work.

I'd already stowed the Christmas presents under our bunk, and packed non-perishable provisions as well as water and fuel aboard during the previous week.

Just before leaving, Ian installed the *Aries* onto its brackets at the stern of the boat. That self-steering gear was way too expensive to leave hanging on the boat at the mooring.

My final task has always been to take the car home, then return to the boat by train, or on this occasion, taxi because there were still a number of last minute things we'd forgotten to bring – like the eggs. I wasn't carrying those on the train.

Eventually, the stowing was complete, the boys were asleep and we dropped the mooring later that night. I felt frustrated when the engine overheated as we motored down the harbour.

'After all the hours of maintenance we've done, I didn't expect anything to go wrong this early,' I said.

Ian took this setback in his stride. My ever competent husband knew just what to do.

'Don't panic - it's just the water pump,' he said. 'I've got a spare impeller. We'll turn the engine off in a minute.'

Before we moved through the heads and out to sea, we raised the sails and then Ian installed the new water pump impeller. Naturally, he had checked that there were spares for every likely occasion.

When the boys awoke next morning, we were already sailing south, the *Aries* steering for us and the boat moving easily to the swell. We didn't plan to stop until we reached Tasmania.

It was a brisk passage down the coast and Ian and I felt really good embarking on a longer voyage again. We had missed the rhythm of life at sea and now we fell into our old patterns very readily. Even my mild sea-sickness felt comfortable! I soon learned to balance on the sloping floor of the galley, moving my weight in time with the motion of the yacht.

On our third day at sea, the *Greenpeace* provided some entertainment for us. Soon after we passed Twofold Bay at Eden, she came out of the bay, moved around in a very large circle, then headed back to land. Overhead, a helicopter hovered, presumably photographing the ship. Shortly afterwards, a small, but quite steep wave lopped over the stern and into the cockpit, wetting both boys.

'I'm going inside,' said Jamie.

'Me too,' said David.

They disappeared into the cabin with alacrity, staying there for most of the crossing of Bass Strait. I didn't mind if they played or read on their bunks, but became concerned about the possibility of concussion when they started jumping monkey-like across the table, using the deck head handholds for support.

*Jamie photographing the Greenpeace*

Jamie would kick at David, then rush back to his bunk and pre-tend to be reading when I stuck my head in from the cockpit. He had a wonderful ability to look innocent when I knew he wasn't.

David would wail his protests. 'Ma-uum, Jamie kicked meee.'

'No I didn't,' Jamie would respond, his nose back inside his book.

What provocation had David provided for this? Sometimes he was at fault; sometimes he would have done nothing to deserve Jamie's assault.

As we approached Bass Strait, a low pressure weather system was stationary over Hobart, bringing south-westerly winds on our nose. The winds were strong and uncomfortable, but not excessive at 30 - 35 knots but enough to raise a small sea which was stopping the boat. It was impossible to make progress on a direct route to Launceston.

'Jan, I'm going to head down the East coast of Flinders Island. That should give us some respite from wind and waves. I hope we'll make more headway, but we'll have to use the tides to make our way west through Banks Strait south of Flinders.'

'And with some luck, the wind will have shifted enough for us to make a clear course for the mouth of the Tamar once we're through the strait,' I added.

We shied off down the east coast of Flinders Island. It was about 2.00 pm when we were nearly ready to turn into Banks Strait between Flinders and Tasmania.

'The wind's picking up,' said Ian. 'I'll need you to help reef the mainsail and change down to a smaller headsail before we head into Banks Strait.'

I backed the sails and loosened the halyard to allow Ian to remove the working jib. He tugged at the sail, but it refused to come down. He returned to the cockpit.

'Damn, damn, damn,' Ian said. 'Something's jammed. I can't get the sail down. We'll miss the tide through the strait if I can't clear it quickly.'

'I hope you don't have to climb the mast, I said. 'I remember all too well you climbing the mast on *Caprice* when we had a broken back-stay half-way across the Indian Ocean.'

When Ian had come down to the cockpit, he was dreadfully bruised, because he'd lost his grip and been swung wildly about up there in the boatswain's chair.

'It's all right. I think the problem's at the bottom of the mast this time.'

Ian went forward again to look for the cause of the trouble. Fortunately, it *was* a block at the bottom of the mast that had failed. The wire halyard strained through the turning block directing the line down from the mast to cross the cabin top. Its nylon sheave had cracked, allowing the wire to jam between the metal cheek and the sheave.

'Do we have a spare turning block? Have a look, please Jan.' Meanwhile, the sail was beating itself against the rigging, its heavy stainless steel clew and the sheet ropes walloping back and forth. It made the whole boat shudder and felt like either the rigging would give way or the sail disintegrate..

'I hate that noise,' I said. 'It always makes me fearful of more damage from the strain inflicted on the rigging.'

'I dislike it too. And yes, more damage is possible. Please look for a replacement block while I try to free the halyard.'

I lashed the tiller and went below to look for a spare block. Work is very slow on a heaving, corkscrewing deck, and more so with a sail flailing about, but Ian mangled the broken block enough to disengage the jammed wire. With the halyard running free, the head sail came down easily. Soon, Ian had replaced the block with one I had found in the spares, and in another half hour, he had hanked on a smaller jib and hauled it up. It was late afternoon by the time the boat was under way again.

'If you pass me the working jib and sail bag, I'll bag the sail and stow it,' I said. 'I feel quite nauseous from the irregular motion, and I need to lie down briefly.'

Ian adjusted the *Aires* and reset the course. With the boat back into a more regular motion, my stomach soon settled and I got up again. 'I'm feeling much better now that the motion is regular again. You rest for a couple of hours while I keep watch and cook dinner.'

'Good,' David interjected. 'I'm hungry.' Jamie kept on reading.

Ian chose to hand-steer much of the night, fighting the east-flowing tide in Banks Strait until it changed direction again. At dawn, I looked outside to see a grey sky, grey spume streaked water and flying spray. We were travelling hard on the wind to close with the mouth of the River Tamar. I ducked behind the bulkhead as a wave splashed across the deck. Soon, the wind increased to forty knots, too much for the sails we had up.

'It's time to try out the new trysail. Can you pull it and the storm jib out of the forepeak please while I gather the lines I'll need.'

I finished serving the boys' breakfast and then heaved the sails out into the cockpit. When they were raised and I'd thrown the others down the hatch, Ian and I both felt pleased. The boat's motion was much more comfortable and we were travelling faster.

'The lines across the cockpit look like a spider's web,' I said. 'We can hardly move for all these ropes.'

'Notice how much better the new trysail pulls than the triple-reefed main and how it balances the storm jib though,' said Ian.

'It does. And look, we haven't dropped our speed. Let me finish my breakfast and then I'll take over watch,' I said, going below to get my porridge.

Ian and I swapped places when I had and then he went to bed for a well-earned rest. The *Aries* was controlling the steering and I stayed in the cockpit, rugged up in my wet weather gear, boots and balaclava. It was cold, and bitter spray regularly flew across the cockpit. Every time *Realitas* hit the top of a swell, I ducked in anticipation. An earful of icy water was something to avoid if possible.

Suddenly there was a noise like a pistol shot in my ear. I thought someone was shooting at us. I looked up and saw the clew of the trysail and its sheet flapping loose. That rope was snapping about like a ninja warrior trying to slash someone's head from their shoulders.

The U bolt we had installed at the stern to hold the turning block for the trysail sheet had snapped in two. I didn't need to call. Ian had already heard the noise and noticed the altered motion of the boat. He'd been so tired, he'd left his wet weather gear and harness on while he slept. Now, he leapt out on deck and clipped the lanyard onto his harness ready to deal with this new emergency.

Between us, we doused the sails and gathered up all the lines from the cockpit. Ian reset the double-reefed main and *Realitas* rocked and churned her way forward again. My knuckles were white as I clung to the cockpit coaming.

Fortunately, it was not long until we tacked our way into the river mouth. The black rocks looked alarmingly close as we came in, but everything looks too close when you have been in the wide spaces of the open ocean. Once into the shelter of the river, we all relaxed considerably.

'You can come outside now kids. We're in the River Tamar.'

I looked back at the rocks we'd just passed at the mouth of the river and shuddered. How easy it would be for a sailing vessel to end up on those jagged black devils.

*Jan keeps watch*

**Realitas** *in the River Tamar*

We motored several miles upriver towards Launceston looking for a spot to drop anchor safely for the night. Once we were past the village of Georgetown, we were into rural countryside and I could smell a hint of cows and their manure on the breeze.

'Haven't we done well? It's exactly seven days since we left Sydney Harbour,' I said.

We were a little battle weary and bruised, but Ian was exhilarated by the sailing, and we were all thrilled to have arrived the day before Christmas Eve.

On the way up the river, we tried to enter a side cove we had identified from the chart as being a suitable anchorage for the night. As we approached, I saw electricity wires passing over the entrance to the bay. They hung in a wide arc from one bank to the other.

'Look Ian!' I pointed up at the wires. 'Will our mast fit safely under?'

My imagination had us all frying from electrocution a few moments hence. We looked for a sign on the shore – nothing.
How high was the clearance? There wasn't anything marked on our chart.

'I think we should look for another spot,' said Ian. 'This isn't worth the risk.'

Eventually, we found a safe place to drop that anchor and at last we fully relaxed and congratulated ourselves on a successful voyage.

For Ian and me, it was good to be able to spread out in our double berth in the forward cabin again. At sea, we have to sleep in the middle of the boat, closest to the centre of gravity.

We slept on the narrow settees which gave the least movement and therefore, the least chance of seasickness. Still, I was very relieved all the motion had ceased.

Next morning, I started unpacking the forward lockers under the vee berth and to my horror, found that the Christmas presents were floating in seawater.

'Ian, how can water have got in here?'

'I'm not sure. Move aside and let me investigate. We'll have to empty everything out to search for an entry point.

'Just as well most things are sealed in plastic bags,' I muttered.

We pulled out everything and dried the parcels as best we could. The books I always buy for Christmas were wet, but fortunately, the remote-controlled car we'd bought for the boys was well wrapped in plastic and it was safe.

'Oh, Ian, our new Honda generator is drowned!'

The generator was stowed lower than anything else.

'I'll have to wash that out in fresh water,' said Ian.

Close examination revealed that the forward bulkhead had moved enough to leak through from the anchor locker while we were sailing hard to windward.

'Come and look,' said Ian. 'See the crack in the edge of the bulkhead just here.'

I squeezed up beside him on the vee berth and peered at the bulkhead.

'Yes, I can see how the fibreglass could have worked enough to allow a leak. The foot end of our bed is wet too.' I said. 'I noticed some dampness there last night and I thought it was just condensation or a trickle from the dinghy while it was stowed down here.'

'It would appear to be more than that.'

Although the leaks had happened only the day before, already the area was starting to smell stale and mildewy. I mopped out the wet lockers and after, Ian drilled limber holes so that if the same thing happened again, the water would drain into the bilge from where it could be pumped out. I tried to dry out the Christmas presents while Ian stripped and washed the generator in fresh water. The relatively new generator never again ran as smoothly as before its dunking, but it did work for many more years.

Later on Christmas Eve, we motored to Gravelly Beach Marina, still some miles from Launceston, and picked up the mooring we'd booked before we left home. That was where *Realitas* would stay while we were ashore.

We phoned the Handlingers to announce our arrival and Mike drove up a couple of hours later to take us to their country property.

We enjoyed a wonderful reunion and Christmas with our close friends. The children played well together and the remote-controlled car was a hit with all three boys.

Seven year old Aletta was more interested in her new kitten, but the boys had a great time. They spent hours on the trampoline too, and Jamie tried riding Aletta's pony. He might have had tight knuckles as he clung to the reins, but the grin on his face told us he thought it was very exciting to be riding so far off the ground. David wasn't game to try – he was still a somewhat timid little boy.

*Ian strips and rinses the generator*

After the New Year celebrations and when we were back on the boat, Ian had a surprise for us.

'I bought charts for the Furneaux and Kent groups of the Bass Strait Islands,' he said. 'I thought we might visit those islands before heading north again to Sydney.'

'The Furneaux Islands means Flinders and the smaller islands nearby, doesn't it?' When Ian nodded, I added, 'What a great idea.'

Our first stop was at East Kangaroo Island, a tiny boomerang shaped piece of land lying a short distance to the west of the southern end of Flinders Island. The seabed consisted of hard packed sand and sea grass and our anchor wouldn't dig in enough to hold the boat against the force of the strong south-westerly wind. 'I'll shackle the Danforth anchor and a few metres of chain in front of the plough,' said Ian. 'That should give a bit more holding power.

Fig. 4. Bass Strait Islands – Deal Island and Furneaux Group including Flinders Island (courtesy The Kent Group Museum)

I hope so, Ian. I'll look for a patch of bare sand. Remember how we've found it impossible to anchor in sea grass at Jervis Bay.'

I was steering while Ian stood at the bow, ready to drop the anchors. I found a patch of sand without sea grass and stopped *Realitas* over it while Ian dropped both of our anchors in tandem as I slowly backed off again. To our relief, they dug in and we were secure.

During the evening, we watched the crew of a Herreschoff Marco Polo yacht trying to anchor. Their vessel was high and narrow, catching the wind across the island. Eventually, the men brought out a huge fisherman's anchor.

'That should work,' exclaimed Ian. 'I don't want their boat drifting down upon us in the night.'

Their anchor didn't set, at least not on the first try. They tried to anchor in several locations, including directly upwind of us. At midnight, after two exhausting hours, the wind dropped a little and their anchor held at last. Ian was still sitting on the foredeck with a knife, ready to cut our anchor line should a sudden gust allow the other boat to drag down upon us. We went off to bed, feeling nearly as tired as we imagined the other crew to be. The next morning, we were still at anchor when they motored past us.

Ian looked out and waved as they passed.

'What have you got down there to hold you?' they called out as they passed by.

'An eighteen pound Danforth in tandem with a twenty-seven pound plough.' They shook their heads.

Before leaving the island, we paid a short visit to shore. The derelict buildings told of mutton birding expeditions. Old feathers and a remnant fishy odour of spilled blood permeated the sheds. Just as in the Foveaux Strait islands of New Zealand, mutton birding in Bass Strait is reserved for the indigenous peoples.

⚓

'I'd like to climb Mt. Strzelecki,' said Ian that night. 'Is anyone else interested?'

'I'd like to come,' I said. 'There should be a really good view out across the islands. What about you two, Jamie and David?'

'How high is it?' asked David.

'It's that hill you can see over there on the big island,' I told him.

'I think I can manage.'

'Okay, let's all go,' said Jamie.

After breakfast next day, we sailed the short distance across to Trousers Point on Flinders Island. This provided the best dinghy landing place for a trek up Mt. Strzelecki. A sign pointed us to the track which started only a few hundred metres from the shore and we took a little more than two hours of hard climbing to reach the top.

On the way up, the views across the straits were breathtakingly beautiful.

'I'm really keen to reach the top,' I said. 'If the view looks great down here, what will it be like from on the top?'

The tantalizing glimpses we'd seen across the strait and its many islands were all I'd anticipated. The boys were racing each other to the summit.

At the top, Ian said, 'Come on you lot. If you line up, I'll photograph you with the view of Bass Strait behind you.'

But seconds before he could push the shutter, a cloud obliterated the scene. Suddenly, we were cold.

We ate our picnic lunch quickly as swirls of damp mist encircled us and then we started climbing down out of the cloud. We were half-way down the mountain before we emerged into sunshine again.

I clearly remember the next day with its azure sky, the sun shining down upon clear turquoise water. We might have been in the tropics but for the sharp temperature of both air and water. Occasionally, we would see a seal lying on its back languidly signalling with a flipper.

'This only looks like a tropical sea. If there're seals in the water, it's too cold for me to wash on deck,' I said. 'I'm going to heat the kettle and bathe in the bathroom.'

Ian braved the elements, but the boys followed my example.

As we sailed north along the west coast of Flinders, Ian commented that we were passing Wybalenna, the remote mission station.

'That's where the last full-blood Tasmanian Aborigines, including Truganini, were secluded,' he said. 'Maybe the last of the full-blood Tasmanian Aborigines died in that lonely prison.'

Our location prompted me to reflect on the cruelty of the Australian white settlers to the Aborigines and the differences with the Maoris in New Zealand, who had fought valiantly for their rights.

In late afternoon, we entered Killiecrankie Bay, the home of Killiecrankie Diamonds, as the locals call their topaz. There was another cruising boat at anchor in the bay. The owners waved as we came in to anchor.

'Come over for a cup of tea when you're ready,' they called. Before our visit to them was over, a strong southerly change blew in.

'I think we're going to have to stay for a while longer,' I said.

'It's impossible to row an inflatable dinghy in forty plus knots of wind.' We'd left our outboard on deck.

We were able to return to *Realitas* once the gale blew itself out about an hour later. Being calmer next morning, we went ashore to see the tiny settlement which consisted of one general store, a small camping ground and the shed which housed the craft shop.

'Would you like me to open the craft store for you?' the lady in charge asked.

'Yes please,' I answered. I wanted to see some of this topaz.

Because we felt we should buy something for the woman's time and effort, Ian chose a tee shirt.

'If you need provisions, I can organise a taxi to take you to Whitemark,' the lady said.

'How far is that, and what's there?' I asked.

'Whitemark, it's about sixty kilometres down there. There are a hotel and a couple of shops,' she said.

We didn't need shops. Instead, we scrambled over the orange lichen-covered rocks, which surrounded the bay, hunting for our own Killiecrankie Diamonds. Needless to say, we didn't find any.

North-west of Flinders, we visited the Kent Group, going first to Deal Island and then to Erith.

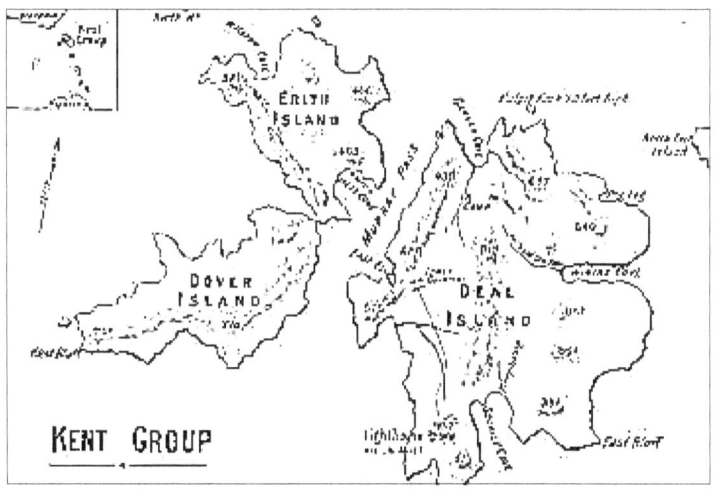

*Fig. 5. Kent Group (Map by* Field Naturalists Club of Victoria, Melbourne, 1890, copy courtesy Museum Victoria*)*

As we approached East Cove on Deal Island, Ian said, 'I need you on the bow, Jan. You're looking for the patches of bull kelp marked on the chart as "dangerous". This weed has thick, large dark green, leathery leaves which can mess up our propeller and also block our anchor from digging in.'

The cove is fairly deep and there were several Victorian yachts already at anchor, making it difficult to find somewhere safe to put *Realitas*. The deeper the water, the more swinging room the yacht requires. Ian was not one hundred percent happy with our anchoring, but we were going to be within sight of the yacht, so we went ashore.

The following is an extract from Wikipedia's entry on these islands:

*The Kent Group of Islands lies in Bass Strait, Australia, north-west of the Furneaux Group near Tasmania. They form the Kent Group National Park. The granite islands were named Kent's Group by Matthew Flinders, "in honour of my friend Captain William Kent, then commander of the Supply" when Flinders passed them on 8 February1798 in the Francis (on her way to salvage the Sydney Cove).*

*The largest island in the group is Deal Island; the others, in order of descending size, are Erith Island, Dover Island, North East Isle, South West Isle and Judgement Rocks.*

*Deal and Erith Islands have long been used by ships to shelter from gales in Bass Strait, but it is a dangerous, partly open, roadstead, and many ships have been wrecked after sudden changes in wind direction and speed.*

*(Rhys Jones, A Note on the Discovery of Stone Tools and a Stratified Prehistoric Site on King Island, Bass Strait.)*

During our visit, we climbed three hundred metres to the top of the lighthouse. Ian and I love looking out from the top of a lighthouse over a vast expanse of ocean. The waves and swell are miniaturised and the horizon seems a thousand miles afar. On a yacht, you are perhaps two metres above water level, and your horizon is usually about two to three sea miles in every direction. In bad weather, with rising waves and swell, you can feel hemmed in, with visibility limited to about twenty metres or even less when the boat drops to the bottom of the swell and maybe half a mile when you rise to the top.

Ian delights in chatting with lighthouse keepers. Theirs is a lonely job and they are happy to converse with any sailors who happen to drop by. Ian had been thinking of the weather reports for the area reported each day on the radio.

*The Lighthouse on Deal Island*

'When you do your reports on weather and sea state, how do you measure wave and swell height?' Ian asked.

The keeper looked a little taken aback. 'You get used to what it looks like,' he said. 'In other words, I give an educated guess.'

Ian had been hoping to hear about some sophisticated measuring device. However, not so many years later, wave-rider buoys came into use to measure the height of waves and swell. Digital and wireless technologies have brought huge changes to many aspects of our maritime environment in just a few years, including control of our lighthouses.

The Deal lighthouse has, like many others been made 'automatic', unfortunately with a lower output and a consequent reduction in light visible from sea. This reduction in the scope of the light is compounded, because no one has yet devised an automatic lens with a window cleaner to keep a clear light. Deal lighthouse was deactivated in 1992, in part because it was obscured by cloud a high proportion of the time. Despite GPS technology, which renders lighthouses less essential, they are still a wonderfully reassuring sight to me when I am on watch on a dark night.

Following our visit to the lighthouse on Deal, we moved across to West Cove on Erith.

'Let's go ashore this afternoon,' said Jamie.

'Yes, we intend to do that,' said Ian. 'After lunch.'

Ashore, we climbed up to a craggy ridge above the bay, where we found fascinating petrified remains. We were puzzled about what they were. My later reading suggests they might be part of the Petrified Forest found on King Island further to the west.

At a time of much lower sea levels, research shows that this forest extended along cliffs from King Island east-ward to Flinders Island which, at that time formed the southern coastline to mainland Australia.

As we were preparing to leave these wild, wind-swept islands, Ian showed me the chart. 'I'm planning to sail straight on north through the Murray Pass here,' he said, pointing to the pass marked on the chart between Erith and Deal islands. 'Of course, we'll have to wait for the north-going tide at 1800 hours.'

Never having adjusted to the twenty four hour clock, I made a mental calculation – 6.00 pm. 'Do you want an early dinner before we leave?' I asked

'Thanks. That would be good.'

Sailing with the tide, we set course to pass between the two main islands and went on to cross the remainder of Bass Strait – a gentle crossing with the wind astern, a clear sky and some moonlight. Bass Strait cruising had been beautiful, with bright sun-shine, sparkling blue seas and sky, but the cold penetrated everything, even though it was mid-summer.

The south-eastern corner of mainland Australia wasn't much better. When we stopped at Eden to top up on provisions and water and revisited the local museum, we were still cold.

Overnight, a front had moved up the NSW coast and we followed it, sailing through the night up the coast to Jervis Bay. Driving rain made the night cold and dark as I huddled in the cockpit for hours, because our course took us right to Georges Point. After our experiences with NSW currents in 1973, I didn't trust them. I couldn't sleep. I visualised *Realitas* crashing onto the rocks at Georges Point. Visibility was, at times, limited to about one boat length, and I peered forward into the black wetness, watching out for danger, but seeing nothing. I strained my ears for any unusual noise. We were navigating by compass, the log and the depth sounder and I hoped the depth sounder would give me warning of shallow water.

Just after daylight, we closed with land. As we sailed down into our favourite corner of Jervis Bay, the clouds cleared and the sun came out, and by late morning, I was lying, half asleep, on the beach, soaking up the sunlight, taking warmth right into my bones. What a contrast.

*Jan gets warm at Jervis Bay*

Once again, we enjoyed exploring the southern reaches of Jervis Bay. On a previous visit, I had discovered that the camping ground laundry had large tubs where I could hand wash our clothes. In the grounds, the owners fed the rosellas to encourage them to stay. There were hundreds of these gaily coloured small parrots nesting in the area and they were extraordinarily tame.

'Can I feed them please, Mum?' Jamie asked. He picked up some seed and stood very still, seed in his outstretched palms while several rosellas landed on his head and body, and then fed from his hands. A magic moment for him. Finding the tame birds was an unexpected bonus to our visit. More recently, we found that the birds were no longer prevalent.

'I think the campground must have changed hands,' I said to Ian. 'The rosellas have gone.'

*Jamie with the rosellas at Jervis Bay*

We left Jervis Bay when the weather was favourable and we had an almost uneventful passage home to Sydney. While we were sailing up the NSW coast, as we often did, I streamed a fishing line behind the boat. I was sitting in the cockpit enjoying the peacefulness of the sailing when I became aware of a fin keeping pace with our hull. Out at sea, I associated fins with dolphins, but this was no dolphin. They come in pods, frolicking and diving, racing and crisscrossing at the bow wave.

'I saw a shark while you were sleeping,' I told Ian, 'the only shark I have ever observed out at sea.'

'Maybe it was after a fish on your line. It wouldn't be the first time you haven't noticed one,' said Ian.

'There was another shark once in 1976 while we were anchored in the Caribbean. Do you remember I had a line over the side and caught a small shark?'

'How could I forget? You blunted both the filleting knife and the galley knife trying to cut through its skin.'

'Yes, well, that skin was like sand paper,' I said, 'but as I commented at the time, a shark wouldn't hesitate to eat me, so why shouldn't I eat shark?'

On that entire trip along the NSW coast, the only fish to take my lure was a small yellow fin tuna. I am allergic to tuna, but I had to fillet and cook that fish for the rest of my family. 'Yuck,' I said, 'I don't even like the smell of tuna!'

'You are the fishing non-expert in this crew,' said Ian. 'I abdicate any role in the matter of fishing, except to wield the net to bring a fish aboard.'

'I'll bet you'll eat some though,' I said.

I love eating most fresh fish, but I dislike killing a fish. I hate the way they writhe on the cockpit floor, with their mouths open in a silent scream. Even so, I force myself to do it for food. My attempts to kill the creature as humanely as possible usually end up making a mess of the job. However, the first taste of a newly cooked, freshly-caught fish is a delight that nothing from a shop or market can match.

Our long summer voyage to Tasmania and the Bass Strait islands ended as we sailed up the harbour, renewing my pleasure in the curved lines of the Opera House and the skyline piercing view of Centre Point Tower. We passed Circular Quay with the familiar green and yellow ferries, to slip under that famous coat-hanger of a bridge on the way up river to our mooring.

We'd had a wonderful, though mostly chilly summer, which left us with some very happy memories – arriving in the Tamar on time, Christmas with our best friends, magical islands, friendly rosellas and long, deserted beaches.

Ian had to return to work the next Monday, but I had a whole week to prepare the boys and me for a new school year.

# 6  Cruising in Local Waters

After our trip to Tasmania, we tried to take the boys cruising every summer. When Ian was promoted to head of his section at the Water Resources Department, he was able to dictate his holiday times.

The boys coped well with ocean passages provided they lasted only a few days. While we were at sea, they both tended to stay in their bunks reading. David never seemed to get seasick. Until he was tall enough to reach things in the galley, I used to provide him with a plastic box full of sandwiches, muesli bars, fruit etc. to keep him happy. During the first couple of days at sea, I was too seasick to provide food for anyone. Jamie took seasickness in his stride. He would eat a peanut butter sandwich, put his head into a book and about twenty minutes later, poke his head out and call to Ian.

'Bucket please, Dad.'

He'd vomit, hand the bucket to Ian for emptying overboard, and return to his reading. An hour later, he'd be hungry again. Ian would also be queasy, but he seldom threw up.

During 1986, most of our sailing was in local waters. Planning to sail to Broken Bay and Pittwater at Easter, we spent a weekend in early March on maintenance.

The pressure kerosene stove needed a thorough cleaning.

'A pressure kerosene stove might heat water and food more quickly, but it blackens the bottoms of my saucepans and kettle, the deck-head above the stove, and the skin under my fingernails.' I said to Ian. 'I'd like to go back to having a *Maxi* methylated spirit stove like we had on *Caprice*. It was so clean.'

Ian replaced the nipples and needles in the jets so that they burned more cleanly. That stove always had a tendency to smoke and I grew to greatly dislike it.

'You grumble about the stove,' said Ian. 'I need to go up the mast early tomorrow. The electrical contacts need cleaning and I need to install new globes for the tricolor and steaming lights. I don't like that job either. The boatswain's chair cuts off my circulation and it's very uncomfortable.

As they often did while we worked, the boys went off in the *Avon* dinghy, motoring in circles so they could jump over their' own wake. They could amuse themselves for a couple of hours or more doing this.

On Good Friday, we set off for Broken Bay. On the way up the harbour, we stopped briefly at Double Bay to see Ian's friend, Richard Cortis, who was working on his 24' Dufour, *Scallywag*. To our surprise, we found *Taria* was moored nearby.

'She looks so sad and neglected,' I said. 'It's over two years since we've set eyes on her.'

'She's been moored here for about six months,' said Richard. 'I haven't seen anyone on her during that time.'

The day-sail north was a pleasant affair for Ian and the boys. As usual, I was seasick until we entered calm waters again.

Those few days in Broken Bay we spent moving from one anchorage to another, exploring the area. When we sailed into Pittwater, we visited our friends, Nick and Ann Reeve, at their home in Little Lovett Bay. Nick and Ann had sailed their Golden Hind 31' yacht *Golden Opportunity* from England during the 1970s, with their two young sons aboard. We first met them in Tahiti and later at Rarotonga, the capital of the Cook Islands. English by birth, they had decided to bring up their boys, Tom and Rupert, in sunny Australia.

⚓

In May school holidays, we slipped *Realitas* at the Gladesville Bridge Marina again. Some factor about Five Dock Bay encouraged marine growth, we realised, because it wasn't yet a full year since the last slipping.

Ian worked long hours for four days so he could take a flexi-day from work on Friday. At high tide, he motored *Realitas* around the corner from our mooring in Five Dock Bay and drove the yacht into the semi-immersed cradle at the marina.

I drove the car, bringing scrubbers, overalls, sandpaper, paint and rollers. After we were tied on securely, the slipway workmen engaged the big winch and pulled *Realitas* out of the water, the cradle sliding up on its rails. Once the bow was securely supported, we started scraping off the marine growth, hosing down the underwater hull and sanding, preparing for new anti-foul paint. We applied the paint with rollers for the first time. What a change that made! The task of painting was so much faster, and we were able to apply the paint more evenly. Paint rollers had been around for a few years and I wondered why we'd been so slow to catch on. This whole procedure of cleaning and repainting the hull normally took us three days and two nights. We paid by the night, so it was prudent to get finished as quickly as possible.

Realitas *on the Gladesville Marina slipway*

'Oh dear, it's starting to rain,' said Ian on Sunday morning. 'Could you drive home and bring back two big tarpaulins and a packet of *Plasticine* please. If we don't protect this wet paint from the rain, it'll flake off when the boat's back in the water.'

Ian used the *Plasticine* to block the drain holes below the gunwales, in the vain hope we could stop runnels of water trickling down and spoiling the paint. It stopped most of the water, but there were still a few dribbles.

The following weekend, Ian's mate, Richard, invited us to meet him on the water.

'You really ought to have a radio on board, Ian,' Richard said.

'It's my choice not to have one,' said Ian.

'Why do we need one now?' I said. 'We didn't have one when we sailed around the world.'

'You've got two kids now. Is it their choice to be without communications? You've got a responsibility to them,' persisted Richard. 'You need a functioning VHF radio,' he insisted. 'That CB radio you have is just crap.'

Apart from his love of racing sailing, Richard was a radio 'nut'. He and Ian had studied engineering in the same class at Sydney University and remained friends over the years.

'I don't want to have a radio on while I'm sailing,' said Ian. 'It just makes a lot of racket.' Ian loved being on the water and sailing for the peace and quiet.

'You have a responsibility to your family to be able to call for help if needed.'

It was difficult to argue with Richard. He was a big man, used to getting his own way. If he said we needed a radio and he was prepared to install an old one of his, Ian decided to allow him to do this.

'Okay mate, you win.'

While the two of them installed the radio and checked its aerial, Richard's teenage son, Andrew, kept our boys occupied. Since he was two years old, Jamie had admired Andrew greatly. Five years older, Andrew was Jamie's first 'hero'.

During the spring school break, Ian took a few days off work, and we sailed to Broken Bay again, where we met up with Richard in *Scallywag*. This time, Dagmar, his wife, and their two daughters were also on board, as well as Andrew, who had sailed north with his father. Dagmar suffers intensely from seasickness and she refuses to go to sea. Instead, she and the girls drove to Brooklyn at Hawkesbury River, where Richard and Andrew picked them up.

⚓

Later in the year, we heard about the Coastal Cruising Club. I made phone contact with the secretary.

Would you like to join us at our next sailaway?' she asked. At the sailaway, we met like-minded people and, more importantly, the Walkers, a family with kids of a similar age to ours.

Joining this club changed the nature of our weekend sailing. The club provided company and new friends when we went out for the weekend. Later, the club changed its name to The Coastal Cruising Club of Australia (CCCA).

Realitas *rafted up at a CCC sailaway*

Ian and I still preferred to be more independent and disliked sailing in a group, though we were happy to join in happy hour and other activities when we reached the outing destination.

'Let's spend New Year's Eve on the harbour this year,' I said, and my family agreed it was a good idea.

On New Year's Eve, we took *Realitas* into Berry's Bay, just west of the harbour bridge, arriving early in the day to obtain a good spot.

'I think we should have a pretty good view from here,' said Ian. 'The breeze is supposed to stay westerly, so it will keep the smoke away from us.'

It was the first time we'd been able to have a close-up view of this spectacular event and I think I was as excited as the boys. We were all entranced during the 9.00 pm event. The night was clear and the view was superb. The spectacular display seemed to go on forever, even though it lasted only fifteen minutes. After it was over, we read stories to the kids and they went off to sleep. We soon followed them to bed, but Ian and I woke up at midnight and watched the second display too.

Fireworks were wreathing the bridge and streaking into the sky with reds, greens and yellows. At the same time, more crackers were exploding from barges, one east and one west of the Harbour Bridge and more still were shooting up above Darling Harbour; they lit up the city skyline in a manner seen only once a year.

⚓

In the middle of January 1987, we set off south again for our favourite spot in those days – Jervis Bay. We stopped at Store Beach near North Head for some sleep before heading out very early in the morning. The wind was so light from the east that we motored until the gauge showed the engine to be over-heating.

'I'm not going to deal with this out here, Jan. Let's get the MPS up and see if we can get some forward motion.'

'Okay. I'll bring the sail up,' I said.

The MPS or multi-purpose spinnaker was our latest addition to the sail wardrobe. Before long, we had it up and drawing.

'I like this sail,' I said. 'It is so much easier and faster to raise than the spinnaker. And you don't have poles flailing wildly on the foredeck as you try to get them set. So much safer.'

'Yes,' said Ian, 'and it can stay up longer as the wind swings. If I sheet it in hard, we can keep it up in light airs with the breeze from the stern quarter through to almost amid-ships.'

We sailed all day and well into the night to reach Point Perpendicular by midnight.

'Jan! Wake up.' Ian said.

'What is it?'

'We're dragging anchor.'

'Bother!'

Ian had anchored *Realitas* in four metres of water off Red Point, in the south-west corner of the bay. The big problem with anchoring in Jervis Bay at night is that you cannot see the patches of bare sand among the heavy sea grass beds. The anchor doesn't dig in properly through the sea grass. Being aware that a south-westerly change was due, we'd anchored in that corner of the bay. We re-anchored at the southern end of the bay, closer to Vincentia, and finally got some sleep.

The sound of a helicopter awoke us a couple of hours after daylight. I looked out the companionway.

'Come and look kids. The navy are practising rescue from a vessel. There's a man being lowered onto a barge.'

Soon, we were all in the cockpit gazing at this action. They were simulating a rescue with two men being winched together back into the helicopter. It was very entertaining to watch them though, just like me, Ian might have been wondering what it would feel like to be the rescued sailor.

Later, when the navy boats had moved away, Jamie, who was eleven by then, wanted to try spinnaker flying. Something about that naval exercise must have sparked the idea. David, two years younger, was keen to try too.

Ian threaded a piece of plastic pipe onto the sheet ropes for a hand hold and checked that the halyard was running freely.

*Ian tries out spinnaker flying while the boys wait for a turn*

'I'll try it first to make sure the handhold works,' said Ian as he allowed the wind to fill the spinnaker and take him out over the water. He wasn't going to let the boys have all the fun.

'My turn now,' insisted Jamie.

'Then mine,' said David. He happily took his turn too. As he'd grown older, he'd grown in confidence too.

When the best weather window arrived to sail north, Ian was suffering from a cold and sinus infection so we didn't leave then. Consequently, he was keen to go at the very next opportunity. The winds flickered about through south, south east and east. Finally there was favourable wind.

'Come on Dad, let's raise the spinnaker,' said Jamie.

'Okay, but you will help me,' said Ian.

Jamie did help raise the sail. Soon the wind was coming in too far abeam and problems arose, as Ian recorded in the logbook:

*Excitement with the spinnaker. So far, the ring dropped off the track and I managed to get it on again with only a few bits of skin missing. The lashings holding the pole downhaul block to the anchor winch came adrift (a puzzle) and the pole shot up vertical. The poles, rings and quarter blocks are all a bit light for this sort of running with the wind forward of the quarter.*

We sailed non-stop back to Sydney because we had a deadline for Ian's return to work. Apart from the early spinnaker difficulty, the voyage home to our mooring was uneventful and took about eighteen hours.

⚓

During Easter, 1987, we decided to visit Lake Macquarie, just south of Newcastle. We hadn't visited Lake Macquarie before this, most likely because of Ian's dislike of crossing sand bars, but we belonged to the CCC now and there was an Easter sailaway to the lake.

'Dad, can Evan come too?' asked Jamie. '

I suppose so, if it's okay with his mum,' said Ian. 'It isn't a long trip at sea. He can swim, can't he?'

'Of course he can. His mum won't mind if he comes.'

We always made sure whether our passengers could swim before taking them out to sea. Evan came with us and no one but me was seasick for the beautiful daysail up the coast. We departed late Friday afternoon, which meant the boys slept most of the trip.

Lake Macquarie is really an enormous salt water lagoon – the biggest in Australia – with a channel in from the ocean. Moon Island, which, marks the channel entry, lies at the southern end of the Newcastle Bight, a large shallow indentation in the coast-line.

Ian double checked Alan Lucas's sailing directions for the NSW coast and followed the instructions for timing a safe crossing of a sandbar at the entry to a channel. He waited for the tidal outflow to stop before we lowered the sails and motored in.

Once up the Swansea channel, we had to pick up a mooring and wait for the hour when the Swansea Bridge on the Pacific Highway would open. We finally came through at 10.00 am on Saturday morning.

We were amused to find Evan was quite agitated.

'When can we go to a shop?' he asked.

We were used to bringing with us everything we thought we'd need. Going to shops was not really on our agenda.

'Why do you need a shop?' said Ian.

'I need to buy a Mars bar and some Coke,' said Evan.

'He's got a caffeine and sugar addiction,' I said to Ian. 'How about that. And he's only eleven years old!'

Ian couldn't accept Evan's agitation, so he decided to motor around to Belmont to let Jamie and Evan go ashore. On the way, we had a surprise. I went below into the cabin for something and found Evan had unscrewed nearly all the bolts holding on the foreward hatch. I hurried back to the cockpit and took the tiller from Ian.

'Evan's taking the forehatch off,' I said. 'You've got to deal with it, Ian.'

'That kid's not coming on our boat ever again after this!' said Ian, as he went to rescue the forehatch.

Evan and Jamie went to the shops, and after his hit of caffeine, Evan settled down and we were all able to enjoy being on the lake.

We spent that night at the southern end of the lake, and woke wheezing, especially Evan, who was asthmatic. I could smell something unhealthy in the air and went outside to check.

'We're not anchoring near this power station again,' I said. 'Look at the smoke from those stacks that's been smothering us. I wonder why we didn't smell it last night? Erk!'

We raised anchor and moved away even before breakfast, going in search of the CCC members whom we knew were anchored at Wangi Wangi. There, we found a large, fairly sheltered bay alongside a small village.

There's an old fashioned quaintness here, I thought, when we went for a walk after lunch, amused by the barbers shop and the lolly shop. The rest of Easter passed relatively smoothly and we stayed several more days after the CCC sailaway was over. I suppose chocolate Easter eggs kept Evan's addiction satisfied.

After leaving the lake, we sailed south to Pittwater and stopped at the Basin, a very protected mooring area on the western shore. After a few days on board, we always enjoyed abrisk walk up the hill overlooking the camping area.

The boys raced each other up the hill.

'Mum, Dad, there's a small dam up here. Can we go for a swim in it?'

'No, you can't,' said Ian. 'That will be the fresh water supply for the camping ground at the Basin.'

The boys were a bit aggrieved, but we persuaded them they shoudn't climb in.

We sailed back home on Thursday, with a minor drama just inside the harbour. Off Bradley's Head, halfway from the heads to the bridge, Ian noticed a diesel leak from the hose connection to the diesel pump. He tried to tighten the bolt but in doing so, he stripped the thread and diesel spurted over Ian's waterproof clothing. He had to turn off the engine yet there was no wind to sail.

'What are we going to do now?' I asked my diesel drenched husband. 'Will we have to anchor while you try to fix the join?'

'I can't fix it now,' said Ian. 'I need special parts and tools that I haven't got on board.'

'Oh. How are we going to get back to our mooring then? Will the dinghy and outboard tow the boat?'

'No. I think it will work better if we tie the dinghy and outboard alongside and Jamie can keep the outboard steady while I steer the yacht from the cockpit.'

Ian and I took the dinghy off the deck and tied it bow and stern alongside *Realitas*. Eager for this new experience, Jamie climbed down and, after Ian had started the dinghy and given him a fixed angle to steer, Ian returned to the cockpit.

While the outboard on the dinghy provided the propulsion, Ian controlled the direction we travelled with the tiller.

'Hey, that works really well,' I said as *Realitas* began moving up the harbour at about two and a half knots. 'How did you know that would work?'

Ian shrugged. It seems he instictively knows stuff that is beyond me.

As soon as possible, Ian purchased the necessary items to fix the fuel hose attachment and he checked out the temperature gauge, sensor and sender as well.

Getting away for weekends and holidays on *Realitas* was our only escape from the pressures of modern city life. Without this time on the yacht, I think our family would have fallen apart. Certainly, Ian would have lost his sanity. At times, I did. Five years of full-time high school teaching and trying to be a super-mum took a huge toll on me. I was permanently stressed and angry. I gave up my "self" to our dream of owning both a house and a yacht so that we could afford the lifestyle of cruising that we had dreamed for years. Everything in our lives became more important than my personal needs, my selfhood. All my creative interests in photography, writing, study, travel, health, sewing and friendships were subjugated to our needs as a family, and that included making enough money to pay our bills.

When the helmswoman of our family wasn't happy, then no one else was either.

⚓

One day when Ian was checking under the house, he discovered that some of the timbers under the floor of our bathroom and behind the shower were becoming damp. We both feared rot setting in, so I decided to renovate the bathroom. Apart from the statutory holidays for Christmas and New Year, Ian didn't have time off in January 1987.

While he was at work, I used the back of an axe to break up the bricks which formed the base of shower cubicle and removed the tiles. When I had exposed the pipe-work, Ian could see how damp the timbers were.

On the second weekend of January, Ian applied *Everdure,* two-pot epoxy, to the timber below the shower taps, to protect them from dry rot.

Within days, I became ill with "acute inflammatory polyarthritis" -- a fancy way of describing what I already knew: many of my joints were swollen and inflamed. Being chemically sensitive, perhaps I should not have been sleeping in the house.

My GP referred me to a rheumatologist and for treatment; he offered frequent injections of cortisone or gold, which I rejected outright. Gold sounded expensive and I had seen what long term treatments with corticosteroids had done to my aging mother. The rheumatologist was somewhat put out that I refused to have his injections.

'I've already injected three people this morning,' he protested, as if that should persuade me.

'If you went out onto the street this morning and shot three people, would that make it okay for you to shoot me too?' I asked.

I managed to continue teaching at Cheltenham Girls High for the first term of 1987, but it was becoming an increasing struggle. When I began to develop panic attacks before going to school in the morning, I knew it was time to take a long period of sick leave. To prolong that time off-duty, I took much of it on half pay. Finally, when my leave was all gone and I still wasn't fit enough to return to full-time work, I had to resign.

What were we going to do without my second income? The mortgage needed to be paid whether or not I was sick, so I registered for casual relief teaching again. The occasional day's pay helped enormously. I also applied to work at the local TAFE college (Technical and Further Education) for part time teaching in the following year's Higher School Certificate program.

Following advice from a naturopath, I kept a food diary and then modified my diet by removing items that aggravated the joint inflammation. My well-being only slowly improved.

Our sons learned important lessons from what happened during those formative years. Today, Ian wonders why neither of them is in full time work. It is obvious to me they have learned that mental health and family come before striving for material things. They are now both playing a very active role in raising their children and teaching them not only about sailing, but all aspects of their lives.

In particular, Jamie and Lisa live aboard their forty-five foot vessel and are planning to home school their two children as they reach school age.

At a Coastal Cruising Club meeting in early spring, Bruce Walker told Ian and me he was planning on sailing with his family to Lord Howe in the summer holidays of 1987/88.

'Why don't we go too, Ian?' I said. 'I think my health has improved enough to manage a short voyage.'

'I don't see why not,' said Ian. And so it was decided.

On the way home, I said, 'I want to climb Mt. Gower to prove that rheumatologist wrong. I want to show him that diet can improve my inflammatory joint condition better than his injections.'

'Just eat a normal diet,' he'd advised. 'You will have to get used to the idea you could be in a wheel-chair for the rest of your life.'

On that score, I was determined to prove him wrong.

# 7  Lord Howe Island at Last

Ian and I had set out to sail from Sydney to Lord Howe Island in August 1973. Fourteen years and four months later, on New Year's Day 1988, we finally stepped ashore at the island.

Waiting at the launching ramp to greet us when we stepped ashore was Bruce Walker, self-acclaimed owner of the slowest cruising boat in the Coastal Cruising Club. Bruce had noticed that we were on board already when he motored *Aragunnu* down the Parramatta River. He had been listening to our radio calls and then watched as our sails could be seen nearing the island.

'Welcome to Lord Howe,' Bruce greeted us. 'What took you so long?'

'Maybe *Aragunnu* is no longer the slowest yacht in the club!' I said.

'There is the small matter of currents around this island,' said Ian, 'though perhaps we should award ourselves the title of slowest cruising couple. We did originally set out in 1973!'

Of course, when we eventually sailed into Lord Howe, it was aboard a different yacht and the crew size was twice that we'd originally started with. Actual sailing time this trip was five and a half days. I think Bruce was rather chuffed to find that his smaller, "slow" *Aragunnu* had made a faster passage than we had on this most recent voyage. Of all the club members at that time, we were the only ones to have completed a world circumnavigation.

The Walkers had departed Five Dock Bay about 20 hours before the Mitchells did on *Realitas* and managed to get themselves moored in the lagoon a day and a half ahead of us.

'The Citation 34 over there close to Dawson Point is *Elke*, with Helmut, John and Sandy aboard. They're all school counsellors – friends of mine,' said Bruce. 'We've all decided to climb Mount Eliza this afternoon and then walk around the cliff top. Do the Mitchells want to join us?' We all nodded in agreement.

'That's decided then,' said Bruce.

That afternoon, we all climbed the smallest of the three

mountains on the island. We could see across the lagoon to Mounts Gower and Lidgbird, and when we came along the cliffs, we could also see the offshore Admiralty Islands which are bird sanctuaries.

*Looking south from Mt. Eliza towards Mts Lidgbird and Gower*

The crews of all three yachts decided to eat together that first evening but although our meal was quite expensive, we departed the table still hungry. Despite that, the setting was very pleasant and we enjoyed the company. We had to remind ourselves that it was New Year's Eve and we were lucky to find a place willing to serve us at all.

That meal proved to be the only slightly negative note in a wonderfully relaxing, thoroughly enjoyable stay on the Island. By comparison, our next experience of eating out was at the Milky Way Friday Night Fish Bake, where we ate our fill for a very modest price.

There is a magic about islands that is absent at other holiday locations. Perhaps that magic lies in the fact that one is separated from normal daily life by sea and air. One cannot simply get into a car or even onto a train to return home; one must sail or fly. Our two weeks on Lord Howe were the best part of one of the best holidays the Mitchell family has enjoyed together. Amid clear skies, crystal water and magnificent views, we spent much of our time bushwalking or swimming. Mountain climbing, hand-line fishing, swimming, snorkeling over coral, hand-feeding fish and bird watching were also on our agenda.

According to the tourist brochure, there are 130 varieties of resident and migratory birds on the island. We were fascinated by how close we were able to approach various nesting sea birds. One bird that fascinated me was the white tern or noddy. On Lord Howe, it 'nests' on a near horizontal tree branch. Many of these 'nests' are on branches that overhang the road.

*White tern and chick on a bare branch6*

*"The White Tern lays only one egg on the bare branch. Incubation lasts 34-36 days shared by both parents. The chick is white and has strong claws which allow it to cling to the branch. It is regularly fed, and for two months more after fledging, which occurs about 48 days a after hatching.' (Wikipedia. Wiki commons).*

Our boys and the Walker's three children had lots of fun dinghy riding in the lagoon and surfing their boogie boards on the eastern beaches. There seemed to be something different to do every day.

Jamie and David also counted as among the more memorable events a flight Ian shouted them out to ball's Pyramid, but swinging on the banyan vines in the Valley of Shadows was their all-time favourite activity.

David was no longer physically timid and he loved jumping onto those hanging roots. Banyans are large fig trees and it was their long aerial 'props' that the children swung on. These grow down until they reach the earth and become part of the root system, the section above ground gradually forming into another trunk. In this manner the figs spread until they form a forest.

*Valley of the Shadows: David swinging on the Banyan Vines. Jamie below, watching.*

Throughout our stay, the weather remained clear and pleasantly warm, although the easterly wind sometimes increased to 30 or 35 knots in gusts across the lagoon. The motion of the boat was not always comfortable, especially if the gusty conditions coincided with a south-westerly swell which rolled over the reef at high tide.

'I want off the boat today – sooner rather than later please. I'm already starting to feel queasy,' I said to Ian one morning, as the boat lurched again with the swell coming over the reef. I was already bustling about packing up food for lunch and the other items we'd need – towels, sunscreen, camera and water bottles.

'I'm just about to lower the dinghy into the water,' said Ian and within half an hour, we were in the dinghy bouncing our way shoreward. We met up with the Walkers again.

'You know, at first I thought the mooring fee seemed fairly steep,' I said, 'but it's a tiny price compared with on-shore accommodation. When the fee covers garbage disposal, clean toilets, hot showers, limited fresh water and a sink where it was possible to do one's laundry, it's not really so bad.'

'It is part of their tourist income. The other thing is bicycles. It seems there is quite a business in renting those to tourists,' said Ian.

'Yes, there is, but in peak tourist season, bicycles are reserved for the tourists in the lodges and not available to yachties,' said Bruce's wife, Cynthia.

'That's no great bother,' I said. 'The main beaches, the shops, post office, weather station and museum are all within a pleasant thirty minute walk from the jetty.'

'Besides,' added Ian, 'the roads are tar-sealed so the few vehicles on the island don't raise any dust.'

Aragunnu *leaves LHI. Bruce on foredeck and Walker children in cockpit*

The Walkers, who had been to Lord Howe before, stayed at the island only one week. Prior to their departure, our two families visited the meteorological station. This was the best way to obtain a glimpse of the weather forecast for the following few days.

When the Walkers departed, motoring through the north channel, Jamie stated in surprised tones, 'Her motor sounds like a Harley Davidson!'

Bruce had installed a marinised Chinese Dong Feng engine, which was originally designed as a tractor engine and he was very proud of the marinised version he had purchased new. He wasn't impressed when Ian later reported to him our son's comment.

Posters about up-coming events on the island were placed on the hall door. One day, we noticed that there was to be a guided climb up Mount Gower the next day.

'We've got to sign up for that, Ian.' I said. The mountain is 865m, quite steep and tourists are not allowed to climb without a guide.

'Don't let on to the guide how sick I've been this year, please. I'm determined to climb that mountain,' I said.

The ascent was a massive effort for me, but I had a lot to prove. The climbing party gathered at Little Island (a large rock on the shoreline at the southern end of the reef) at 9.00 a.m. Four hours later, after a lot of hard climbing, some of it with ropes, we emerged at the summit.

'Hey, I made it.' I grinned with satisfaction as I looked at my family standing on this secluded mountain top. 'The hard effort was worth it, eh? I need someone to take a photo of me up here, please. That rheumatologist told me nine months ago that I'd never walk properly again and now I've climbed a mountain!'

Unfortunately, I seem to have lost that treasured photo.

I had been doubtful of my ability to manage such a mountain climb using ropes, but there I was on top of Mt. Gower, where we shared our lunch with the resident wood hens, until some rats stole their portion.

After my initial impression of a damp, humus smelling area, the mountaintop cloud conveniently cleared to expose a magnificently panoramic view of the entire island. We took photographs, explored the flora and signed the climbers' book before our guide, Ray, indicated it was time to begin our descent.

As I feared, the roped sections were scarier going down than up, but by 5.00 pm, without accident we were back at the shore, feeling both weary and exhilarated at the same time.

*David descending Mt. Gower*

The fifty minute dinghy ride across the lagoon each way made it a long day, but we wouldn't have missed it. I felt deep satisfaction at having managed that climb successfully.

Another day, we rode the dinghy those eight miles back to Little Island. This, we found, was the best place on the island to snorkel. It is amazing to me now that I had never learned to snorkel earlier, and that in 1976, Ian and I had not explored any of the coral reefs in the West Indies.

For our visit to Lord Howe, Ian had purchased a see-through bucket for me. If he'd had the time, I am sure he could have made one. It was a normal plastic bucket with its bottom removed and a circular piece of *Perspex* stuck into its place with silicone. While the others donned masks and snorkels, I floated about on the surface looking through the bucket. What I could see was absolutely tantalizing.

There was a magical, colourful world beneath the surface of that water and I wanted to see it properly. Never mind that I'd had a fear of putting my face in water ever since my brother had held me under almost too long when we were children.

David came out of the water, looking cold. I saw my chance to try a mask.

'David, you're shivering. Wrap yourself in a towel from there on the rock, and lend me your mask and snorkel please.'

I fitted the mask over my face and swam off. After looking down once, I was hooked. Snorkeling over coral was the most exciting visual activity I had ever experienced- better even than those warm, moonlit nights when we sailed downwind across the ocean that sparkled with starlight and bioluminescence.

'Now I know what I've been missing!' I said when Ian and Jamie emerged from the water.

I was reluctant to leave, but I had no wetsuit and I was shivering violently. Ian wrapped a towel around my shaking body, helping to dry me off. I put on my nylon spray jacket and we set off in the dinghy back to *Realitas*. By the time we had traversed those eight kilometres and reached the yacht, I was suffering from hypothermia. I was no longer shivering, just very, very cold.

'Give me your hand, Mum.' Jamie helped me over the rail into the cockpit.

Ian tied up the dinghy, then came aboard and stripped off my wet bathers for me, and wrapped me in a down sleeping bag. Several hours later, my body temperature returned to normal, but I was shocked how quickly hypothermia had taken hold.

⚓

We departed Lord Howe Island with a 35 knot easterly on our stern and rising seas.

'I'm going to set the course for Port Stephens, Jan. I thought we might stop there for a few days,' said Ian. 'What do you think about doing that?'

'It sounds good to me,' I said. 'That also gives us the advantage of allowing for southerly currents. Do you think the westerly current we experienced on the way out might still be running? It would be a great boost if it were.'

However, in the perverse nature of currents around Lord Howe, the favourable current had gone, possibly affected by Cyclone Aggie, which was centred somewhere near Noumea and there was another weather disturbance off Brisbane.

Consequently, the seas were moderately rough and the weather conditions overcast and gusty. When the wind backed to the S.W. and increased, we lay to for several hours for the skipper to rest. It was only on the fourth day, as we approached the coast that the wind and seas moderated to what we would call reasonable cruising conditions.

The bucketing, corkscrewing motion had me very sick again. After three weeks on board, I had not expected to
be sick on the return voyage.

When we had departed Sydney, it seemed my family expected it of me. At dinner the night before we set sail, David looked at his vegetable stew, a dish he's often rejected, and made his declaration.

'I'm going to eat all of mine. We mightn't get another hot dinner for a few days if Mummy's seasick.'

Needless to say, he retained an excellent appetite all the time at sea, while the remainder of the crew experienced queasiness. None of my usual remedies had worked this trip, and it was not until the fourth day at sea that I gained my sea legs. By then, we were already in sight of the mainland. After a close examination of the chart, we decided to put into Esmeralda Cove on Broughton Island, rather than Port Stephens itself.

Realitas *at anchor in Esmerelda Cove, Broughton Island*

A really sheltered anchorage was impossible because of all the moorings, so we picked up a vacant one then went ashore to meet the locals who were holidaying in huts and tents near the beach. Ian approached one man outside his holiday shack.

'Is it okay to use that mooring for a while, Mate?' '

'She's right. That bloke's not out here at the moment, so you can stay there as long as you want.' We spent two lazy days rambling over the island and beachcombing. Swimming seemed a little chilly after the warmth of the lagoon at Lord Howe.

A gusty cold front was predicted and duly arrived, so we decided to drop the mooring the following morning in hope of a gentle south-easterly breeze by which to sail home. We duly set off about 7.00 am under motor in a dead calm. The breeze, when it finally did come, was about 5 knots dead ahead so we motored on and seventeen hours later, dropped anchor in Manly Cove. It was almost Saturday, 23rd January, 1988. We were in time for the Bicentenary weekend festivities on the harbour.

'That was the best holiday ever,' said Jamie, who was now twelve.

'I had a really good time too – Just the bestest,' said David.

'But getting there and back again - that's as boring as cutting your toenails,' Jamie declared. 'I really liked the trip home on the catamaran though.'

The owner of a large cat had invited both boys to sail on his boat from Broughton Island back to Sydney and they had both loved that experience. He let them steer – his boat had a wheel in a very sheltered cockpit. Maybe David's current love of multihulls was initiated that day?

For Ian and me, it was wonderful to have been to Lord Howe Island at last and even though I didn't expect a rough passage and seasickness on the way home, it was still all good.

⚓

The Australian bicentennial celebrations of January 1988 were centred on Sydney Harbour. There was a re-enactment of the landing by Captain Cook as well as the arrival of a fleet of tall ships.

We contacted Horst and Tilly, who came down to Manly with Anja and Paul, to join us on board *Realitas*. Together, we sailed out of the heads we'd entered only a couple of days before. This time, we turned south, but only for a short distance. The tall ships were already nearly upon us. What a thrill to turn about and sail back into the harbour in their company. With eight people on board, and boats everywhere, my job was to be bow-lookout in those churning waters.

'Ian, did you see that fellow in a kayak sweep past our bow with about two metres to spare?' I asked Ian.

'Do you mean that little orange one over there? What's the fool doing out here? Does he want to drown himself?'

*Tall ship outside Sydney Heads, Australia Day 1988*

We followed the ships right into the harbour. The waterways boats and staff were kept very busy guiding boats away from areas restricted for those vessels taking part in the action. We managed to anchor in a spot that gave us a reasonable view of the proceedings.

'This is a very good place to be,' said Tilly, and Horst nodded in agreement. 'Now we are stopped, how about some wine?'

She pulled out a bottle from her picnic basket and handed it to Horst, while I went to the galley for glasses. We sipped our wine and ate lunch while we watched the entertainment and the other people and boats crowded onto the harbour. There were water displays from the fire tugs, a race by the old ladies of Sydney's ferry fleet, a parade of dressed ships and other excitement.

The evening's official festivities culminated with the 9.00 pm fireworks display. Outside of China, Sydney has the most expert pyro technicians in the world. The displays they engineer are always magnificent and this one was no exception

Many boat crews stayed on partying, waiting for the second fireworks display at midnight. Unlike the previous year's display we had watched on the harbour, this night some of the smoke drifted over us but that hardly dampened our exhilaration.

Blooms of red and white lights filled the sky, rockets whistled heavenwards, to burst into showers of multi-coloured sparks, and a waterfall of white light flowed off the harbour bridge into the water below. There were special effects over the top of the bridge and Opera House too.

After that magnificent performance, those with children aboard pulled up their anchors and moved off. This was another rather hair-raising effort, because so many motor boats were not displaying lights. Most people had been drinking alcohol and, unlike Ian, many skippers had drunk too much. Under motor, cautiously we wended our way back towards Manly, where we were to drop Horst, Tilly and their children ashore.

'Thank you very much for a wonderful day,' Tilly said, hugging me before she climbed into the dinghy.

Horst gave me a peck on the cheek. 'This was a very good day,' he said.

I helped Anja and Paul over the rail into the dinghy with their parents. Soon, it was very quiet. Our boys dropped into their bunks and fell fast asleep without any squabbles. When Ian returned from shore and we had secured the dinghy with double lines and checked that our anchor lights were showing at the top of the mast as well as on the bow and stern, we too went to bed, tired, but very relaxed and happy.

'What a wonderful summer holiday we've all had,' I said to Ian just before we fell asleep.

The next morning we sailed back up the harbour to Five Dock Bay and our mooring.

'Have you noticed how little rubbish is left? ' said Ian.

'That's really gratifying considering the number of boats that were out. Maybe at last people are getting the message about littering.'

For such a large crowd on the harbour, that was remarkable. Civic pride in the European history of Australia had made its mark on this Bicentennial Australia Day celebration.

Aboriginal disgust at such a celebration of the loss of their lands was barely mentioned on the news.

# 8  Voyage across the Tasman

We sailed to New Zealand in December 1988, the year Jamie completed his first year of high school and David was in year five at Normanhurst Primary School. I had wanted to take a week off work in February of 1986, to attend the wedding of my youngest brother. My application for leave was refused. I felt aggrieved. I would have been eligible for family leave by that time, except that the rules had been changed since I began full time teaching for the NSW Department of Education. It was years since I had spent Christmas in New Zealand.

'Ian, I want to be with all of my family this Christmas. Since we can't afford for all of us to fly to New Zealand, why don't we sail across the Tasman?'

'I'll think about it and make a list of what we'd need to do in preparation.'

'Good idea. Thanks,' I said.

Ian assessed what tasks were required to prepare *Realitas* for such a voyage and agreed that we should sail, leaving at the beginning of December. This was nearly three weeks earlier than primary schools ended for the year and two weeks earlier than high schools finished.

During 1988, with my health much improved, I had picked up casual work at the local TAFE College, teaching two Higher School Certificate classes in English. My teaching duties for the year were over when my students left towards the end of October, and began their HSC exams in early November.

Our kids were happy to miss the last few weeks of their school term, so early December was a good time to depart.

'They'll learn more coming to New Zealand than they will in school at this time of the year,' said Ian.

'I heartily agree. We need to do something about the water tank though. I don't want that fibreglass taste anymore.'

'I don't think I've got time to epoxy the tank,' said Ian. 'Work's pretty busy right now and I've other things to think about. Maybe there's a paint product you could use?'

We checked in the chandlery catalogue and found that the New Zealand company *Epiglass* made a product called "O and T" (standing for odourless and tasteless) for water tanks. We decided to try using it.

During November, I spent many days down at Five Dock Bay preparing and painting the water tanks. I checked and double checked with the paint company via the telephone help-line, that I was doing everything right. I checked with Ian too.

'You know, I rang the *Epiglass* help-line again today and the person I spoke to gave me slightly different advice than I received last time.'

'If you're following the instructions, I'm sure it'll work fine,' said Ian.

'But I opened the *O and T* paint today. It looked and smelled foul, so I put the lid back on and came home to call them yet again. It's a yicky brown colour. When I told them, they said that's how it's supposed to look.'

'Well just put it on if that's what they said.'

'Okay.' I sighed. 'So much for odourless and tasteless! I hope they mean when the paint has dried.'

Ian had more things to think about than the tasks I had set for myself. The next day, I went back and painted the interior of the two water tanks, leaving them to air dry. Three days later, I was back to apply the next coat and three or four days later, recoated the surface again - exactly according to the instructions. When all was finished and dry, I still had misgivings. Certainly the surface was dry, but the paint underneath was still soft. I had followed every instruction, so we screwed down the lids and filled the tanks.

As usual for our summer holidays, I had the boat fully provisioned by the weekend before we were due to leave. Just the fresh fruit and vegies, eggs and bread had to go on board with us and our clothes. Over the years, despite my philosophy of equal opportunity, Ian's technical superiority meant he looked after the tools, engine, spares etc., and I did the water, food and clothing.

Since I also cook faster and more efficiently in terms of utensils used, it didn't take long for Ian to suggest that if I fed everyone, he and the boys would do the cleaning up. I quite enjoy cooking, but dislike washing up, so I was easily persuaded to follow this pattern.

While they washed up, I read aloud to them. The boys enjoyed this and each sailing holiday, we would choose a novel to read aloud. Even now, as adults, they spend time reading aloud to their partners and their children.

Two days later than our planned departure time, on the first day of December 1988, we sailed to Watsons Bay near Sydney Heads for our final clearance from Customs and Immigration. Much of the paper work had already been completed when I visited the Customs House in York Street in the city during the days before our departure. In the shipping office at Watsons Bay, our passports were stamped and we were free to sail out of Sydney Harbour. I also collected the cameras I had bought duty free for the children for Christmas.

It seemed that *Realitas* was rearing to go as much as we were. We were all excited to be setting off on a trans-Tasman crossing. Ian set a course for Cook Strait. With the wind just east of north, fully laden as she was, *Realitas* seemed to gallop away from the coast at 7 - 8 knots. With a little help from some current, we covered 180 nautical miles in those first twenty-four hours!

The wind remained north- east, coming over our port bow for the next three days before easing to the beam. Just like the pilot charts had shown, December was the right time to go east across the Tasman.

This longer voyage created a challenge for me: I had to find ways to keep the children occupied on board. Jamie had just turned 13 and David was 11. Jamie had always been an avid reader, David more reluctant. It was a gamble trying to get books that would appeal to David's zany sense of humour and that would keep him interested for more than a few minutes.

Later, we finally found that the reason he had trouble with reading was that he had a large degree of astigmatism in his eyes, but despite many consultations with the optician and also an eye specialist doctor, we were unaware, at this stage, of his difficulty being any more than slight short sightedness and a problem with concentration. I knew David liked Roald Dahl's sense of humour and his children's stories. I took the adults stories along as well.

David also had some Lego with him. I had given Jamie a harmonica for his thirteenth birthday in November and he was making excellent progress in playing it, even reading simple music scores. Also, he happily chose his own books and was busy reading the first of them when we set off.

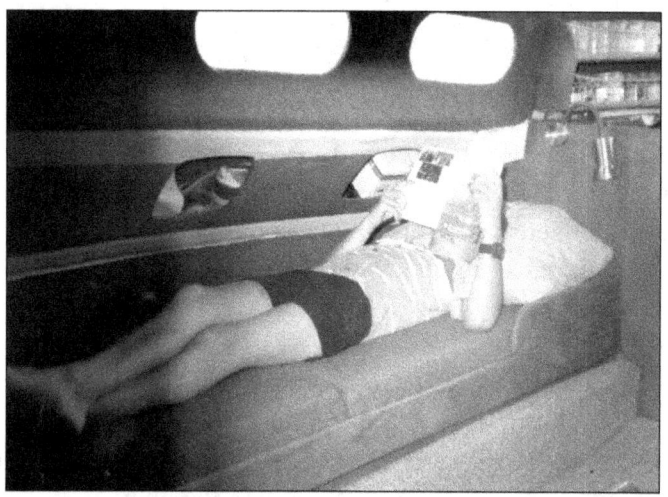

*Jamie reading in his bunk*

We were all settling down to life at sea and falling into the rhythm of the boat and sailing, when we faced a serious problem. Only two days after our departure, I realised that the brown flakes coming through the galley tap which looked like tea leaves, were probably sticky flakes of paint.

'Look at these flakes, Ian. It has to be the O and T paint coming off the inside of the tank.'

'I don't think we can continue to use this water pump, 'It is going to become gummed up if much more paint flakes off.'

Obviously the problem was the product I had recently used to coat the water tank. Despite my best efforts, the stuff was coming off in sheets and breaking up inside the tank. We held a family conference about what we should do.

'Do you think we need to turn back, Jan?' Ian asked.

'I don't want to do that. We've made really good progress so far,' I said.

'Don't turn back, Dad. How much other water have we got?' asked Jamie.

A good point, Jamie,' said Ian. 'Let's measure how much other water there is, apart from the main tank. We need to estimate the risk of running out.'

'We're already more than 200 nm off shore,' I said. 'We're all over our initial seasickness and starting to really enjoy the voyage. Let's check how much uncontaminated water there is and then decide if it's safe to go on.'

We had a fifty litre flexible tank of water supplying the bathroom basin and a further thirty litres in two fifteen litre jerry cans in the cockpit locker. There was also the chance of some rain en route.

'It will be tight, but I think we can carry on. We must restrict our fresh water usage,' Ian told us.

'We'll need to save the bathroom water for drinking and use salt water for cleaning our teeth and for washing ourselves. Jan, can you use half salt water and half fresh when you're cooking? '

'No problem. I won't need to add cooking salt. We do have some other liquids for drinking too - packets of UHT milk and juice. I won't use the dried peas and beans that require rehydration,' I said. 'And there's water in our canned fruit and vegies, soups and jars of preserved meat. There's also moisture in the fresh fruit and vegies.' We had plenty of those.

Just over half way across the Tasman, the wind came round to the north, turned light, and then dropped off altogether. The temperature rose, and by early afternoon it was a hot sunny day.

'We're not going anywhere. How about a dip over the side?' suggested Ian. 'I'm going in.'

Ian stripped off and jumped in.

'Don't swim too far from the boat,' I said. 'If the wind comes back suddenly, I want you on board.'

When Ian came back, I was in my bathers ready to go over the rail. I didn't like the idea of swimming nude in front of the boys. Once I was standing there looking down into the water, I had second thoughts about swimming. The blue seemed to go down for ever. Maybe five thousand metres - that seemed like an abyss because I couldn't see the bottom. I jumped in cautiously and immediately grabbed hold of the side of the boat, finding it really difficult to make myself let go. Rationally, I knew I was being stupid, but I couldn't make myself swim free. When I swim mid-ocean, I am extremely aware of the depth below me. If I look down, the blue continues until it is swallowed by blackness.

David passed my shampoo to me and I washed my hair, ducked under the water long enough to rinse it clean of soap, then I was back on deck, toweling off.

'Your turn boys,' said Ian.

'I'm not sure I want to,' said Jamie.

'Why not?' asked Ian. 'Tell you what, you can go over with a line around your waist and I'll attach it to the stern cleat. Will that make you feel more secure?'

Jamie was persuaded, but not David. After my display of caution, I wasn't surprised. I don't understand why swimming in the open ocean is so intimidating. It should be like swimming in a salt water pool beside the beach; the only difference being that you cannot see the sandy bottom.

The very warm, calm day was the prelude to a southerly change. When the front passed over us, it brought some welcome rain. As it began to rain, Ian said, 'Who's going to be first into the cockpit for a fresh water shower?'

*Tethered to* Realitas, *Jamie floats on his back mid-ocean*

Of course, Ian was first. Instead of just washing himself, he dug into the locker for a couple of buckets to catch the water flowing off the end of the boom next to the mast.

I stripped in the forward cabin and wrapped in my towel, climbed outside past the canvas rain curtain hanging over the companionway. The rain water was colder than I anticipated, so my shower was very brief and, shivering, I returned to the shelter of the cabin where I stood dripping a puddle onto the floor from under my towel. The two boys didn't volunteer to get wet, and I decided not to push the issue.

After a few hours lying hove-to for the passage of that front, we were on our way again with an additional couple of buckets of water. It wasn't fresh enough for drinking because the sails and boom were salty, but it was excellent for a sponge bath and to rinse some clothes.

There was a downside to the rain. The companionway was damp from droplets blowing in and as I went to climb out into the cockpit, my hand slipped on the wet handhold. With the roll of the boat, my body was flung backwards, still upright, onto the support pole for the deck. I hit my lower spine. Ian heard my groan.

'What have you done to yourself?'

'I think I'm okay,' I answered, 'I don't think I've damaged anything. My hand slipped and maybe I've got a bruise.'

I was thankful that I hadn't fallen and that I was protected by the padding of my heavy wet weather coat and trousers. I
I thought no more about it until the next day, when I twisted slightly to enter the bathroom.

'Aaahhhh!'

'What's wrong, Mum?' asked Jamie.

'I can't move without it hurting. Ooooo!'

I was suddenly in agony from a pinched nerve, but I had to use the toilet. I screamed at every movement I made in that cramped space and I felt exhausted from the pain by the time I emerged. For about thirty-six hours, I couldn't lie down, and nor could I climb out into the cockpit. Every movement hurt. I placed a pillow over my stomach, and sat behind the table, laying my upper body over the cushion and onto the table in an attempt to gain some traction on my spine and ease the pain. Occasionally, I managed to sleep a little.

At times like that, I would have really appreciated a fridge on board so that I could have something cold on my back to reduce the inflammation. We didn't even have any oral anti-inflammatories in our medical kit. So long as I didn't move, the nerve didn't hurt. But that was impossible in a yacht that was continuing to sail towards the coast of New Zealand.

Two nights before we closed with the north-west coast of the South Island, I awoke to hear Ian talking on the VHF radio. At 2.00am, he had seen lights a few miles off, and called up the ship to check if they were aware of our position. After a little hesitation, a Scottish voice came over the air waves.

'How do I show upon your radar?' asked Ian.

'Ahhh, I see a light due north. Would that be your wee boat?'

After a few minutes of chat, the Scot said, 'I can see a blip on the radar. What do ye estimate your position to be?'

Ian reported the co-ordinates he had estimated for our position. The Scot wanted to chat on, especially about the difficulties of maintaining a marriage when he was away from home for such long periods. Ian listened to this for fifteen minutes before claiming that the radio was dropping out.

'What's going on, Ian?'

'I saw the ship's lights well up on the horizon. I just tried calling on VHF to see if anyone on board was awake.' Ian said. 'He didn't have the radar on. That first burst of chit chat was to fill in the time it took to start up the radar.'

'Sounds like they didn't know we were here,' I said.

'No, but they do now. I think the watch-keeper received a shock when he heard a voice on the VHF radio.'

We were also a bit taken aback, because with *Caprice*, when we sailed without navigation lights away from most shipping, any ships we did see changed course when they were about two miles off, which gave us the assurance that our radar reflector had been seen. Here, we were in a bigger yacht with a taller mast and with a bigger version of the radar reflector, and we weren't being seen because the watch keeper didn't have the ship's radar turned on. We were using our masthead navigation lights too. With a diesel engine in *Realitas*, we had more reliable battery charging than we'd had on *Caprice* with her 12 horsepower temperamental petrol engine, so we were able to carry lights all night.

The following night, about two hours after dark, we noticed a huge glow of light ahead.

'I think this has to be a cruise ship,' Ian said.

'That's about the only thing I can think of that'd have so many bright lights,' I said, looking out the cabin window.

Ian turned on the VHF radio, which sailors use for short distance, line of sight communication. He called on channel 16. There was no response. We left the radio on and also turned the HF radio to 2182 MHz. We could hear no traffic at all except for some voices speaking in an Asian language. Worldwide, radio traffic is supposed to be in English. As we came closer to the source of the lights, they seemed to stop and start, following an erratic course.

'This can't possibly be a cruise ship. The lights are too erratic. A cruise ship would be off over the horizon by now,' I said. 'They travel at fifteen to eighteen knots, don't they?'

'Even faster. These lights are a mystery to me,' said Ian.

Finally, the lights moved in one direction and we sailed past in another. We still had no inkling what these intense lights were about.

The next morning, the north-western most corner of the South Island was visible in the distance. The day dawned clear and bright, the light grey early morning cloud lifting off the land as the sun rose.

Soon after breakfast, we entered Cook Strait. I think I was more uptight than the others because, being a New Zealander, I was more aware than they were of the fearsome reputation of this strait. It has seen some vicious storms and claimed the lives of many sailors.

At long last, the nerve swelling in my lower back had reduced sufficiently that I could step up and out into the cockpit. The area was still very tender, but I no longer gasped with pain at every move. Maybe having reached my homeland had something to do with an increase in my feelings of wellbeing too.

As we were about to enter the Queen Charlotte Sound, I noticed a churning of the water, as though it were flowing rapidly over rocks just below the surface. I hurried below to look at the chart. Were we about to run into a shallow patch I looked at the chart. 'There's nothing marked to indicate any danger,' I said.

Ian turned on the depth sounder. 'The gauge is recording plenty of water.' It continued to do so as we sailed through this area of turbulence. 'I think it is merely the confluence of two tidal streams,' said Ian.

The weather continued to be perfect, with a gentle breeze that gave us a beam reach of five knots all the way into Queen Charlotte Sound. Sailing up the sound was like being inside a picture book. The scenery was magnificent; the sound is lined by deep green, tree-covered, gentle hills. Overhead that day, the blue sky was dotted with fluffy, light grey and white clouds, reflected back into the deep blue still water.

*Figure 5. Cook Strait and the Marlborough Sounds*

Picton lies close to Blenheim and at the head of Queen Charlotte Sound the interisland ferry passed us, and we followed it into port. The big ferry had just completed berthing when we pulled into the town wharf, our yellow quarantine flag fluttering at the starboard spreader underneath the New Zealand courtesy flag. Our excitement at arriving in excellent time - ten and a half days across the Tasman - was somewhat dampened when a port officer approached.

'Picton isn't a port of entry. You'll have to wait for Customs and Immigration to come over from Nelson tomorrow. You'll have to be confined to your boat until you've been cleared.' The customs officer saw my face fall. 'You are not really confined strictly to your boat,' he said. 'You're allowed to use the amenities block. There are showers and toilets and a laundry.'

'Whew! Thank you. I was really looking forward to a fresh water shower and a hair wash. But since when has this not been a port of entry? Our pilot book says it is.'

'It used to be, but no longer. How old is your pilot book?'

'A few years,' said Ian, knowing full well he had bought it in 1973.

With my back so tender, I had been outside only for the past day and a half, and hadn't been able to give myself an all-over wash because the movement of the yacht caused me too much pain. I was so looking forward to a long shower in an adequate space. By the time Customs and Immigration had cleared us in the next morning and we were free to explore the town, we were all showered, with hair washed free of salt spray, and wearing clean clothes.

Realitas *at the wharf in Picton*

When we did get into town, we were fascinated to see the lifeboat of the Russian cruise ship *Lermontov* decorating the shopping centre. The event had been well-publicised, even in Australia.

About a year before, the ship had been involved in an accident, which resulted in her sinking in a nearby sound.
The details had not been fully reported in Australia, so we asked the locals to tell us what had happened. They were more than happy to oblige.

'The Captain managed to steer into a narrow slot between a rock and the mainland,' one old timer told us. 'The water was shallow and rocky. The rocks tore a hole in the bottom of the hull. No one knows why the New Zealand pilot didn't stop him.'

'Rumours had it that the Pilot and the Captain were both drunk,' added his friend. 'The Captain drove the ship close enough to shore for the passengers to climb off, before backing into deeper water where the vessel sank. There was a huge scandal at the time about the role played by the Pilot.'

⚓

Christmas was just four days away and there were three important matters to attend to in town: it was imperative to find a chiropractor for me; to make travel bookings to Ashburton; and talk to *Epiglass*, the makers of the water-tank paint.

I searched the phone book for a chiropractor to give me treatment for my back. There were none in Picton, but I found one in nearby Blenheim, a larger centre, where an appointment was available the next morning. I could fit that in if I travelled by an early bus over to Blenheim. The rail line also passed through the town, but the train left later in the morning after the ferry had arrived from Wellington. I had time to receive treatment by the chiropractor in Blenheim, and then walk to the railway station to meet Ian and the boys, who would already be on the southbound train from Picton, along with my luggage. The timing was perfect!

How the internet and mobile phones have transformed the way we seek information and make travel bookings. I had to find a phone box in town to call the chiropractor and a travel agent to book tickets on the train to Christchurch the next day, as well as for the coach on to Ashburton.

Ian did manage to make a phone call to the paint company and found that, being a New Zealand manufacturer, it had a local representative. However, the company was shutting for the Christmas break and they advised Ian to call the representative when we returned from South Canterbury after Christmas.

The safety of *Realitas* and our expensive inflatable dinghy were weighing on Ian's mind. He was much relieved when he saw the people at the Ports and Harbours Authority in Picton and they allocated us a temporary mooring for the yacht.

First thing after an early breakfast, Ian saw me off on the coach into Blenheim. After that, he had to sort the boat and the dinghy. He motored *Realitas* out to the mooring. When he and the boys were ready, he took them and our bags ashore, then rowed the dinghy back to *Realitas,* where he brought it up onto the deck, deflated it, rolled it up and put it out of sight inside the boat. Leaving his old clothes on board, Ian dressed in his bathers and swam ashore, where he changed into his travelling clothes.

My back was incredibly better after the chiropractor treated it. I had twisted my pelvis, putting pressure on the sciatic nerve and injured some other aspect of my lower pelvis. It was a great relief not to experience pain every time I sat down or moved in a hurry. After all, we had a six hour journey ahead of us.

Soon the scenery out the train window gained the attention of us all, and we turned thoughts of the sea and boats towards a land-based Christmas at my brother's farm.

# 9. New Zealand and Home Again

Although still sore, I was able to sit for the six hour journey south. Jamie and David thought it a wonderful adventure to travel in this old diesel train down the east coast. Often the line ran very close to the coastline, especially where it skirted the edge of the Kaikoura Mountains. David, in particular, delighted in seeing the seals that proliferate on the rocky shore. There was so much to see out the windows, and the scenery was such a contrast to the ten days on the ocean, the two of them didn't fight much at all.

*View from train on Kaikoura coast (Photo: NZ Government Rail)*

The train didn't reach Christchurch until very late afternoon. Trains used to travel from Christchurch to Invercargill when I was a child, but no longer. We had to get ourselves to the coach station to continue our journey south. That evening, the coach pulled into Ashburton, where Mother was waiting to greet us and drive us to my eldest brother, Peter's, farm. Mother lived there in a tiny one-bedroom cottage.

'Hello Ian. Hello Jannie.' She kissed and hugged me, always thrilled to see her well-travelled elder daughter. Mother was not a very strong swimmer, so she worried constantly about us when we were at sea.

'My, how you boys have grown since I last saw you.' She hugged her grandsons and then we piled into her little car for the half hour drive to the farm near the foothills of the Southern Alps. In the big old farm-house, my sister in law, Barbara, had two spare bedrooms ready for us.

Jamie and David were very excited to arrive. They were shy at first with their cousin, eleven year old Richard, but they were all close in age, Richard being five months older than David. Jamie had turned thirteen the previous month.

My eldest brother, Peter, took Richard aside.

'Remember that your cousins are city kids. Show them around the farm.'

Peter and Barbara have two adult daughters. Richard was a late addition to their family. At the time of our visit, their elder daughter, Karen, was working in Europe.

'Sarah's working at the local nursery,' Barbara told me. 'She's just completed her diploma in horticulture.'

'Where did she do that?'

'Up at Lincoln,' Barbara said.

Lincoln is the agricultural college, part of the University of Canterbury. Peter had completed his degree in Agricultural Science there in the 1960s.

It was very good to be able to get to know Sarah as a young adult. Karen had visited us in Australia, but Sarah hadn't travelled overseas and we hadn't had a chance to know her as a young woman.

The day before Christmas Eve, we borrowed Mother's car and drove to Twizel, a village in the high country, where my father was living. He and Mother had divorced about eight years earlier. His attitude to our visit reminded me why I was not fond of him. Following complaints in his letters about his sore back, I thought that a vibrating cushion would be a useful Christmas present.

'What did you buy that for?' he said, giving it back to me. 'A pair of socks is all I need.'

Taking the cushion away with us, we went to the local shop, bought him his socks and received no thanks. I was pleased to leave again, having done my daughterly duty.

'That cushion will be useful for my sore back,' I said.

It was a wonderful reunion with some of the other members of my family though, and Christmas day was a happy affair. We all gathered in the big farmhouse. My sister in law's parents joined us for Christmas dinner, bringing the number around the table to eleven. I love a large family Christmas, with the women all pitching in to help prepare the food. It was easy in Barbara's large farm house kitchen.

The three boys were happy together in Richard's playroom, where he had lots of Lego set up, including a train track. The three of them played happily together for hours. Ten days on the farm gave our boys time to get to know something about a different way of life. Richard took the lead in their activities. He had much to teach his big city cousins, like driving the three-wheeler farm motorbike, as well as Richard's Honda CT 90 and the Suzuki farm truck. They also climbed trees, built car-racing tracks across the playroom floor, swam in the pool and played tennis on the grass court. Also during that time, Jamie forged a bond with his Nana.

All too soon, our family time was over and we retraced our journey by coach and train back to Picton and *Realitas*. However, more fun was in store, because this was the time to begin our cruise of the Marlborough Sounds.

Before we set off to explore the Sounds, we re-contacted the *Epiglass* representative, who visited us at the boat. He was appalled by our experience, explaining that his company had removed the product from the market in New Zealand because of problems with it. The representative was unaware it was still being sold in Australia.

'My advice to you is to contact the Australian distributors to demand compensation upon your return home,' he said.

We did this a few months later, receiving promptly a large can of paint remover delivered to our door. Only later did I regret not having asked for more, such as having a professional re-glass the tank for us. Every time I looked at the empty space which should have been a functioning water tank, my heart sank. I couldn't find the energy to tackle it again. We took the easy way out, installing jerry cans in the tank. The disadvantage of this was that every twenty litres, we had to unscrew the top of the tank and rearrange the jerry cans so that the hose reached the water in the closest can. However, all that was in the future. We were in the Marlborough Sounds, determined to have a good time.

Bush walking in New Zealand is very different to Australia. The damp ground consists of layers of wet humus, which squeaks under your boots, and the forest smells of decomposing foliage and ferns.

The nearest I've experienced was in the Daintree rainforest in Far North Queensland. But I'm jumping ahead. The weather was mostly fine with light to moderate winds, just perfect for summer cruising. The Sounds provide the most spectacular land and seascapes, with very little human habitation and lots of natural vegetation on the coastal fringe.

We cruised more slowly through Queen Charlotte Sound on our exit, stopping off at Captain Cook's landing place, from where we walked the trails in the vicinity.

Back in Cook Strait, it took less than a day to sail west to the Marlborough Sounds, a more complex set of drowned valleys on the northern coast of the South Island. During the afternoons, the sea breeze funnelled through the channels, cooling us all from the heat of the day. We learned it was better to swim or sail in the mornings, before the wind became too brisk, and to be anchored with a stern line to a tree ashore by mid-afternoon.

Realitas *anchored stern to tree ashore, Marlborough Sounds*

Ian dived on the steep, rocky shoreline, finding paua for a special dinner that reminded me of preparing conchs in the Bahamas. Conchs live in large trumpet shaped shells, but the flesh is tough and muscular, just like that of the bivalve paua, which is the Maori name for abalone. The meat needs to be tenderised and cooked quickly to be edible.

'Look at the inside of the paua shell boys. See how it's smooth, shiny and multi coloured. That's what the Maori people use to make the eyes in their carvings.'

'It's pretty,' said David.

'Yes, it is. Nowadays, there's a lot of jewellery made using paua shell.'

Two small paua, below the legal limit to harvest, became temporary pets for the boys. For a day, they lived in a bucket of water in the cockpit. David and Jamie 'raced' them up the side of the cockpit, in a game reminiscent of racing snails. When the paua had been 'raced' a few times, Ian told the boys, 'Time to return these ones. I'll get you a couple more tomorrow.'

After several days of this relaxed lifestyle, it was time to move on.

'We'll start off for Nelson tomorrow,' Ian decided.

We sailed through Cook Strait for French Pass, a shortcut entry to Tasman Bay, and so to Nelson. It was the alternative route to sailing right around moderately large D'Urville Island. Near the entrance to French Pass was a small cove with a general store on the shore. We stopped there to refuel. The boys and I headed to the shop.

'Do you have any tide tables for French Pass?' I asked.

'Sorry dear, I'm not a sailor,' said the shop keeper. 'I don't know anything about tides.'

'Oh, that's a bother. Never mind. My boys would like a hot pie each please.'

He heated the pies in his microwave. As I paid for them, he wished me luck.

'You'll have to figure it out for yourself,' I told Ian, 'or ask one of the other skippers.'

We anchored with several other yachts to await the right time, but Ian was too diffident to ask anyone. With Cook Strait on one side and the large Tasman Bay on the other, the tidal flow through this narrow, rocky pass was considerable. We needed to go through when the flow was minimal, between the two tides. The level of water in Tasman Bay is nearly a metre higher than the level on the other side of the pass, meaning that we were about to motor our boat 'uphill'. This uphill 'step' would be lowest at the change of tide.

We were waiting for an indication from the other boats that someone knew the timing of slack water in relation to the tide at Nelson. Ours was the largest of the yachts waiting. Eventually, we realised everyone else seemed as ignorant as our-selves about this narrow water way and its tides.

'I think they're all waiting for us to make a move,' I said.

Ian decided that we should go. 'I hope we haven't left it too late,' he said.

With trepidation, we raised the anchor and motored towards the pass. The other yachts fell into line behind us. The passageway seemed even narrower than it appeared on the chart.

On the left side of the pass was a steep cliff and to the right, a hundred metres away was shallow rock-strewn water, with some sticks concreted into rock crevices to mark the starboard limit of the passage. Ian pointed the nose of the boat towards the middle of the pass and gunned the engine.

We moved about halfway through before the current spun us about. We tried a second time with a similar result.

Next, a small yacht with an outboard motor tried a lot closer to the cliff. They succeeded in moving further towards the throat of the pass than we had managed powered by our twenty horse-power diesel.

'There's some counter current over there,' said Ian. 'With our bigger engine and the help of the counter current, we might just make it. But I don't fancy a swirl of current flinging us against the cliff.'

Ian moved *Realitas* closer to the cliff and gunned the engine.

We sped forward. As we neared the throat of the pass, the current slowed us. All four of were willing *Realitas* forward. Ever so slowly, we inched closer. Seconds seemed like minutes and minutes like hours. Eventually, like a cork eased out of a champagne bottle, we popped over the top and out into Tasman Bay.

*Looking back at French Pass with its strong tidal flow*

We'd just motored against the tide, up and over a 300 mm step. In the distance, far across the bay, we could see sand dunes and the skyline of the small city of Nelson.

When we had relaxed again, Ian said, 'I think that is the most stupidly risky thing I have ever done in a yacht! We could have lost the boat back there.' But we had done it and his fears were not realised.

A pleasantly brisk sail across the bay brought us close to the channel entrance of the well-protected harbour. Having relaxed for an hour or so, I became tense again. The chart showed a narrow winding channel into the town marina. At first, I couldn't even make out the harbour entrance.

'Jan, would you steer please.'

'Where am I aiming?'

'That gap in the rock wall ahead.' '

I can't see any gap!' Panic edged into my voice.

I'd had enough stress for one day.

Impatiently, Ian gave me a compass course to steer by while

he attended to other things. Eventually, I made out the entrance. Now, I wonder why he hadn't asked Jamie to steer. He was old enough at thirteen and he has excellent eyesight, not short sightedness like both his parents.

Eventually, it all became clear. We made several turns,

passed the commercial fishing boats and came at last into the private boat owners' marina, run by the local council.

There were some floating docks, but not where we were instructed to tie up, just high piles with rings bolted on for tying up the boat and a long, vertical steel ladder to climb up to the road. Once we had secured *Realitas*, we locked her and clambered up the ladder to investigate our surroundings.

We all needed to uncoil our tensions from the time aboard and to let some adrenalin loose. The boys set off, racing one another to who knows which goal. Nearby, we found all sorts of small businesses operating industries related to boating: there were welders, tank makers, boat builders, riggers and so on. I spotted a business that dealt in manufacturing stainless steel tanks.

'Why don't we order a tank to fit the space under the aft end of the port berth? You've often said we should have a day-tank for diesel. That area's useless space, unless we make it available for extra fuel,' I said. 'Storing our entire spare diesel in the aft locker puts too much weight in the stern,' I added.

'I *have* been thinking about installing a day-tank,' said Ian. 'I think if we placed a tank there, it could hold about thirty litres of fuel and would bring a heavy weight closer to the centre of gravity in the boat.'

Ian ordered the tank, and after he picked it up he showed it to me. 'That was much cheaper than I expected and look what a great job they've done,' he said. 'The welding is excellent.'

We were both very pleased and stowed the tank into its space under the bunk, planning to connect it up on our return to Five Dock Bay.

As we explored the port, we noticed some boats with huge lights burning brightly in full day light.

'What on earth...?' I said.

'Aha!' exclaimed Ian, pointing at those fishing boats. 'That explains the strangely moving lights out at sea.'

'How do you mean?'

'They're squid fishing boats – from Taiwan by the look of the details on their sterns. They were out there fishing for squid and chatting to each other in Taiwanese.'

I wanted to take my family to see the tobacco farms in the Nelson hinterland near Motueka - something they wouldn't be able to see anywhere in NSW. Unfortunately, there wasn't time to hire a car and tour the surrounding district, because we had to be home by the start of the new school year, and time was running out. Life is full of compromises.

Ian notified Customs and Immigration of our planned departure, set a time and filled out all the forms. Formalities completed, I bought fresh provisions for our voyage home.

A couple of days later, after the immigration official had stamped our passports, we took in our mooring lines and motored out into Tasman Bay.

Realitas *heads across Golden Bay, Ian and Jamie in the cockpit*

As we crossed the bay, I prepared snacks for the boys and Ian so that I could rest when we reached the open sea.

'I'm glad we don't have to return via French Pass,' I said.

'Not sure I'd like to go back that way either,' said Ian.

The western side of D'Urville Island is wide open to Cook Strait. Before long, we rounded the long sand spit separating

Golden Bay from the western end of Cook Strait and before nightfall, we had entered the Tasman Sea, setting course for Sydney.

Fortunately, the return voyage is usually kinder to me than the outward one, because we have been on the water for several weeks. Even so, I was mildly queasy for a few hours. It really depends on how calm the anchorages have been, and that marina in Nelson was *very* protected.

Our trip home was as comfortable as the voyage across the Tasman to New Zealand, or more so for me, because I was no longer in pain. Our return also took ten and a half warm, sunny days, with a few hours of calm mid-ocean, during which Ian filled the cockpit with water for a bath. The boys considered that much more fun than going over the side for a swim.

*Ian and the boys cooling off in the cockpit mid-Tasman*

Approximately thirty nautical miles from Sydney, we spied Centre Point Tower clearly dominating the upper Sydney skyline. We passed out of the south bound current and when we moved into the north-going counter current closer to the coast, Ian noticed a small whale taking advantage of its assistance.

After sailing one thousand, six hundred nautical miles from Nelson, we picked up the designated mooring in Watsons Bay to clear in with Australian Customs. Ian was happy to have brought our family safely home again.

The boys were sorry that their New Zealand adventure was over. And I was very grateful to have been able to spend time with my birth family over Christmas and then to cruise in the magnificent Marlborough Sounds. We were all refreshed for the coming year.

Penta Comstat was a private business run by Derek and Jeanine Barnard, who kept daily schedules, night and morning for cruising yachties in return for an annual membership fee. After fitting an HF radio, we had joined their club in 1988 before setting off for New Zealand.

We listened in every morning at eight o'clock and every afternoon at four as the yachts at sea gave their positions and weather reports. Each yacht was called in alphabetical order.

I liked the service this couple provided and like many cruising yachties, we came to feel we knew them personally. Even Ian, who had resisted marine radios and position reporting for years, found Penta Comstat agreeable. Unlike on the Coastguard service, there were no runabouts and people out fishing making their reports. It was all people cruising the coast like us, and in early January, also the race boats returning from Hobart.

Using Penta Comstat during our voyage had created the feeling of a special bond with this lovely couple who kept watch over our position each day.

A few months after our return from New Zealand, we decided to drive to Firefly on the Central Coast near Gosford. We wanted to meet the Barnard's at home and see the office from where they broadcast to yachties up and down the Australian coast and out into the Pacific.

I was intrigued to find they had a son called David who was close in age to our younger son. In 2012,, all cruising yachties who had used the Penta Comstat service were saddened to learn of Jeanine's untimely illness and subsequent death. Subsequently, Derek closed down Penta Comstat's position reporting service. No similar business has replaced that efficient and friendly service. *Vale* Jeanine.

# 10  A Second Visit to Lord Howe Island

We had all enjoyed our first visit to Lord Howe Island so much that we had vowed to return. Two year later, on Boxing Day 1989, we left our mooring to do just that.

We were determined to keep Jamie out of Sydney as much as possible that summer because most of his mates were getting into serious trouble. Jamie had just turned fourteen and David would turn twelve soon after we returned home. Both boys were to change schools later that summer – David was entering High School; and Jamie was enrolled to board at Chevalier College in Bowral.

'We need to refuel before we leave the harbour, Jan.'

'Where do you want to do that? Birkenhead Point Marina?'

'I think so, and we'll go over to Balls Head Bay for the night. How does that sound to you?'

'Sounds fine.'

After filling up with both diesel and fresh water, we crossed the Parramatta River to anchor. The idea was to give us time to develop our 'sea legs'. Balls Head Bay received a little more wash from passing ferries than we received in Five Dock Bay.

Early the next morning, 0730 on the twenty seventh of December, 1989, as recorded in our ship's log, we pulled up anchor and motored right out to the heads. By then there was a little bit of breeze, and together we raised the sails and set a course towards Lord Howe.

'You've made sure our course will miss those two sea-mounts?' I asked. 'I don't want to be any more seasick than necessary.'

The currents swirl around those under-water mountains, making the seas higher and steeper. Of course Ian had set a course to miss them. He is always a very cautious navigator and we didn't experience adverse current until we were fairly close to Lord Howe Island. As we approached the island, Ian called Clive

Wilson, the Harbour Master, on VHF radio to notify him of our proximity.

I felt unhappy when I overheard the conversation.

'*Realitas*, the tide is unusually low and the supply ship has gone aground in the northern passage into the lagoon. Please anchor on the eastern side of the island until the tide rises and the lagoon entrance is clear,' said Clive.

'Leave your radio turned on so that I can keep you informed. Do you copy?'

The eastern anchorage is in an open bay and the swell and waves can make the boat pitch wildly, bringing on seasickness, especially for me.

'Damn! I'd rather not be seasick at anchor,' I said. 'I'd rather not be seasick at all, especially having just got over it on the way out.'

Fortunately the supply ship floated quite soon with the incoming tide and we were in the open roadstead for only a few hours before Clive guided us into the lagoon and directed us to a mooring near Rabbit (aka Blackburn) Island.

*David photographs Clive Wilson leading* Realitas *into the lagoon*
6

Being close to the island in the lagoon gave us the opportunity to visit ashore there, which we hadn't done previously. The ground was full of shearwater nests and therefore a protected place. In fact, you had to be careful where you put your feet. It was possible to sprain an ankle in one of those holes and at the same time you risked being pecked severely by an angry shearwater for injuring her baby.

Fleshy-footed shearwaters are also known as "mutton birds" because of their oily flesh. In New Zealand, harvesting of mutton birds used to be restricted to the Maori people, and in Tasmania and the Bass Strait Islands, the Aborigines. They are protected now.

When I was a small child living near Invercargill, a few were sold, and my mother used to cook them as a special treat.

"It bit me!' Jamie squawked indignantly. He held up his bloodied finger for me to inspect.

'What did you do to it?' I knew my son too well.

'Nothing. I just tried to pat it,' said Jamie.

'I didn't get pecked,' said David sanctimoniously.

*Supply ship at the wharf in Lord Howe's lagoon*

One day, we noticed a sign outside the hall saying that the resident naturalist was giving a talk for visitors the next morning about life on the foreshore – the littoral zone.

'Let's go to that,' said Ian.

'Yes, let's. It sounds interesting. Good information for the boys too.'

The naturalist's talk was both engaging and informative. I hadn't observed sea squirts before, nor looked closely at a sea cucumber. David eagerly watched the naturalist hold a sea squirt in the shallow water while it ejected its cloud of emissions.

The naturalist also showed us a crown-of-thorns starfish, giving us a better understanding of why their overgrowth was causing so much coral devastation on the Great Barrier Reef.

*Scotch Mist* arrived the day after we did. Janet White and Barry Gow were members of our Coastal Cruising Club and we particularly liked their company. Janet had a very easy manner with our boys, and they really liked her too.

The crew of *Scotch Mist* had been delayed near the start of their voyage out from Sydney Harbour. Janet was decanting some methylated spirit inside the cabin of their boat at the same time as she had the oven going, cooking some goodies. Even though she wasn't standing next to the oven, the fumes caused a flashover fire, which ignited the bottle she was holding. In a second, the cabin was on fire. When she dropped the bottle, methylated spirit splashed on Janet's arms and legs as well as her clothing and in a second she was alight too. She told us she called loudly to Barry, who was in the cockpit. Once she managed to catch his attention, he came to her aid and soon had the fire under control.

As an ex-nurse, Janet knew she didn't have sufficient first aid materials on board to be able to dress all her wounds for the several days until they reached the island. They decided to return to Sydney, where she had her wounds properly assessed and dressed and she gathered enough dressings to last her for some days.

Janet is a very practical, hardy woman, with a wonderful sense of humour. We all felt for her to be suffering and in pain, but typical of her spirit, she didn't complain. She insisted on heading out of Sydney again to have her holiday on Lord Howe.

While we knew of *Scotch Mist's* position as we sailed, we were unaware of their predicament or why they had returned to Sydney. Ian had been tuning into Penta Comstat and he was monitoring the location of both *Scotch Mist* and *Wine Dark*, another member of the CCC.

This visit, I'd come prepared for coral viewing. I'd bought a spring suit (a light, short-sleeved wetsuit) at the end-of-summer sales the previous year and had purchased a snorkel and mask just before Christmas.

On our bushwalks together with Janet, Barry and some of the other CCC members, we appreciated Janet's long talks with Jamie. She had a magical way with him that I could never emulate. She managed to allay much of his fear of the unknown school year ahead, and he went off to start at boarding school in a calm and accepting frame of mind.

David too had a big change approaching. He was starting at Turramurra High School, the school Jamie had just left. I remembered how my two brothers had been compared at their high school, so we had offered David a different school, but he insisted he wanted to go to Turramurra High.

Janet and Barry's good friends and work colleagues, Dave Davey and Annick Anselin, had also come to Lord Howe in their lovely 34 foot yacht, *Windclimber*.

'Could we have New Year's dinner together?' I asked the other CCC women.

'We've got room in *Wine Dark's* saloon for everyone,' said Margaret. 'Can you all bring something to share?'

'I preserved some turkey meat in jars this year. We can share that hot with some gravy,' I offered.

From L to R: *Dave Davey, Annick Anselin, Hayden Rough, Ian Mitchell in saloon of* Wine Dark *on New Year's Day*

'I've got plenty of potatoes on board. I can roast some in the oven,' said Margaret. *Wine Dark* was owned by her partner, Hayden Rough. Having an oven on board was a luxury I had yet to experience.

Janet and Annick offered snacks, other vegetables and salads and cheeses.

'I've also made a plum pudding that will be enough for everyone for desert.' I added, 'We might need custard or cream to go with it.'

Ten of us gathered around the table in *Wine Dark's* cabin on New Year's Day – eight adults and our two children shared dinner. We had a really enjoyable party that New Year's day.

One morning, we walked across the island to Ned's Beach armed with plenty of bread. The fish were accustomed to being fed mid-morning and I was thrilled to watch them from under water.

'Look! I am putting my face under water. It doesn't frighten me anymore,' I told my family. I was more impressed with my having overcome my phobia than they were.

When we swam at the nearest coral hole near *Realitas* to look at the brightly coloured coral and tropical fish, I was less sure. Closer to the outer reef was a better section of coral, but sharks came in over the reef occasionally.

'I can't swim out there on my own. Reef sharks still scare me,' I said as I prepared to go snorkeling. 'I want someone to swim with me.'

Jamie agreed to come and he stayed close beside me, pointing out things of interest while I viewed the coral and the fish. When I indicated that I was becoming cold and needed to return to the boat, he swam beside me. This was behaviour that heralded his growing up and I was very grateful to him.

A visit to Little Island was what I had been waiting for. That was where I had become enamoured of the sights under the water during our last visit to Lord Howe Island. We took the dinghy across the lagoon one morning.

'Hey Mum, would you like to use the bits of wetsuit that Janet gave me?' said Jamie. Janet had decided she didn't want the arms and legs on her wetsuit and had cut them off. Jamie had asked for them and she happily obliged. I slipped into the water. I felt somewhat silly with the pieces of wetsuit I now used to cover my arms, but much warmer. I was delighted with what I could see under water. To date, Little Island was the best coral viewing I had been exposed to. What a wonderful underwater world I had been missing out on. 'I can't believe we spent weeks in the West Indies in the 1970s and I didn't try snorkeling,' I said to Ian. 'All that coral and fish, and I was unaware of them right underneath our boat.'

*Jan, Jamie and David in wetsuits after snorkeling*

Jamie had a day when he didn't feel very well. A couple of days later, he came out in spots. It was chicken pox. What to do? After a consultation with Ian and also with Nurse Janet, we decided it was too hard to isolate him.

'You can go ashore as usual whenever you feel well enough,' I told Jamie. 'Just keep the hat pulled well down to hide the spots on your face.' After more consultation, we told David our verdict.

'Both Dad and I feel it is healthier for you to catch the chicken pox too,' I said. 'You will gain immunity to this mild childhood disease, rather than risk having it when you grow up.

If you get chicken pox when you're an adult, it is much more serious.'

To protect Jamie's eyes, which were sensitive to the very bright light, the boys often stayed inside the community hall playing pool together

Time passed quickly on the island. There was always something to do and laundry was one of those things. There was now a washing machine available for the use of crews from the cruising yachts, and the islanders had strung a clothes line between two trees. The clothes dried very quickly in the sea breeze, which was mostly gentle enough to not include sea spray.

Yachtie visitors were allowed to hire bicycles too. That was another change since our first visit. Ian hired two for the boys one day and they went off for a long ride together.

When we returned home, Richard Cortis explained. 'Do you know the reason why they wouldn't let yachties hire bikes?'

'No.' 'A few years back, after the Gosford to Lord Howe race, some blokes got drunk and wrecked a few bikes,' he said. 'Of course, many of the islanders are Seventh Day Adventist and disapprove of drinking alcohol.'

*Barry Gow and Janet White of* Scotch Mist *cycling on Lord Howe*

Apparently, yacht crews from the mainland were forgiven by the islanders– or at least given another chance. While the boys went off on their bikes, I relaxed on the beach with a novel.

When high tide occurred in the middle of the day, we would pack up lunch and all we needed for the day, then go ashore in the dinghy. At the swimming beach that year, the locals had anchored a life raft for swimmers to sunbathe on. 'You've seen the life raft someone's tied to the swimming platform? We should all try climbing into that raft,' said Ian. 'It could be a life-saving experience to know how to get into one.'

As we were still not able to afford to buy our own life raft, we were in the habit of borrowing Horst and Tilly's one when we sailed offshore.

We all swam out, but David and I struggled to pull ourselves inside. It was difficult to get my foot even onto the lowest rung, and the rungs of the short fabric ladder were too far apart. Even in the very slight waves in the bay, I found out that, like so many things in this world, having short legs was a severe disadvantage. The footholds to climb into the raft were designed for adult men, not someone who stands only 160 cm tall (five foot two and a half inches). And David was even shorter than me. Once I did manage to get inside I felt claustrophobic and slightly nauseous from the confined size and the rubbery smell.

I swam lots that summer. I was losing my fear of the reef sharks, but not enough to swim alone yet. Besides, the wet suit I had bought was only a spring suit, and not really warm enough for me.

Still, it was a cheap entry suit for me to learn about snorkeling and what I liked to do in the water. This was a big change for me. Before this holiday, I had been happy to swim a few lengths of the local swimming pool, but beach swimming had never been part of my program.

The lagoon was different. I found it partly calm like the pool, but with salt water for buoyancy. If the breeze came up, tiny wavelets washed into my face. That encouraged me to put my head down and use the snorkel. Looking about the underwater world, I began to lose my fear of it. After all, fear is usually related to the unknown. Once we can see something, we start to understand it, and with understanding, the fear goes.

We left Lord Howe the same day as *Windclimber*, two weeks after our arrival. They followed us out of the pass. By this time, David had also succumbed to the chickenpox. He was only at the beginning of it and feeling unwell. His spots developed as we sailed home.

'Let's carry on with our book,' said Jamie, as soon as we were through the pass.

'You continue reading, Jamie' said David, who was resting in his bunk.

As a family we had been reading aloud a Stephen King novel that Jamie had chosen. I don't like horror stories of that nature, but like so many things we do as parents, we have to let our kids learn to choose stuff we ourselves don't particularly like. No sooner had Ian set the sails and the course than he came below and Jamie started reading aloud.

Because we were all below decks, we were unaware of a small drama unfolding close to us. As Dave and Annick were pulling up their sails, a line caught around their life raft, pulling on the emergency line attached to it. Suddenly, they had an inflating life raft on their deck, interfering with the working of their yacht. Together, they tried to push the raft down their companionway to clear space on deck to set their sails and course.

Apparently they called out to us as we sailed past *Windclimber*, vainly hoping we could help somehow. We were oblivious. The incident was reported to us in detail at the next yacht club meeting, which caused us to gain a reputation in the club as being careless about watch keeping.

'We have to accept your criticism,' said Ian. We should have been keeping watch close to the island and with another yacht nearby.'

I nodded in agreement. We had to accept the ribbing in good part.

Our trip home from Lord Howe Island was brisk – our fastest between the island and mainland yet. Jamie was quite old enough to participate more in the running of the boat too, which was helpful to Ian. After only three and a half days, we sailed into Broken Bay. The yacht club was to hold its Australia Day gathering at Dangar Island, and we wanted to be there.

One night during that voyage home, on watch by myself in the cockpit, I began contemplating my future. Jamie was about to go to boarding school and David was entering high school.

For me, high school teaching had become a "Catch 22". I could have part-time teaching if I wanted to apply by a date in November the previous year. I had to name the school that needed a part-time teacher. Schools couldn't apply for a part-time teacher until the first day of the school year in February, when they knew definitely the number of students enrolled. Ergo, the Department didn't really want part-time teachers. I didn't want to continue school teaching either, but there was still that mortgage to be paid and I hoped to continue teaching part-time at Hornsby TAFE.

During a long night-watch, I decided it was time for a change of career to something less stressful. I had long held an interest in nutrition. Why not find a college where I could study to become a naturopath? This notion was partly related to the help I'd found from a naturopath for my autoimmune illness, partly to my long-term interest in nutrition. I made up my mind that was the path I wanted to follow. I needed a little bit of "me time" for a change.

When I told my family I intended to enroll part-time at a naturopathic college, they were somewhat shocked. I had made the decision without consulting them. Perhaps they had no idea how alienated I felt from my own self, having given my all to them for the past fifteen years.

Their needs, wants and demands had always come first. Now, I felt, it was my turn.

# 11  Big Changes

At the start of the nineteen nineties, all of us were entering a new phase in our lives. Both boys were starting at new schools. Ian had been promoted and was working in a more administrative role which was more stressful for him, and I enrolled for naturopathic study. This meant we had different priorities and were not able to spend every weekend on the boat.

Ian and I were concerned about how Jamie would cope at boarding school and tried to reassure him that it was up to him to create a new reputation.

'Jamie,' I told him, 'you will be an unknown quantity at your new school. Private schools don't receive any kind of record from your public school without our permission. You will be able to decide what sort of impression you want to make.'

I gave David advice too. Despite his more equable nature, I was concerned that Jamie's reputation for troublesome behaviour would influence how the staff at Turramurra High School would treat him.

'David, when you start at Turramurra, I suggest you don't tell anyone you are Jamie's brother. Make your own mark. I don't want teachers comparing you.'

On the day we delivered Jamie to his new school in Bowral (Southern Highlands of NSW) in late January, we first made a brief visit to Ian's mother in the aged care home at nearby Mittagong. Mrs. Mitchell senior had been there only a couple of years and her slowly developing Alzheimer's disease was not yet serious.

'Hello Grandma. Have they put you in prison too?'

Jamie's grandmother looked bemused.

At the boarding school, we left Jamie sitting on his dormitory bed. I have an image of him with legs crossed and a large mop of very curly hair that he'd allowed me to trim only so far. As I hugged him goodbye, I gave him a key to our back door.

'If you are too homesick and can't wait for us to come down for you, you'll be able to get in at home.'

'Thanks Mum.'

Ian hugged him and David gave his brother a friendly pat on the shoulder.

When we climbed back into the car and set off, it was with very mixed feelings.

'It's really hard leaving Jamie there,' I said, tearfully.

'I know,' said Ian in a strange voice, 'but it is for the best.'

'I know that. I also feel very relieved that we know where he is. I've had enough of chasing around the countryside looking for him and his no-good mates. The hardest part is not being allowed to visit him for six weeks.'

'I'm sure they know from experience how best to settle new kids into the boarding house,' said Ian.

'I guess so. I suppose I don't want him to feel we've thrown him out of home. That's why I gave him the key.'

After that conversation, it was a very quiet drive back to Sydney. David sat in the back playing with an electronic game. He wouldn't miss being ordered around by his older brother.

The next morning, the first day of the school term, I sorted David for Turramurra High School and photographed him in his new uniform. He looked very small to be going off to high school.

When I'd seen him off on his school bus, I caught the train into the city to find and evaluate the two naturopathic colleges in the central city. Neither appealed to me, but when I walked into the third one, Nature Care College in Artarmon, I felt like I had come home. I belonged there. Artarmon is five suburbs north of the city centre and I was able to reach the college easily by train.

I went into the office to find out about enrolment, only to discover term had already started the previous week. I enrolled, bought the large anatomy and physiology textbook and set about catching up.

Upon arriving home, I found a message from the local TAFE College, asking me to call back. The Head of English had a teaching job for me – four hours a week face to face with a class of adult Higher School Certificate students – English of course. Within a couple of days of accepting that work, Maureen, my boss, rang again.

'Jan, would you be willing to take a second HSC English class?'

'Will they be studying the same texts as the first class?' I asked.

'Yes, all classes study the same texts.'

She continued, 'The only difference is that these students work during the day and come in two evenings a week from 6.00–8.00 pm; would that pose a problem? '

'No. That sounds wonderful,' I said. 'No extra preparation, just extra marking. I think I can manage that. Thank you very much.'

This work gave me an income to support both my study fees and also Jamie's fees for Chevalier College. Having a regular part-time job helped me feel I was contributing to the family's income, not leaving the entire provider's role to Ian.

In the typical fashion of a fourteen year old, Jamie hadn't replied to my advice about setting his own reputation, but he must have listened because, as we had hoped, he took the opportunity presented to him and started to turn his life around. By end of term, he had become accustomed to the new routine, and began paying attention during lessons and settled in to boarding house life. The friends he developed that first year were of a totally different calibre to those he left behind. Ben, the son of a Sydney gynaecologist and obstetrician, became his best mate. They were part of a group of fine young people, which included the daughter of the Deputy Head-master. These kids became his friends for many years after his school days were over.

We were able to relax as far as Jamie was concerned. We knew where he was. He knew we had not cast him out of the family, but were paying boarding school fees for him as an investment in his future.

Jamie joined the Cadet Corps while he was in year nine, soon after his arrival at the school. The following year, he enrolled in the year ten wilderness course. These two activities let him out of the school on camping expeditions. You weren't supposed to do both cadets and wilderness studies because of the time spent away from class, but Jamie managed to persuade the principal, Father Irwin, to allow him to do just that. Jamie could be very persuasive, and he thrived on getting out into the bush, especially on the wilderness course.

'On a cadets' expedition, we clear the ground, dig a latrine, and when we pack up, you know exactly where we have camped,' Jamie laughed. 'A couple of weeks later, we go out for wilderness studies, Mr. X makes sure we don't destroy anything, not even a sapling. He says that when we are ready to leave, there should be no sign we were ever there. What a contrast!'

Our son was already benefiting hugely from his change of school environment. We were growing very proud to see him moving in a more positive direction.

It was different for David, who was struggling academically at high school. Did he have Attention Deficit Disorder (ADD) as had been diagnosed the previous year – or just poor eyesight? At the beginning of his second year of high school, he was in the bottom class for English, barely middling in other subjects and shining only in Manual Arts. However, he was making friends of his own and seemed relatively happy.

That was when I heard on ABC radio about another kind of eye problem – a developmental one that arose from a neurological processing difficulty. I found an optometrist in nearby Pennant Hills who specialized in developmental optometry and booked an appointment for David. He knew he wouldn't be leaving that clinic without a prescription for glasses and he had selected his frames before he was called in to be tested. When he emerged from the office, the optometrist smiled at me.

'David doesn't have a developmental problem with his vision,' she said.

My heart sank. 'If that isn't the problem, do you know what is?' I asked.

'Oh yes. He has a fair degree of astigmatism in both his eyes.'

'And that would account for his difficulties with reading books and the blackboard at school?'

'Most definitely. Astigmatism means that the muscles don't pull evenly on the eyeball, making the eyeball distorted. That's what is causing problems with his vision.' '
I can't believe this has never been picked up before! Today's test must be at least the fifth eye exam he's had.'

'Well, you know now. David tells me he has already selected some frames. Do you want to try them on David?' She continued, 'Those ones are a good choice. What do you think, Mum?'

'Yes,' I said, 'I think those look fine.'

'They will be ready in about a week. Our receptionist will phone you when they come in.'

I had taken David for eye checks regularly and even to an eye doctor while he was in primary school. I knew he was not mentally slow and had always suspected there was something wrong with his eyesight. Because he hadn't worn glasses, his education thus far had been seriously impacted. His low academic performance led us to believe he would probably attend Technical College (TAFE) after leaving school, and be apprenticed in a trade. He would prove us wrong in that assumption.

During 1990, we tried to spend as many weekends as possible on the boat, as well as taking both boys with us on school holidays. At Easter that year, we felt it was imperative to keep Jamie away from his old mates who were now so much bad news, though we were happy for him to continue his association with Peter, his friend from Wahroonga. His parents owned a yacht, so Peter was familiar with sailing and came along with us that holiday. We sailed down to Gunnamatta Bay and Jibbon Beach at Port Hacking (south of Cronulla), leaving late on Thursday evening to avoid the southerly predicted to arrive overnight.

The weather on Friday was unpleasant, with persistent rain, but little wind. When we motored over to where the rest of the CCC members were anchored near the beach, our engine seemed a little sick.

Ian checked the oil and he was not pleased to find a whitish emulsion on the dipstick.

'Look at that,' said Ian. 'The oil's emulsified'

'That's a funny colour for the oil to be,' I said. 'What do you mean by "emulsified"?'

'It means there's water in the oil,' Ian stated.

'Oh. That's not good, is it?'

'Definitely not.'

Straightaway, Ian started trying to find out where the water was entering the crankcase. He spent nearly all Good Friday bent over that engine, head down and his backside in the air.

The engine covers were blocking up access for the rest of us to move about. Bowls of nuts and bolts sat on my galley bench top and he spread tool boxes on the floor, along with bits and pieces of engine. The boys and I were restricted to curling up on the bunks and settees with books or electronic games.

The atmosphere inside became heated, the humidity rose, condensed and trickled down inside the windows. All our tempers were fraying. Outside, the weather wasn't much better.

The sky covered us like a grey army blanket, oozing water. I wanted out, but Ian wasn't prepared to move. The cover over the front engine provided the steps out to the cockpit – it was blocking the middle of the boat.

*Ian searches for source of water in engine oil*

'Is there any way I can get out?' I asked. 'Maybe go ashore or to visit on another boat?'

'No, I don't think so. You won't be able to step out over the engine.' '

Isn't there anything to step on?'

'No. I've removed the air cleaner bracket you usually stand on when I'm servicing the motor.'

Ian's only concession to move was when I needed to get into

the galley to provide a meal.

After hours of investigation, he concluded there was something seriously wrong with the engine. On Saturday morning, he packed up all the pieces and stowed them ready for the mechanic. We were all fed up, so while the wind was favourable, we sailed out of the bay in a fifteen knot southerly and returned to Port Jackson.

'If I drop you and David ashore at the opera house, you can go home and bring the car down to collect the rest of us,' Ian said. He anchored in Farm Cove, took the dinghy off the deck and rowed David and me ashore.

Jamie and Peter remained on board to help Ian take the engineless yacht back to her mooring.

By this stage, the wind had turned easterly and become very light. Ian tied the dinghy amidships to *Realitas*.

'Come on, into the dinghy you two.'

Jamie and Peter sat in the dinghy, Jamie using the outboard handle to keep the little motor heading in the right direction, while Ian steered the yacht.

They returned to the mooring where Ian further dismantled the engine. That was when he found that the head was cracked. It required an expensive repair, well beyond Ian's mechanical abilities.

He and the boys took the engine head ashore to the car and delivered it to our marine mechanic, who lived close by, before returning home. Later, when the head was repaired, Ian put the engine back together again.

At one of our yacht club meetings, Bruce Walker approached us. 'When I was out sailing the other week, I went up the Lane Cove River and I spotted *Caprice* up there moored in Tambourine Bay,' he said. The Lane Cove River flows into Sydney Harbour a few kilometres north-west of the Harbour Bridge.

We had not set eyes upon the boat we'd sold after our world circumnavigation. One weekend during spring, 1991, we sailed up the river and found *Caprice* just where Bruce had told us. For twelve years. Now, we'd found her again.

'I don't like the dark green they've painted her,' I said. '
It looks like house paint,' said Ian. 'Still, it's probably better

than the blinding "aqua" colour we painted her in South Africa.'

We wrote a note for the owners, giving our details and left it in a weighted plastic bag in the cockpit.

A couple of weeks later, there was a phone call from Mark, the current owner. He invited us to meet him and his wife Trish at their home. Mark was keen to show us the original RCA Dolphin motor that had frustrated us so much. We'd never known whether it would start or not when we really needed it. Mark brought out a large board on which he'd mounted the engine. He'd polished the brass bits until they glowed. He glowed with pride.

As a replacement for that engine, Mark had bought and installed a more modern RCA Dolphin.

Mark and Trish invited us to visit on board *Caprice* one Sunday. In early November, we did just that. With Jamie and David on board, we sailed *Realitas* into the Lane Cove River and motored upstream to Tambourine Bay, where we rafted alongside *Caprice*.

When we stepped off *Realitas* onto the side deck of *Caprice*, we were astonished at how much she heeled. Of course, we'd had a ton of gear, food, water and fuel on board when we were living on her. Trish and Mark kept her relatively empty.

'We sold *Caprice* to a doctor in 1978,' I said. 'When did you buy her?'

'We bought her from that doctor,' said Mark. 'I think he'd had her for only about six months. We bought her in early 1979.'

Trish and Mark were most gracious hosts, but I was surprised to find they'd never taken *Caprice* out to sea in the eleven years they'd owned her.

To us, *Caprice* was almost a person. We'd loved her and in return she'd taught us much and kept us safe. She seemed very much alive when we took her to sea, bounding across the waves. Yes, we'd romantised her, and we felt sad that after all the thousands of sea miles she'd covered with us, now she was mostly tied up to a mooring in a quiet, secluded bay.

We never felt quite the same about *Realitas*. She was a compromise, utilitarian, a means to an end, but very competent in fulfilling her role as a holiday boat. We did love her, but we had another home.

# 12 Fun on the South Coast

We had more engine troubles on *Realitas* during 1990. In October, Ian found a crack in the dipstick tube to the gear box. Once more, he dismantled the engine and delivered the gearbox to the marine mechanic. It wasn't until early December, when we were at the Gladesville Bridge marina slipway for antifouling, that Ian had a chance to replace the repaired gearbox. Until then, we'd had to use the dinghy alongside *Realitas* to move her when the conditions were unsuitable for sailing.

About this time, Judy Handlinger rang me.

'We're spending Christmas with my sisters in Melbourne this year and we've booked to bring the car over with us on the ferry.'

'Hey, that's great news. Our engine is back in the boat. Perhaps we can come south and meet you somewhere after Christmas.'

I checked with Ian.

'Why don't you ask Judy if we can meet them at Eden and we can sail down? That way, we can take them all sailing on Twofold Bay.'

'Good idea.'

I rang Judy back.

'Do you think you could all come to Eden? Ian suggests we sail down there to meet up with you.'

'That sounds fine. We'll book somewhere to stay in Eden. You can't cope with four extras sleeping on board the boat. And you know Michael. He'll insist on sleeping in a proper bed.'

'All right, but we'll be able to take you out day-sailing. There are lots of places to visit down there.'

Not wanting to be on the coast with the Sydney Hobart racing yachts which leave on Boxing Day, this time we departed from our mooring about 6.00 pm on Christmas Eve. Our plan was to sail to Eden without stopping en route. The Handlingers were due to arrive on Boxing Day and we didn't want to waste any of the six days we could spend with them.

We made excellent progress south, first hard on the wind

with a light south-easterly which eased to an easterly, and later in the morning the wind came in from the north-east. By daylight on Christmas morning, we were already off the northern part of Jervis Bay.

*Realitas* was sailing on a broad reach, and on that afternoon's 'sched' with Penta Comstat, we reported our position as fifteen nm NE of Montague Island. Moving over the ground at a consistent 5 – 6 knots and with the aid of the southbound current, we had already covered 170nm through the water. The good wind didn't last, turning to the north-west and dropping off to almost nothing.

'I think we'll use the motor. The batteries need charging too,' said Ian. 'They are very low at the moment.'

I went off to sleep to the drone of the motor. I would take watch later, after sleeping for a couple of hours.

*At sea south of Jervis Bay*

On deck, Ian kept a close look-out for any shipping, because we were well off shore in the east Australian current (EAC) that sweeps down the entire east coast of Australia. Occasionally a ship heading south would pass to port (left) of us, or one heading north would pass inshore.

The wind died in the early hours of Boxing Day morning, so we began motoring again. A weak southerly change arrived just after 0300. We tried to sail for a couple of hours, before the wind failed us yet again.

Just before daybreak, Ian spotted the loom of Green Cape lighthouse. Green Cape lies south of Eden, so we were becoming very close to our destination. Shortly after noon, we dropped our anchor off a small beach in the northern part of Snug Cove.

It was good timing – Judy, Mike and kids were due to arrive in Eden the same day. We met up with them in their motel room after their arrival later that afternoon.

'There's a forecast for a southerly to arrive very early on Friday morning,' Ian told us all. 'My suggestion is that on Thursday, you should all come on board and we'll take you across Twofold Bay to Boydtown.'

The Handlingers were keen to come along and, before lunch time, we were anchored in East Boyd Bay on the southern shore. We all went ashore to view the old buildings that had been restored. There, we learned that Benjamin Boyd was the European pioneer of the area, arriving in the mid-1800s. His earliest endeavour was in whaling, and he set up a full scale whaling operation in Twofold Bay.

Deep in the bay, he built a 'factory', where mostly right whales were brought ashore. There, they were flensed and the blubber was rendered in huge iron tri-pots. Importing sandstone from Sydney in 1843, Boyd built a small town. All that is left now is a sandstone building, which was abandoned only a few years after it was built.

In the 1930s, the building was restored as the Sea Horse Inn, which is a tourist venue today.

Out on the headland of the southern shore, Boyd built a stone tower, which he planned originally to be his private lighthouse. The government of the day refused him permission to have a lighthouse which didn't operate all night, and every night. Boyd altered his tower into a watchtower from which a lookout could spot whales that had come to the surface to blow, so he could send his whaling boats after them.

Today, most of the area from the southern headland of Twofold Bay to Green Cape forms Boyd National Park.

On Friday, after the southerly had passed and the weather

was fine and warm again, the Handlingers came aboard a second time. We crossed the bay to anchor near the wood chip mill in the southeast corner.

*On board Realitas: From L to R: Mike Handlinger, Judy Handlinger, Jan Mitchell, Aletta Handlinger, David Mitchell, Jamie Mitchell*

*The Seahorse Inn, Boydtown*

Ashore, we walked through an area of felled pine trees to reach the tower out on the cliffs.

The rest of our few days together, we spent under a beach umbrella, on the beach or frolicking in the water. Jamie and David's boogie boards and sailboard provided hours of fun for the kids. They tied either the sailboard or a boogie board behind the dinghy and 'waterskied' or pulled up the sail and practiced getting up on the sailboard.

Jamie has always found skating, surfing and skiing easy activities, so he was the most proficient, but of course, he was also the oldest of the four children.

*Boyd's Tower, lookout for right whales*

*L to R: Aletta Handlinger, Ian Mitchell, Jamie Mitchell, Nick Handlinger, Judy Handlinger and David Mitchell at coastal lookout*

Our week together flew by. Judy and Mike couldn't extend their stay because they had a booking for the Bass Strait ferry with their car. Reflecting our mood, New Year's Day weather was dreary when we farewelled our friends.

To cheer ourselves up, we decided to visit a locality not far distant that we'd heard about a couple of years before. It is a tiny, place called Bittangabee Creek. Fellow CCC members had written about Bittangabee and how to find it in our club newsletter, *The Mainsheet*. The creek lies within the Boyd National Park, between Eden and Green Point. We were sailing south towards Green Point when, suddenly, a pod of small dolphins appeared and began frolicking at our bow.

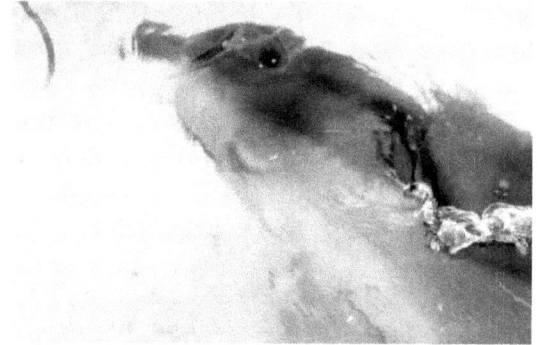

*Small dolphin swimming in our bow wave*

At Green Point, we turned about and began sailing close in to the shore, looking for the entrance to Bittangabee. The creek was reputed to be difficult to see, but by scanning the shore with binoculars, Ian eventually spotted the entrance. We edged in closer, cautiously watching our depth sounder. When we were quite close, the way in became obvious and soon we could see several boats at anchor.

'It's not crowded over there near that small yacht,' I said.

'I think we will anchor there,' said Ian. 'There's more room than over to port.' He continued motoring towards the small boat, when suddenly, we touched bottom.

'Damn,' said Ian. 'So that's why there's no one else here.'

'Hmm. Only 1.1m on the depth sounder. That boat must have a centreboard,' I said. 'How high is the tide?'

'It's just passed its peak,' said Ian. 'We'll be here for a while. It's a nice afternoon to be in the water. Let's pretend we went aground deliberately and we'll clean off the hull while she's leaning over.'

When the tide returned and our floating holiday home was upright again, we moved closer to the other anchored yachts for the night. We had intended to go into the water anyway, so Ian and I scrubbed the exposed hull, while the boys rode on the sailboard.

*Jamie on the sailboard*

Realitas *aground at Bittangabee Creek*

'Let's explore ashore today,' I said over breakfast next morning.

'David and I have already found some ruins,' said Jamie. 'There's a small camping ground too.'

'Good, you can show us where to go,' said Ian.

We found the concrete foundations and a few blocks of building stone that might have been a home or business. We walked along a well-made track into the camping area where a few cars and four wheel drives were parked. There was little in the way of modern camping ground facilities, just the basics – pit toilets and rubbish bins.

After a swim and early lunch, we spent the afternoon chatting with some of the other boaties.

'This really is a delightful nook,' I said. 'I'm so pleased we found it.'

'Let's stay another night,' said Ian.

'Yes, let's,' chorused the boys.

By the next day, Saturday 5$^{th}$ January, it really was time to leave. The tide peaked at 6.00am and we motored out into a quiet sea, the coast sheltering us from the light north-westerly wind.

When David awoke at sea that morning, he was feverish and had a very sore throat. I was concerned that if we didn't see a doctor and get some medication for him he might become quite ill. Ian decided that rather than turn back to Eden, we should pull into Merimbula, a town a few miles further up the coast. It was already mid-morning and I became concerned we wouldn't get in before midday, when everything closed down for the weekend.

A Maritime Services boat was entering the port and since we had never been there before, we followed it in over the bar. Ian called the VMR on the radio.

'Where do you want to tie up, mate? The town wharf or the services club?'

'Which is closest to a doctor's surgery?'

'You'd better go to the town wharf.'

As soon as we touched the town wharf, I hurried David off the boat, leaving Ian and Jamie to tie up. I found a doctor whose diagnosis was tonsillitis, and the chemist sold me the prescribed antibiotics just before he closed his shop for the day. The antibiotics quickly started to take effect and to my relief, David's fever began to drop.

'We might as well go for a walk this afternoon and check this place out,' said Ian. 'There's a southerly due later today.'

Soon after our walk, the southerly came in with rain. We played cards, read aloud, read our own books and wrote up our diaries.

Late on Monday morning, we departed with a very light westerly breeze and clear skies. Soon, we changed to the starboard tack as the wind strengthened and Ian set a northerly course. With the wind off the land, the seas were very calm and we had excellent sailing, averaging four knots.

In the dim light of early morning Tuesday, we approached the Tollgate Islands, near Batemans Bay.

'Where are you thinking of anchoring, Ian?' I said.

'Here, behind one of the Tollgate Islands until the tide rises,' he said, pointing to the chart. 'Probably in the lee of Snapper Island.'

Before Ian came below to rest, he noticed dolphins arcing across the water as they fished by teamwork for their breakfast. 'Hey, all of you come out and look. See the dolphins fishing – probably for yellow fin tuna. They form a line and herd the fish into a smaller corral, until they are so frightened, the dolphins can gorge on them.' I had seen this action by dolphins once before out in the middle of the Pacific Ocean.

The day remained overcast. When the tide was right, we were able to enter the town basin. Ian moored in a pen at the town's tiny public wharf, which made it very handy to go to Woolworths for fresh groceries.

We also walked up to the VMR base, just a little way east of the shopping centre. Ian wanted some local information about opening times for the bridge over the Clyde River. Ian put in a request to travel upstream on Wednesday morning. We stopped downstream of the Nelligen Bridge at 1.00pm and the bridge opened for us.

We motored up river until we found a congenial spot to anchor. The river was pretty with weeping willows and other trees lining its banks. The boys tried 'skiing' on their boogie boards behind the yacht as we motored along.

Jamie and David were keen to fly on the spinnaker again, so they helped Ian set it up and then he and I retired below for some peace and a cuppa.

*Nelligen Bridge over the Clyde River at Batemans Bay with the central bridge span raised to let* **Realitas** *pass under*

*David 'skiing' on his boogie board*

The wind was gentle and the boys were enjoying themselves. They had enjoyed so much fun with their boards and the spinnaker that cruise, we were unprepared for the sudden cries of alarm.

I was surprised to note it was Jamie, not David, who was shrieking. When Ian and I emerged from the cabin, David had helped Jamie back on board.

Jamie had his hand over his eyes and was already pale with shock. Ian helped our son inside and I wrapped a towel around his shaking body.

'What happened?' asked Ian.

'I swung out on the spinnaker and bombed into the water on top of one of those great big brown jellyfish,' said Jamie. 'It stung me on the backs of my legs and across my face.'

His legs were coming up in small blisters and he had his hands over his eyes. Hurriedly, I searched the first aid kit for something to soothe the stings, but Ian went to the galley for vinegar. He gently wiped the mild acid across Jamie's face, over his eyelids and on the backs of his legs, removing the remains of the jellyfish tentacles.

'What about my eyes?' said Jamie. 'They're stinging too.'

I looked in the bathroom for eye wash, but didn't find any. It was four thirty in the afternoon and I had noticed a small general store on the shore nearby.

'If you hurry ashore Ian, you might find something like eyewash or drops at that store before it closes,' I said.

'Good idea,' he said, taking his wallet and climbing into the dinghy. Before long, he was back with some eye drops, which soothed Jamie's eyes.

The next day, when Jamie was more comfortable, we motored back down the river and under the open bridge, this time picking up a mooring on the northern side of the bay opposite the main shopping centre.

Before sun-up on Friday, at high tide and in the utterly grey stillness of early morning, we motored over the bar and out to sea. The stars had twinkled out and the planets were fast disappearing as the sky started to develop pink streaks over the horizon. Seven hours later, we picked up a mooring in Ulladulla harbour, moving on again the next morning for Jervis Bay.

'This is one of the most unspoiled beaches I know of in NSW,' said Ian after we'd anchored off Hole in the Wall. 'Where else can you walk for nearly two kilometres and see no one, just a few rocks, driftwood and dead sea grass?'

'I love it too,' I said.

We took a long walk along the beaches which led to the caravan park, then back to where we'd left the dinghy.

We weren't alone for long. Two club members were also moving up the coast and came in to anchor – the Walkers in *Aragunnu,* and *Jimbun,* with Graeme Solomon. Our two were happy to catch up with the three Walker children and exchange news of their holiday activities, while the adults did a similar thing over afternoon coffee.

On Monday morning, *Jimbun* headed off for the Crookhaven River and Nowra. We followed Graeme out. We had five knots of 'wind' and Ian was not happy with the forecasters. The breeze that did arrive late that morning was from the SE, so we were able to sail up the coast comfortably, the wind on the beam.

By mid-afternoon, we were off Wollongong, the wind behind us and the sails wung out either side. The *Aires* won't handle sailing like this, so we had to hand steer for an hour or so, until the curve of the coast allowed us to alter course a few degrees and bring both sails to port, the genoa poled out and a preventer on the main to stop it from gybing.

It was just on midnight when we slipped into Quarantine Bay behind North Head, Sydney, and anchored off the beach there.

'That was one of the best cruises,' I said to Ian, as we drifted off to sleep.

⚓

During Easter of 1991, we sailed to Broken Bay and Pittwater. It was a fun weekend even though the weather was quite dreary. We joined the CCC club boats anchored in America Bay, just around the corner from Refuge Cove and its famous waterfall. The boys went off in the dinghy for a couple of hours and I asked them to drop off our garbage while they were out.

For the holiday weekend, the Waterways Authority had moored two large barges with skips on them, so visitors could leave their waste.

Jamie could see the laziness of people and capitalised by giving the yachties the convenience of a personalized pickup service. Only when they returned, smelly and waving some money, did we realised what they had been doing.

'Most people were keen for us to remove their garbage for them,' said Jamie. 'Most of them gave us five bucks.'

'Should we be ashamed of them or congratulate them on their enterprise?' I said to Ian.

'I don't know. I do want them to wash out the dinghy and shower themselves under the waterfall though,' said Ian.

Herein lay a source of some of the problems I had with my elder son. I admired his quick mind, his energy and his resourcefulness. At the same time, I was slightly embarrassed by some of his actions and often had to 'hide' a grin while I told him he shouldn't be doing whatever he had been up to.

Eventually, a psychologist explained to Ian and me that we were giving our son double messages and that he was opting to take on board the message giving him leave to break rules.

Another pointer I learned too late in life to apply to my own children was the notion of giving children boundaries. Most people it seems, including the lecturers at Teachers College, considered this concept so elemental, they didn't mention it, despite my difficulties with disciplining school children. I was a grandmother before someone explained it to me.

'What do you mean by "boundaries"?' I asked.

She said, 'You've got to set boundaries and stick to them.' When she realised I still didn't understand her, she explained the concept and I realised that such boundaries had been haphazard during my own somewhat dysfunctional upbringing.

# 13  Coastal Cruising North

At the end of 1991, the bi-polar roller coaster kicked in again and I became severely depressed. I was stressed from studying hard for my naturopathic exams. I suppose I should have gone to hospital, but Ian knew I was terrified of that scenario. He decided that the best solution for us all was to take me on board *Realitas* that New Year and day-sail up the coast.

Jamie persuaded his father to let him take his sailboard with us. Ian was less keen than he had been the previous summer. He was intending to take *Realitas* over several bars that were more unpredictable than those on the south coast.

The only place to stow the sailboard was to strap it to the starboard railing. A wave rolling over the deck could take the whole railing with the board. Ian reluctantly agreed to have it on board, only because we were day-sailing and not making any overnight passages. That meant it was less likely we would be caught out with bad weather.

I was in no state to help with the sailing, but Jamie was fifteen and well capable of assisting Ian. David, almost thirteen, took his turns on watch too. We day-sailed north as far as Port Macquarie, stopping en route at Port Stephens, where we joined with yachting friends celebrating New Year in Fame Cove.

One day, when we were anchored in Salamander Bay, (convenient to showers on the beach and within walking to a large shopping centre and industrial hub), a mastless yacht came in and anchored.

'That's *Tarraleaha*,' said Ian.

Janet White and Barry Gow had sold *Scotch Mist*, and *Tarraleaha* was their new 34 foot yacht (UFO design).

We climbed into the dinghy and went over to greet them.

'What happened to you?' I asked. 'How did you lose your mast?'

'We were sailing along quite comfortable yesterday when it suddenly fell down,' said Janet. 'Fortunately, it was in daylight.'

'Conditions were good yesterday, so what happened?' asked Ian. 'Did something break?'

'Yes,' said Barry. 'The stays are fixed to the deck with "U" bolts. One failed and the whole lot came down. This is the bolt that failed.'

Ian turned his attention to the broken "U" bolt Barry was holding out to him.

'Ahh, you can see how this has cracked some time ago, progressively weakened and then suddenly let go,' said Ian. He turned to me. 'See Jan, you can tell by the changes in colour where it has broken off. The early crack is stained dark and the bright metal is the final break.'

In discussion with Barry about how this might have happened, Ian suggested the most likely scenario was that someone had used the "U" bolt as a fixing point for a spring line when mooring the yacht. Constant surging in strong winds while moored thus could have weakened the bolt.

'So how did you get the mast back on board?' I asked.

'Janet did that,' said Barry. 'The mast was banging into the side of the boat. I was about to cut it free, but she insisted we try to get it back on board.'

'I'm hoping we can reuse it,' said Janet. She went on to describe her herculean effort to bring it all back on board. Our admiration for this woman grew.

The following day, Richard came in with *Mistress*. Ian told him what had happened to Janet and Barry.

'I'd have been pleased to get a mast back on board with a strong crew of six,' he said.

A couple of days later, we set off north. There was little wind at first and we motored the eight miles over to Broughton Island where we anchored overnight in Esmeralda Cove. On the fourth of January we had some good sailing, reaching Cape Hawke by early afternoon and entered Cape Hawke harbour beside the town of Tuncurry.

The next day, Sunday, we walked across the bridge to Forster. Forster-Tuncurry is a pleasantly quiet holiday town for Aussies. It has no big resorts and is not a mecca for foreign tourists, but rather sports a large, well-kept caravan park. The tall bridge allows shallow draft vessels to enter the Wallis Lakes, coastal lagoons which lie behind the town.

*Figure 6. Northern Coast of NSW*

From Forster we moved on to Camden Haven and its town, Laurieton, where we needed to visit the supermarket. The boys did the grocery shopping, while I went along to pay for our purchases by debit card. How we managed to take any groceries back to the boat, I don't know. Every time the boys put something into the trolley, I removed it.

'We can't afford to buy that,' I said, putting a salami sausage back into the fridge.

'But Mum, we've got to buy some food to eat.' David put the salami back into the trolley along with the bread and eggs.

When really depressed, I lose my appetite and become very mean with money. My sons were exasperated with me but managed to take some food back to the boat.

The next day, Ian and the boys decided to hike up to the top of North Brother – a hill behind the town. There was no question of my staying by myself on *Realitas*. I was too unwell to be left alone. I walked slowly up the hill track to the lookout, dragging the pace.

On the way back, Jamie led us through the bush – he loved to go cross country. By the time we returned to 'civilisation' I was hot, torn and scratched by branches, dirty and crying. We were all thirsty and entered a shop to buy drinks. I don't know what the shop keeper made of this rag-tailed party with Ian trying to console me. At the time, I didn't even care. Somehow, my family endured my illness and, rather than throw me overboard, they took me home again.

The weather was unpleasant for a couple of days with rain squalls and gusty winds. We stayed put at Laurieton, mostly reading. When the sky cleared we headed north again, sailing as far north as Port Macquarie, Ian's planned destination.

Although the town and marina are attractive, the river entrance is not so very friendly. The mouth is wide, but it is well known in boating circles to have a difficult bar. Ian was very cautious to follow all the known rules for crossing a bar when we entered. We waited a mile or so off shore until the tide was both high and at slack water, before following a local fishing boat in.

When we were preparing to leave Ian walked up to the top of a knoll to the north of the town from where he could look down on the river bar. He watched as a powerboat headed out to sea. The bar looked calm for several minutes, then a wave reared up in front of the powerboat. The driver increased speed and forced his way through. The boat's bow soared up about thirty-five degrees, before pushing through the crest. It seemed the tide was still rising and there were occasionally very steep waves forming against the outflow from the river.

Back on *Realitas*, Ian insisted that Jamie's sailboard should be stowed inside the boat and the companion way boards locked in place. He also insisted we all wear lifejackets. At that time, there was no ruling on the wearing of lifejackets for crossing bars.

'Aren't you being a bit over cautious, Dad?' Jamie scoffed.

'No. You will do as you're told for once. Now get that lifejacket on and done up.'

The tidal current into the port had abated. We motored out towards sea and all felt good after the boat had crossed the bar. Jamie opened his mouth and was half way through saying "I told you so, Dad,' when a large wave rose up behind us and broke very close astern. Both boys were silent for the next fifteen minutes. Those waves gave little warning. There must have been some irregularity in the sea floor just there to make it happen. We turned south – homewards.

Crowdy Head provided an uncomfortable overnight stop. The anchorage in behind the fishermen's wharf is very tight and the swell crept around the breakwater and rocked us more than soothingly.

The next day, aware that a southerly front was imminent, we stopped at Broughton Island again, dropping anchor in the northern bay of the island which would provide the best shelter from southerly winds. Ian was happily talking to some other yachties while David and Jamie were mucking about with the sailboard. David returned to *Realitas* and Jamie set off on his board. I thought he'd said he was going to visit the two small islands close by.

When Ian and I realised that Jamie had disappeared, we asked David. 'Where's your brother gone?'

'I think Jamie intends to sail his board right around Broughton Island,' David said.

We became concerned. A cold front was forecast to arrive within the hour. What should we do? Just then, a member of our yacht club came over to our boat.

'The locals have reported that Jamie is in trouble on his board on the other side of the island. Someone is going out to rescue him,' he said.

Ian became very angry that Jamie should do such a foolish thing as to put himself in a dangerous situation on the water and involve someone else in a rescue attempt. Both of us climbed into the dinghy and went ashore. We climbed up to a lookout and scanned the horizon for our wayward son. Soon, we saw him being brought to shore in a fishing runabout. Briskly, we walked down to the cove. Fifteen year old Jamie had a beer bottle in his hand.

'What were you thinking? You didn't know how strong the southerly would be. The forecast was for thirty knots. How were you to know it wouldn't be that strong, or even more like forty knots? You could have drowned out there.'

Ian's concern was betrayed by his anger. He feared he could have lost his elder son.

'I was fine. I wasn't in any trouble,' said Jamie.

'So why did the locals think you needed rescuing?'

'I dunno. I was just sitting on my board having a rest when they came out and insisted I should go ashore with them. I told them "No." I wanted to finish my circumnavigation of Broughton.'

'And?'

'They offered me a beer if I would get into their runabout. I could see they weren't going to give up, so I thought I'd better come in with them.'

'Did you thank them for rescuing you?' I said.

'They didn't rescue me! I didn't need rescuing. I wanted to keep sailing.'

Jamie was being very truculent. He hated being thwarted. (How like his mother he can be.) We took him and his sailboard back out to *Realitas*.

Ian and I felt embarrassed. We didn't go ashore at that bay again on this visit to Broughton. The next morning we sailed around to Coalshaft Bay on the western side of the island, where we swam and snorkelled. I didn't enjoy Coalshaft Bay. In my mental state, I wasn't able to enjoy anything.

After my experiences at Lord Howe Island, and despite Ian putting his wetsuit top on me, I found the water cold and there were few fish to see. Those I saw were dull and grey and silver – nothing like the wondrous tropical colours I liked. The warm east coast current brings the coral spore and warm waters to the Lord Howe Rise, but that is the southernmost area of tropical coral in the Tasman Sea.

It is only eight miles from Broughton Island to the Tomago Headland at the entrance to Shoal Bay in Port Stephens. That afternoon, we sailed that short distance and entered the port. Just as we cleared the entrance, Jamie prepared his board and declared his intention of sailing by himself from there.

'Let me off with my board, Dad.'

'No.'

'Let me off, Dad.'

'No.'

'I'll throw the board over and swim after it.'

'Why are you so keen to sail?'

'Cos those blokes didn't let me finish my circumnavigation of the island.'

'We're heading in to Fame Cove. Do you reckon you can follow us right in there?'

'Yeah.'

'All right then.' Ian gave in less than gracefully.

When Jamie had made up his mind about something, it was no use trying to make him budge.

All the way up the harbour, I kept staring back to check on Jamie. I suppose Ian was checking too, but he didn't let on. Jamie was standing on his board and seemed to be having no trouble at all. We continued round the corner into Fame Cove, the keyhole hideaway, where Ian anchored. We'd just finished tidying everything away, when our son "sauntered" around the corner. He was still upright, his tee shirt and shorts as dry as when he'd climbed off Realitas several miles back. He was wearing his sunhat with a feather stuck into the brim and he was whistling.

'See, I *can* do it,' he seemed to be saying.

We spent two days at Port Stephens, then moved on again, sailing straight back to Sydney Harbour, where we arrived in the early hours of the following morning. Ian took *Realitas* around North Head and tucked her into Little Manly Cove, where we could relax and get some sleep before heading on up the harbour to our mooring in Five Dock Bay.

Gradually, my depression eased, and in late January 1992, I enrolled again at Nature Care College in Artarmon, studying more subjects in Natural Therapies while, at the same time, continuing to teach Higher School Certificate English at Hornsby TAFE.

Starting to practise meditation helped moderate my tendency to anxiety. It was not all plain sailing though. Because I had not yet found any medication to help my bi-polar condition, I was still experiencing the roller coaster of high moods and severe depressions. When I realised I had become a very good massage therapist, I went looking for work. After going to three interviews in small upstairs 'clinics', it dawned on me that these were brothels.

In frustration, I went to the college office. 'How do I find a massage job that's not in a brothel?'

'Have you tried the clinic in Sage Street?'

'No. Where's that?'

Given directions to the north shore suburb, I set off to find the clinic. The crowd of cars parked in the suburban street alerted me to the clinic's presence. This was a very professional set-up, with six treatment rooms and another small office set up for iridology and colonic irrigation. The owner's daughter was also a natural therapist and this small office was her domain.

I was delighted when the boss employed me there three days a week. What a lot I learned working at that clinic! My faith in my ability to massage well was justified and I also learned more from my fellow massage therapists by watching, copying and experimenting.

⚓

By the time David reached fourteen, he was often not keen to accompany us sailing on weekends. He was developing his own interests, especially in motorbikes. A boy at his school was selling his off-road motorcycle.

'Hey Dad, this kid at school's got a Kawasaki, a KX80. I want to buy it. I've got enough money saved up.'

He was sure he wanted it, so we were preparing to hook up our trailer to the car before going to see the bike.

'Why are we doing this, Jan?'

'So that David learns to control a motorcycle in a safe environment and not by riding on the road. Inevitably he'll want a road bike. You ride one, and I still have a licence to ride. How will you manage to convince David he shouldn't ride a motor bike?'

David bought the Kawasaki and joined the Mount Ku-ring-gai Motocross Club. We took him to the off-road club most weekends to practise riding or compete, except when we visited Jamie and Ian's mother in the Southern Highlands.

For the next couple of years there was little time to think about boating, except during school holidays. We antifouled *Realitas* in early April and at Easter, Ian sailed with David to Broken Bay in the Hawkesbury.

I didn't fancy being seasick that Easter, so I travelled up to Hawkesbury River train station and Ian brought *Realitas* there to pick me up. Jamie also arrived by train at the Hawkesbury River station in Brooklyn the day after me.

Dagmar and Richard did a similar thing, with Richard sailing *Mistress* up the coast accompanied by Andrew, while Dagmar and the girls drove up from their home in Clovelly.

*Mistress* and *Realitas* met up again in Jerusalem Bay, a large bay and a favourite spot that is well-sheltered from the wind in most directions.

After a long weekend of chocolate munching, reading and socialising, David and I went home by train and Jamie remained on board; he and Ian motored across to Dangar Island. There Ian discovered that *Realitas* had water in the engine once again.

Richard dropped Dagmar and the girls off at Brooklyn too, and then he anchored *Mistress* beside *Realitas* off Dangar Island. Together, the men examined our engine.

No water came out of the exhaust when the motor was running. Ian reversed the sealing plate in the water pump and replaced a piece of hose he thought might be leaking. Although according to Richard, the engine sounded very rough, they agreed that it should get Ian home.

Work demanded both Richard and Ian return to Sydney, so they set off next morning with Jamie still onboard *Realitas* to give Ian a hand bringing the boat back to her mooring.

The following weekend, after pulling the engine down enough to examine the head and the exhaust manifold, Ian found no cracks. The only explanation he could find for the problem was that we needed a proper siphon breaker to prevent water flowing in through the exhaust and then draining back into the engine.

Once Ian had installed the siphon breaker, we had no more problems with water entering the engine.

# 14  Cruising to the Lord Howe Rise

Jamie turned seventeen in November 1992, and had only one year of school left to complete.

'Where would you like to go for our holiday cruise this summer, Jamie?' we asked him.

There was, unusually for Jamie, little hesitation. 'Lord Howe,' he said.

Jamie was hoping to enter the army in February, 1994, so we knew he could be sent anywhere after that.

'Why does Jamie get to choose?' asked David.

'Once Jamie's finished the HSC next year and left school, he'll probably be in the army. He mightn't join us again for a family holiday,' I said. 'You can choose before you leave school.'

Once again, we moved to the boat on Boxing Day. This time, we took all day to organise ourselves and slept overnight at our mooring in Five Dock Bay. The next day, we still had chores to complete, so we motored to Manly Cove, where Ian and I went into the water to scrub the hull.

Ian's friend, Richard, was always keen to buy new yachting technology.

'How'd you like to borrow my GPS for your summer trip to Lord Howe Island?' he asked.

'Are you sure you won't need it in January?' Ian said.

'No. We're not sailing this summer holidays. Take it now,' said Richard.

Ian set about learning how to operate this little wonder gadget. It was fairly easy to use, he discovered. Wow, what a difference using GPS made to our voyage. We took along the sextant and tables as back-up of course, but they stayed packed away.

'I can't believe we can know exactly where we are, just at the push of a button!' I said. Suddenly the real advantage dawned on me. 'Hey, now I understand how it shows current. If we have moved over the ground faster than the log shows, the extra is current in our direction. Before, I didn't fully understand the implications for reading the strength of currents.'

'And if the log indicates more distance than we have actually covered over the ground than shown by our position on the GPS, the current is holding us back,' said Ian. 'Having the loan of Richard's GPS means we can safely visit the Lord Howe Rise. That's something I've long wanted to do but it was too dangerous without accurate navigation.'

The tiny cays and reefs to the north of Lord Howe form part of an underwater ridge that sweeps up into the Coral Sea, and the currents around them are notorious for drifting boats onto the reefs.

'That sounds like a really interesting addition to our usual Lord Howe Island visit,' I said. 'We'd better do some research about the reef.'

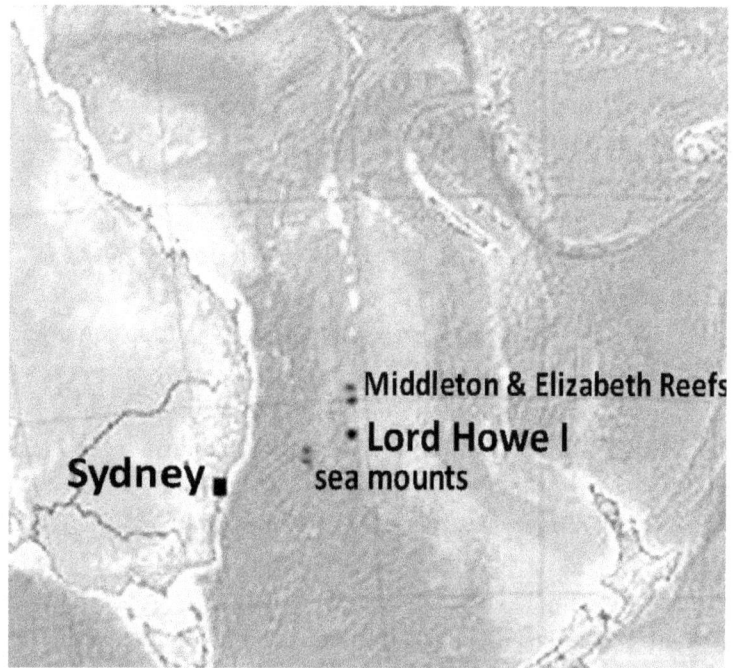

Figure 7. The Lord Howe Rise

'Yes. And I'll probably need you to visit the hydrographic chart office at Boat Books in Crows Nest.'

Lord Howe Island lies at the southern tip of that mostly underwater ridge. Much of the area consists of shallows, reef and wrecks, all of which only show above the horizon at low tide.

These cause the unpredictable currents. Our plan was to sail to Lord Howe first, then go north to stop at Elizabeth and Middleton Reefs.

In preparation, I visited Boat Books and made notes of all the recent updates about the suspected inaccuracies on the Lord Howe Rise charts.

'There's a note on the chart that the south-eastern end of Middleton Reef extends one nautical mile east of where it used to be shown,' I told Ian when I came home.

Our passage was much faster than on previous voyages out to the island. We were able to adjust our course whenever the current started affecting us, so that we took a much more direct course this time.

However, because we had started off forty-eight hours later than usual, we were still at sea on New Year's Eve. On earlier visits, we had enjoyed New Year's Eve on the island. The islanders always have a big beach party and invite all visitors. During the day, the young people gather an enormous pile of flammable material, building it into a small mountain on the beach. They set it alight about eight pm.

We arrived very early on the second of January after waiting for enough light to enter the southern pass, which is usually reserved for bigger yachts. This entrance is more complicated, so the Harbour Master, Clive Wilson, usually brings smaller yachts in the northern end of the lagoon. We found ourselves moored next to a 54 foot Radcliffe designed yacht, which had made the 400 nautical mile passage in only two days! Ian was impressed and accepted the skipper's invitation to go on board.

This mooring was only temporary. The next morning, Clive guided us out of the lagoon again, instructing us to motor to the northern pass, where we re-entered and picked up a mooring near Blackburn Island and close to *Tarraleaha*.

We were not long settled at the mooring, when Jamie asked if he could have the dinghy to go ashore to climb on Mt. Lidgbird. Jamie took a backpack and bottle of water with him and David dropped him ashore and then brought the dinghy back. A couple of hours later, Janet called us on the VHF radio.

'I can see Jamie through the binoculars. He is half way up Mt. Lidgbird, but not on the track to the Goat House,' she said.

We became concerned for Jamie's safety, and also that that his actions could affect all visiting yachties. Jamie was a survivor, but what he was doing was forbidden. People had died trying to reach the summit of Lidgebird, which was why there were no tours up there and no path maintained. The maintained path went only as far as the Goat House, which was a cave about half way up the mountain.

I spent a tense couple of hours watching for Jamie through our binoculars. Eventually, he returned, grazed, tired, hungry, and disappointed he hadn't been able to reach the top.

'How did you do this?' I asked, pointing to his grazed forearms.

'I tried to scale a rocky cliff,' said Jamie. 'That's when I had to turn back. I ran out of hand holds.'

We were relieved he was back relatively unscathed and that there were no repercussions by the island authorities from his actions.

This trip, I decided I would hike up to the Goat House cave. Not requiring a guide, Ian, the boys and I walked to the base of the mountain and set off up the track. There were ropes tied to trees in places to help pull ourselves up.

It was a lovely climb, not nearly as arduous as the Mt. Gower climb we'd done on our second visit to Lord Howe.

However, the final ascent to the Goat House, just fifty metres up a rope, defeated me. When the others came down, Ian had something to report.

'There's a tropic bird on its nest up there,' he said.

*Tropic bird in a rocky nest on Mt.Lidgbird's Goat House Cave*

'I'd like to have seen that,' I replied. I couldn't. Given the specialist's prediction three years before that I would never walk properly again, I was very lucky to have managed to climb all three mountains on Lord Howe.

We had scaled Mt. Eliza, the third and smallest peak at the northern end of the island, easily on our first visit to the island and Mount Gower on our second visit.

Not only was I fitter, I was also better prepared for this visit to Lord Howe, having bought myself a full wetsuit and proper snorkel and goggles to fit my narrow face.

I was serious about snorkeling. The underwater world had captured my imagination and nothing was going to stop me exploring it. There was magic down there, not dreamed of from the relatively dreary surface. Despite our intrusions into their milieu, those colourful fish went on living their lives, swimming in and around the coral outcrops, feeding, keeping a lookout for predators and generally going about their business. I loved it.

'Don't let yourself get too cold, Jan,' said Ian.

'There's no way I'm going to forget my brush with hypothermia,' I said.

My confidence in the water now extended to swimming off the boat at our anchorage. There were a couple of interesting holes in the reef close by that were well worth a visit. I still wasn't used to the idea that reef sharks were not interested in humans though. A shark was still a shark to me and whenever I saw one, I hastily retreated to the dinghy.

We anchored the dinghy near where we wanted to snorkel at Little Island where the best coral is really close to the stony beach.

Another preparation I had made was to buy a proper dinghy anchor for this voyage. Dinghy anchors are designed without sharp points, a useful attribute in an inflatable dinghy and perhaps less damaging to the coral too. They fold up, and therefore it is not nearly so easy to stub cold bare toes.

Getting into the water from the dinghy while kitted out in wetsuit, mask, snorkel and fins is not easy either. You need to make sure your fins don't catch on anything that you want to remain in the bottom of the dinghy. I swivel my body and slosh over the side; Ian just sits on the inflated side tube and falls backwards, but I prefer to face where I am going.

To get back into any dinghy from the water is difficult, but the inflatable has fabric handles on the interior sides of its floatation tubes. By kicking your fins and grabbing for the handles of the tube on the opposite side, it is possible to slither into the dinghy on your belly – rather like an ungainly seal might.

Several Coastal Cruising Club boats were present on this visit. One was a large catamaran, the crew of which invited us to accompany them on a trip out to Balls Pyramid. This is a pinnacle of rock that rears up out of the sea about twenty miles from the main island. There is nowhere safe to land on this steep, grey-black monolith, but nearby, the water is shallow enough to anchor.

The two young crewmen on board the catamaran had brought dive tanks with them and to jet themselves about they had a *Scudo* (an underwater motorised scooter). The machine had a 'back to the future' aspect to it, I thought.

Balls Pyramid

While they were preparing the machine for the water, Ian, Jamie and David donned their masks and snorkels and jumped into the water where Ian duck dived down to the bottom.

'Do you want to have a try?' the young men asked Ian. Ian and both boys tried out the *Scudo*. It was a fun novelty for them.

'Doesn't the noise from that machine scare the fish away?' I asked the crew when they came back on board.

'Perhaps a little,' one answered. They weren't going to admit to any negatives about their new toy.

On the sail back, the young men told Ian, 'We lost the knack of free diving when we bought scuba tanks.' Ian was quite surprised by their admission.

I stayed safely on board. I wasn't ready for swimming off a boat out there. There were ocean sharks out there, not just reef sharks. Besides, I was still queasy with sea sickness. The motion on a catamaran is very different to that of a mono-hull and I was mildly seasick going both ways.

Before leaving Lord Howe, we made our usual pilgrimage to the weather station, which had been relocated to a position beside the airfield.

This time, we were allowed inside to look at the screens on the computers, which were filled with colour pictures beamed from satellites. Each employee had a PC on his desk. We were fascinated. Only Ian was familiar with computers, which he used at work. I used to feel alienated when Ian and our neighbour started chatting about computing, throwing about terms like FORTRAN, programming and spreadsheets. Back then, spreading a sheet meant making a bed to me. It had nothing to do with data.

*Lord Howe I. met officer about to launch weather balloon*

We watched one of the officers preparing a weather balloon for its flight, and then sending it aloft. As it soared skywards, it appeared smaller and smaller until I could no longer see it.

'Ian, do you remember the balloon we saw come down in Harold Park a few years ago? As it descended, I momentarily thought it was a UFO and wondered to myself how many weather balloons people reported as UFOs when they saw them drifting back to earth.'

⚓

This time when we exited the pass from the lagoon, we had another adventure planned. The forecasters predicted suitably mild weather for us to go searching for mid-ocean reefs. We left Lord Howe late in the afternoon, turned north instead of south-east and sailed all night so that in the morning we could look for Elizabeth Reef. About eight am Ian pointed out to the north-east.

'If you look over there you can see the wreck on the southern end of the reef,' he said.

'Strange sight, a wreck rising out of the ocean like that,' I said. 'Fancy that being the highest landmark, and now it's little more than a rusted hulk.'

Until GPS became affordable for ships and yachts, ocean navigation had been a much more difficult exercise involving sextant sights, navigation tables and long calculations.

No wonder ships hit these reefs which lie en route between northern New Zealand and Queensland, especially when those reefs were not even located where shown on the charts and had unpredictable currents circulating around them.

Sailing on, we made our way to the northern shore of the cay, where we found the entrance to the lagoon and wended our way in to a secure anchorage. Soon after, we were just considering leaping into the warm, crystal clear water when a US military aircraft came over the reef. Two fighter planes followed. We knew that Australian and US naval manoeuvres were being held, but we thought they'd be closer to the mainland.

'Perhaps they are on their way home after their exercises,' I said.

We waved as they passed, but soon they were back. They seemed to be using our mast as target practice, swooping low over it every time they passed. For at least half an hour they roared overhead. Ian tried calling them on the VHF radio but they didn't respond. The noise was painful on our ears – truly deafening and we had no idea how to make the planes go away!

The boys jumped into the water trying to escape the noise, but found no relief there.

'It's just as bad under water. Even the fish seem distressed. They're rushing about, trying to escape the noise,' said Jamie when they came back onboard.

I contemplated taking the dinghy to the nearest sand and writing 'STOP' in large letters. Finally, they departed. Once the planes had gone, our ears still ringing, we began to relax into the peace of this magical place in the middle of the ocean.

Realitas *anchored at low tide in the lagoon at Middleton Reef*

We swam and snorkeled, gazing at the brightly coloured corals and fish. I didn't know what most of them were, but I loved their underwater world. David found a squid and brought it on board to examine more closely. As squid do when afraid, it squirted black ink onto our deck. Those stains took several months to fade.

At low tide we walked on the beach, seeing pieces of timber and steel wreckage half buried in the sand. I wondered how it would feel to be shipwrecked somewhere like this. We saw it as a kind of paradise. But what if your arrival was unintended?

Ian reminded me about a lone sailor who had entered the New Plymouth (NZ) to Gladstone single-handed yacht race. 'Do you remember Bill Belcher's description on TV of how his yacht was driven onto one of these reefs?'

'I suppose the currents took his boat off course,' I said.

'Fortunately, he still had his yacht for shelter and had access to his stores on board,' said Ian. 'However, he didn't know how long it would take for someone to find him. Do you remember how he described eating baked beans from a can, savouring each bean, carefully chewing it and finally swallowing it?'

The next day, we sailed to Middleton Reef, a short distance to the north. A large part of Middleton Reef lies barely under the water's surface. In bad weather, the reef is largely invisible from the deck of even a large boat. Like Elizabeth Reef, the entrance to the lagoon was on the northern side.

'The wreck down on the southern end of the reef is supposed to contain emergency supplies,' said Ian. 'How about we go down and have a look?'

'Will we be able to get on board?' asked Jamie.

'I want to go on board too,' said David.

'Okay,' I said. 'How long do you estimate it'll take? What will we need to take with us?'

'Sunscreen, drinking water, maybe some fruit ... 'said Ian. 'We'll probably have to wait until the tide is rising again, so we'll be gone a few hours.'

We left *Realitas* at anchor in the lagoon and crossed the reef in the inflatable at high tide. Our *Avon* inflatable is flat bottomed not a RIB (inflatable dinghy with a keel). Even so, at places, we had to lift the outboard propeller to avoid hitting the coral.

The reef is quite extensive and the dinghy ride across to the wreck of the smallish cargo ship on the southern shore took nearly an hour. In very large letters on the side of the ship, someone had sprayed the words, 'Emergency Food Here'.

'I wonder who places the supplies in the ship? How often do you think they are checked for accessibility and fitness for consumption?' I said.

'It's possibly looked after by the Australian Navy,' said Ian.

'Let's go and see what they've left up there,' said Jamie. 'Come on David.'

'I'd better keep an eye on them.' Ian followed the two boys.

They climbed up into the rusting hulk to examine the supplies. What would I do in an emergency if I needed to get myself up into that ship? The sides were high and the deck was severely rusted. I could see no way up for me though I suppose a rush of adrenalin would help me if I was really in need. I'm not sure how David clambered up.

When my family came down, Jamie reported, 'As well as cans of food and fresh water, there're some blankets, Mum. The inside of the ship is pretty rusted, but.'

'We had to be very careful about where we stepped,' added Ian. 'The deck is mostly rusted out.'

'This place feels like paradise to me,' I said, 'but I don't think I would feel so happy if I had to wait here to be rescued. It would be very frustrating if I knew there were food, water and blankets up there and I couldn't reach them easily.'

After a few more days of relaxation, the pressures of ordinary life - work for Ian and me and school for the boys - demanded that we set off for home. This was the way our summer holidays always ended. Just when we were most relaxed and all tensions between us were gone, it would be time to return to the city, work and school.

The weather was incredibly calm, as it had been ever since our arrival at the reefs. After motoring in a south-westerly direction for a while, a light breeze came up, so Ian decided to set the spinnaker. The boys were eager to help. Any sort of action interested Jamie, while David loved sailing fast.

At first, the breeze barely swelled the sail, but slowly, the wind increased. Soon the big red, orange and white sail was drawing strongly. Our speed increased a little more. David and Jamie were taking turns on the tiller, alternating with the job of spinnaker trimmer. *Do they think this is a racing yacht?*

An hour or so later, we were sailing at five knots. After another hour, I noticed our *Sumlog* indicated eight knots. Ian was struggling to hold the tiller. Jamie was grinning and still happily taking his turn to steer, using his feet as well as his hands to keep the boat on course. The tiller on *Realitas* was always a little heavy, even with Ian's earlier modification it was too much for David. 'Hey, we're going great guns,' he grinned. 'Think how many miles we're covering. If we take the spinnaker down, we'll get only about three knots.'

Feeling the wind on my face, I looked at the whitecaps.

'I think we'll still get five knots with just the mainsail.'

The boys agreed with their father, who turned back to his struggle with the tiller.

Realitas *under spinnaker*

Shortly after our conversation, there was a ripping noise. We all looked up to see the spinnaker flying loose. It had torn completely out of its side tapes. The grins disappeared and Ian dropped the halyard.

I looked at Ian meaningfully, and then nodded towards the knot meter. I looked at Ian and held my lips firmly together. We were still making five knots! That spinnaker was going to take a lot of mending – by me.

'Come and help, boys,' he said as we started to gather in the sail that was drifting under the keel.

'Just let it go, Dad,' urged Jamie.

'Yeah, let it go,' echoed David.

They didn't know how much it would cost to buy a new spinnaker. I brought up the sail-bag. As we dragged up the torn, wet sail, I carefully stuffed it into the bag.

We went back to the cockpit and I looked at the knot metre and then at Ian, my lips held firmly shut.

The wind stayed. We sailed into Broken Bay in under three days, making excellent time – an average of five knots from Middleton Reef. That was probably one of the fastest passages we ever made in *Realitas*.

We had arrived just in time for The Coastal Cruising Club's Australia Day rendezvous at Dangar Island on the Hawkesbury River near Brooklyn.

# 15  Summer Holiday in Broken Bay

In his final year (1993) at Chevalier College, Jamie was made House Captain, a duty he took seriously. He also studied hard and performed well in his Higher School Certificate exams. He had more than fulfilled our expectations and we felt that the struggle to pay boarding school fees was well worthwhile. He turned eighteen about the time he was finishing his final exams.

When Jamie came home, we hosted what he called a 'gathering'. We invited all his friends as well as all the adults who had known him well as he grew up. It was a 'pot luck' event. Everyone brought food or snacks to contribute to the party. The adults gathered inside the house; the young people gathered in the backyard, on the veranda or in the boys' bedrooms, which were in a separate building just behind the house.

I remembered the key to the house I had given Jamie when we left him at boarding school – symbolic that we hadn't abandoned him, that we always would welcome him home. Now he needed a different kind of key to celebrate his official entrance to adulthood. At school in the manual arts workshop, David made a wooden key about 400mm long. We varnished it and in gold paint I wrote on it Jamie's name and "Key to the World".

*Jamie on his eighteenth birthday*

That party was also a celebration for Ian and me that our son had done well. He had gained a worthwhile education and our family was still complete. Jamie wasn't living on the streets or with anti-social people. These were all the things I'd feared when he was mixing with his former friends four years before.

At the end of the school year, we all wanted to have a boating holiday, but the results of Jamie's Higher School Certificate exams were due to be posted on the tenth of January. These days, 'posted' means available on the internet; back then it was 'snail mail'. Jamie had to be at home to collect his letter from our mailbox at the front gate.

'If we go up to the Hawkesbury River,' I suggested, 'Jamie can go ashore from Jerusalem Bay to Cowan station and travel home by train to collect his exam results. That way, we can join the club members for New Year's Eve in America Bay.'

'Good thinking, Mum,' agreed Jamie.

During that year, we had seldom had time to visit the boat. Ian, Jamie and I went down to Five Dock Bay and found that due to our long neglect, the batteries had lost so much charge we couldn't start the engine. When Ian realised the electric starter would not turn the engine over, he tried hand-cranking and Jamie helped too.

'I don't think that's going to work, Jamie,' Ian said.

'Shall we go ashore and bring the car battery back?' asked Jamie.

'No. I've got one more trick up my sleeve before we do that,' said Ian. 'We'll try using *Aerostart*.'

Jamie turned the crank handle while Ian squirted the *Aerostart* into the combustion chamber. There was a loud bang and after that, the engine refused to budge any more.

When Ian dismantled the engine, he discovered that when it had fired, the camshaft gear had slipped, mis-timing the pistons and so bending the rockers and push rods. No wonder nothing would move and it required more than Ian's abilities to fix. There was no way we could afford to pay the mechanic to repair such serious damage, so Ian put all the pieces into a box and delivered the box to the mechanic.

'I'll let you know when I can afford to pay you to fix it,' Ian told him.

With no engine, it was difficult to use the boat. We never had learned to manoeuvre *Realitas* under sail in confined waters, so Richard lent us an old long-shaft outboard motor. If we could use the outboard on *Realitas*, we could move her when there was no wind.

Ian decided to build a steel bracket for the stern of the boat to hold the motor. After working at the back of the house for an hour or so one Saturday morning, he came inside, holding his right hand.

'I think I've broken it,' he said.

'How on earth did you do that?'

'The drill grabbed in the metal hole and twisted my hand severely.'

I went to find elastic bandages, then picked up my car keys.

'Come on, let's take you up to the hospital for an X-ray,' I said.

'Not yet. I'm going to finish drilling the hole first.' He saw the disbelief on my face. 'I'll use my left hand.'

At the hospital outpatients, the radiologist confirmed that the fourth metatarsal was indeed broken. Ian's osteoporosis had been diagnosed when he was in his mid-thirties. He well knew when a bone was broken.

'I'm not going to be much use sailing the boat with a broken hand,' said Ian.

'I could sail her up for you, if you'll let me,' suggested Jamie. 'I'm sure I could find a couple of friends from school to help.'

Ian looked doubtful, but I thought Jamie, now eighteen, was responsible enough.

'Why not, Ian?'

In the end, we all went on the boat after Christmas, with Jamie doing the bulk of the sailing. We still had no engine, but Richard's outboard on the stern bracket worked if both boys sat on the back of the boat. That kept the propeller deep enough into the water for the blades to bite. The assembly probably looked a little crazy, but it functioned – just – and we could move the boat when there was no wind.

In those days, the two boys had become much better friends than when they were younger. Jamie's four years at boarding school had broken his domination over his brother and, of course, they had both grown up a lot.

The wind was very light as we sailed up the Hawkesbury River, drifted into America Bay and over to our Coastal Cruising Club mooring, where we rafted up with several other club boats.

We had a very social holiday that year. Nearly all our friends with boats were in the area – *Mistress, Sapphire, Mr Percival,* as well as *Tarraleagha, Aragunnu* and lots of other CCC club boats too.

We called at Pittwater on our way back. The Reeves were home at Little Lovett Bay in Pittwater, with their boat, *Golden Opportunity*, on their newly built jetty. Nick moved his boat out to its mooring for the night we visited, and we tied *Realitas* alongside the jetty.

We had first met the Reeves in Tahiti. They and their two young sons were sailing out from England in their 31foot twin bilge keeled Golden Hind yacht. We had met up with them again in Rarotonga (see *Two in a Top Hat* p.123) and maintained our friendship when they settled in Little Lovett Bay. Their sons had grown up and Tom had married a Russian girl. Her parents were due to visit from Russia.

Another day, we met up with friends, anchoring our boats next to each other in Towlers Bay. That day, the atmosphere became cracklingly hot and dry, with buffeting blustery westerly winds. The humidity dropped to twenty percent, while the temperature soared to over forty degrees. It was bushfire weather.

Roslyn and I sat in the shallows of the luke-warm bay chattin desultorily, frequently sipping from our water bottles
which floated beside us. I had met Roslyn at Nature Care College, where she was also studying Natural Therapies. She lived in the northern suburbs with her family where I'd visited her, but this was the first time both families had met on the water.

As the heat of the afternoon waned a little, we motored from Towlers Bay to The Basin, where I had a verbal altercation with a power boat owner. This self-righteous, beer-bellied man had moored his big power boat on the CCC mooring. I hailed him.

'This is a private club mooring. Would you please vacate it so we can tie up.' I was using my best manners.

'Sorry love, I'm busy.'

I repeated my request, firmly, but still politely. His next words revealed he knew very well that this was a club mooring.

'I'm a member of the CCC. I've a right to use this mooring.'

He was lying. There were no power boats in our sailing club. Mostly, our members were disdainful of big power boaters.

'Really? When did you join?'

'Oh, we haven't joined quite yet. Friends who are members invited us to use the mooring.' More lies.

I went below and picked up our club membership booklet. Outside, I waved it.

'Which friends are those? This is our membership list. Your friends' names should be in here.'

Ian had been steering the boat and keeping station while this conversation proceeded. At this point, his embarrassment grew so deep, he disappeared below to join the boys and stayed there. I had to steer as well as argue.

'Give me half an hour to finish barbecuing and I'll move,' Mr. Smarmy conceded.

'No. You'll move now. We want to use our club's mooring.'

I was being very insistent because, being early New Year, there wasn't another mooring to be had. We had no wish to anchor out and row half a mile to shore. Ian's hand was still not healed. Besides, we paid our membership dues and we had the right to use the club mooring. I was becoming very annoyed with this prig.

'I tell you what love, why don't you tie up alongside.'

'I'm not your love!'

Grrrr! How stupid was this man. Our stanchions would catch under and damage the flared hull of his boat if there was the slightest rocking.

'No. You'll move and move now!'

Finally, he gave up, put down his beer bottle and started his motor. He moved off and we picked up the mooring. When we turned off our engine, I received applause from all round the anchorage. Everyone had been listening to this exchange.

The owner of one small yacht nearby called to me. 'Good on you! We tied up there and he told us the mooring belonged to the Confederate Cruising Club and asked us to move off.'

Now, I felt even more justified in my hard stand. It was time people stood up to his kind of behaviour. Being the woman who had done this, I felt proud of myself. I detested his arrogance. It reminded me of men who call their wives "the little woman". I hoped our sons would have more respect for the women in their lives. Certainly, Ian had given them a good example to follow.

At The Basin, we had access to fresh water. Next morning, we filled jerry cans for the boat and did laundry, as well as climbing the track up the hill to the road, before moving off to Yeoman's Bay for lunch. By the time we had finished eating, the tinder-dry wind was increasing from the north-west. We could see smoke on the horizon.

I tuned into ABC radio news. Many bushfires were breaking out around Sydney. Ian decided we should move, afraid we'd be caught in one. The national park was likely to catch fire too. A lightning strike was frequently the spark that ignited.

We were towing our inflatable *Avon* dinghy, with the outboard motor on it. Of course, we should have lifted the motor off, but Ian had decided to risk leaving it on. Bad move. As we left the bay for Cowan Creek, the wind whipped the dinghy upside down, drowning the motor. Not only was this not good for the motor, it made *Realitas* more difficult to control. With difficulty, Ian managed to steer to Looking Glass Bay, across the creek from Cottage Point. By late afternoon, we were securely anchored, but the sky was dark with smoke.

There were fires on the ridges surrounding Cottage Point. Together, we watched as the wall of flames creep closer to our anchorage, and then the four of us retired to our bed. Areas of Ku Ring Gai National Park burned to the water's edge that January night while we slept soundly.

Bushfires have changed in the twenty years since then. They are no longer just angry – now they are enraged, rampaging and livid, violently destructive. Ember showers arrive kilometres ahead of the front, igniting more fires. Back then we felt safe because we were on Pittwater.

It was a disastrous season for fire. Lane Cove National Park in the north of Sydney was also burning and the Commenara Parkway was closed, houses were burnt and the freeway was cut between Hornsby and Gosford. I spent a lot of time listening to the ABC reports on the radio.

'Stop worrying, Jan. There's nothing you are going to be able to do about it if our house is burned.'

'I just want to know what's happening,' I said and went back to listening to ABC local radio reports about the fires. Ian was more philosophical about such things than I was.

The next morning, Jamie rowed the dinghy ashore while Ian fiddled with the outboard motor. Jamie was determined to see if he could find any surviving animals. His Cadet Corps and wilderness courses had developed in him an affinity with the bush and its wildlife. He returned rather grubby from smoke and charcoal.

'I couldn't find animals alive or dead,' he reported. 'What's for breakfast?'

'You can help here with the outboard.' Ian didn't have much sympathy for Jamie's trip ashore.

After drying out all the outboard parts they could, and washing important things like the carburetor in fresh water and then in methylated spirit, Ian finally managed to get the motor running again. Just as well, because Richard's spare outboard was not the most reliable and our alternative motor propulsion in light conditions was to tie the dinghy amidships and use the little Suzuki to move *Realitas*.

We heard reports on the radio that houses had burned in Lovett Bay. We sailed back into Pittwater and down to Lovett Bay to check on our friends. Fortunately, they had saved their house, but others in the bay were not so lucky. We saw the Maritime fireboats spraying water upon some of the still smouldering buildings and decided that in a place where the only access was by water, it was better to take ourselves out of the way.

Nick told us their tale later. 'Our Russian guests had never experienced bushfire before. They became very excited, rushing about trying to help save things,' said Nick.

'We were putting all our valuables – photos and things like that, onto *Golden Opportunity*.

We had her moored at our jetty,' said Ann. 'I had to stop our visitors putting the lounge chairs aboard. They had no idea about boats either,' laughed Ann. 'How could we have motored the yacht to safety with our lounge chairs in the cockpit?'

'Luckily, it didn't come to that and they helped us carry the furniture back inside after the fire had passed,' added Nick.

After the weekend we moved to Jerusalem Bay. To our surprise, we found Richard and his wife, Dagmar, in *Mistress* moored alongside a Cavalier 32. On board the Cavalier were Richard's sister and family. Richard had seen us approaching and quickly put out fenders for us to raft up beside *Mistress*.

When *Realitas* was secure, David rowed Jamie to shore to catch a train home. We hoped the mailing of his HSC results had not been affected by the fires and that he would find his exam results in our letterbox. Jamie had to cross hot, burned ground on the track up to Cowan station.

Some hours later, we were on the alert for Jamie's return. Without radio or mobile phone communications, we had to wait for a signal from him. We scanned the shoreline frequently with the binoculars, looking for a sign. Eventually, we heard his whistle. He had scrambled through the bush before getting close enough for his signal to alert us. David rowed over to pick him up.

'Well Jamie, come on. What score did you get?' I asked before he was out of the dinghy.

'Good enough Mum.'

'What's "good enough"?'

'It should be enough to get into the army course.'

Jamie could be very irritating when the mood took him. I was itching to know his actual score out of a hundred. The HSC was scaled to try to make all subjects of equal weight, then averaged, so that the final score was out of 100 and called a student's Tertiary Entrance Result. Later this was changed to 'score' so TER became TES. What they call it now, I have no idea.

We eventually found out that Jamie had achieved a respectable score of 78. He was correct. He was accepted into the new army program, the Ready Reserve, where the cadets would not only train, but also study at university on army pay. His score was also high enough for entry to Duntroon Military College if he wished to go there. Those holidays, sixteen year old David stunned us by announcing he intended to continue into senior high school.

He had been in the lower streamed classes for English and instead of studying foreign languages for the first two years of high school, had received lessons in remedial English from another Mrs. Mitchell! By the time most of the poorly performing students had left school, David was able to concentrate better in class. Being able to read the board and text books clearly made a difference too.

'You can leave school if you have a job or an apprenticeship to go to,' Ian and I had told him.

'No. I want to sit for the HSC. Obviously I want to do Industrial Technology, and Tech Drawing, but I want to do three unit Geography too, and I've got to do Maths and English.'

'How are you going to cope with three unit Geography?' we asked in unison.

'I want to give it a go.'

We agreed he should have the chance to follow his plan. Once David had decided for himself that gaining his Higher School Certificate was his goal, he became a different student.

Just before he turned seventeen, David met Emma and their relationship lasted for the next three years. Emma's love and encouragement significantly helped David turn into a confident young adult.

In February 1994, the army sent Jamie to the training camp at Kapooka, near Wagga Wagga. While there, the recruits were told they could apply for officer training at Duntroon. Those who applied were flown to Melbourne for interviews. Jamie and two new friends decided to go to Melbourne for the Duntroon interview, just as a lark.

'Hey, if the army wants to pay for us to fly down to Melbourne for a weekend, we'd be mad not to go,' Jamie told us on the phone.

After completing his three months in the Ready Reserve, Jamie came to Sydney to the Holsworthy base. Only a few weeks later, he and his two mates received notice they had been selected for officer training at Duntroon.

'My mate Chris and I didn't take the interview seriously. Maybe they took our relaxed attitude for confidence.'

All three accepted, but later Jamie and Chris regretted their decision to take this option. Their other mate was very happy to become an officer, but Jamie and Chris both wanted to go to university. Jamie had originally decided that having the army pay for his studies was a good way to go and that was why he had enlisted in the Ready Reserve. Now, the boys were on rather a different trajectory and I was fearful Jamie would be sent to serve in North Africa or the Middle East. I need not have worried though. He has always had a very good sense of self-preservation, and he used the army to his advantage.

After eighteen months at Duntroon, Chris had already resigned and Jamie signed out too, shortly before he would have committed himself to being an officer for the next five years. By then he had saved a considerable nest egg. Jamie and Chris had six months before university started the following year. Together, they went on a very long bike tour, starting out from Coffs Harbour, from where they cycled north as far as Rockhampton which lies on the Tropic of Capricorn.

After returning home by train, Jamie took a job in the city as a bicycle courier. He managed to stay in that job without injury for four months – quite an achievement. When he was the only one from his starting cohort who remained uninjured, he left, claiming that his luck might run out very soon. He sought gardening jobs after that. Jamie was saving as much money as he could, with the aim of buying his own boat. Now that he had left the army, he had to pay his own way through university and Jamie planned to live on board a boat while he studied. In the army, the recruits had been given lectures on saving. Jamie had taken this advice to heart. He was not interested in spending wildly on TVs, four-wheel drives and booze, as many of his fellow recruits did.

'Food, clothes and accommodation are all provided. What do I need money for? Five or six dollars a week buys petrol for my motorbike and gives me a beer on Friday night. I've even got enough to visit the theatre occasionally or see a film. I can save the rest.'

⚓

During this time, Ian was perpetually tired. All through 1995, he hid from me the slow encroachment of his illness. I was aware that the NSW government had a moratorium on staff replacements and knew that Ian seemed to have an ever increasing workload. He frequently brought home a briefcase of work, but always seemed too tired to do any of it.

'Why do you bring work home when you know you're not going to do it?'

'Because I've always got so many reports to write,' said Ian. 'There's always the hope I might find the time and energy to do some of it.'

'In my opinion, the weekend is family time and work belongs at work,' I said.

What I didn't know was that Ian was visiting Parramatta Park most lunch times, lying under a tree and sleeping for over an hour. Flexi-time allowed him to take up to two hours for lunch.

One Monday morning in mid-August 1995, as Ian was going out of the door, he kissed me goodbye as usual. I looked a second time at his face.

'You look unwell. I think you should take a sickie today.'

'I can't. The work just keeps piling up. I don't have time to be sick.'

I shrugged. It was his decision. He put on his motorcycle helmet and rode off. I thought no more about it until the phone rang about nine o'clock.

'Nothing's working, Jan,' said Ian's tired voice. 'I'm coming home.'

I didn't quite understand what was happening until a ghost walked in the back door. Ian took off his motor cycle gear, undressed and went to bed. The next day, I took him to see his GP. Ian, who usually bounded upstairs, went by lift from the medical centre car park up to the waiting room. I held him upright as we progressed into the doctor's consulting room.

The doctor looked questioningly from Ian to me.

'He's got adrenal exhaustion,' I explained.

Bad move for most doctors. They like to make the diagnosis. This one took it in his stride. He asked Ian to lie on the couch. *Lie down? That was a good idea.*

After several visits and a thorough examination, the doctor looked serious.

'I'll have to rule out a few other things first,' he said, 'but to me, this looks like Chronic Fatigue Syndrome. I've never seen a case before, Ian, but your symptoms fit the pattern I've read about. We can't make a definitive diagnosis for six months. In the meantime, you need lots of rest. There is no question of returning to work for a while. I can write you a medical certificate for only a week though. Come back in another week and we'll see how things are.'

Ian's life centred on bed rest for the best part of the next three months, and frequently, he was barely able to struggle to the bathroom. We also began a round of visits to various specialists, who ruled out Myasthenia Gravis, Multiple Sclerosis, severe depression, and a few other illnesses.

⚓

By 1995, David was in his final school year. He decided he wanted to build a landsailer for his practical HSC project in Technology. While Ian had little energy to help David as much as he would have liked, I tried to encourage our younger son and drove him to industrial suppliers to buy the materials he needed to build his masterpiece.

Ian and I had some of our rare disagreements over that project. He was being very negative.

'That won't work,' Ian told David.

'You can't expect David to make a perfect machine using your knowledge. This is his project and his learning experience!' I said.

I didn't have much technical knowledge, but I could see David was very frustrated by his father's attitude. Illness was making Ian grumpy. He was worried he would be forced to return to work, when he knew his aching body and foggy brain were not going to co-operate.

In that final year at high school, David, a hands-on learner, proved himself by, once again, topping his year in Industrial Technology. For his HSC project, he was Highly Commended, and received an offer to have his 'vessel' included on the train that tours NSW each year with the best art and technology works. What an honour!

I would like to have included in this book a picture of the landsailer David built, because I was very proud of his accomplishment. However, I gave him the best photo I had and now, sadly, we can't find it.

It was a double achievement for David because he also gained a sufficiently high mark to go to university if he wanted.

A lot of my attention was devoted to looking after Ian's health rather than supporting our son. While emotional support was limited from us, David did have many of those needs met by Emma.

David didn't want a big party for his eighteenth birthday. Instead, we hosted a dinner party for him, Emma and her parents joined us, as well as Travis, David's best friend, and his parents.

Ian's mother had died towards the end of 1994. She'd been in a nursing home for ten years, the dementia from Alzheimer's getting worse and worse, until she recognised no one. After the disease had slowly taken her from us, there was little grief left.

More than a year after her death, Ian's brother, Lindsay, who was executor for her estate, rang him. Apparently, their mother had investments tucked away that her family didn't know about, and which she had probably forgotten.

'The sale of Mum's house has finally been settled,' said Lindsay, 'and now the estate has been wound up. There's X dollars for you from the settlement of the estate.'

'Aha,' said Ian. 'And that gets split between Shirl, you and me.'

'No mate, that's your share.' Ian almost dropped the phone. What a welcome windfall. 'It'll be a while before the cheque comes through,' Lindsay added.

For months, we had been living on Ian's sick pay, our savings and my meagre, part-time earnings. Before long, our savings were gone, and we were reduced to an income less than half that we'd been used to when we were both working full time.

We were still paying a mortgage and, to make ends meet, I was teaching massage and aromatherapy at the local evening college.

Nearly six months after Ian's final day at work, he had to attend an appointment with a government doctor, who was assessing him on behalf of his State Government employer. The journey into the city by train was extremely tiring for him and Ian nearly fell asleep during the hour-long interview, which exhausted him. However, he was finally granted a medical discharge from his work.

In mid-1996, the Water Resources Department permitted Ian to draw his superannuation at its full rate. One day, not long before Ian officially retired and he was allowed to draw on that superannuation, a letter arrived for him.

'It doesn't look like a bill.' Ian took the envelope from me. 'Look at this Jan. It's the cheque from Mum's estate. Now we can pay off the mortgage!'

I stared at the numbers on the cheque, etching them into my mind. Until I saw the amount on paper, I hadn't really believed it.

We felt positively flush. What an enormous load of stress that money removed! What a wonderful change it would make to our lives. And we could afford to have the boat engine fixed at last, more than two years after Ian had pulled it apart.

Early the next year, 1997, Jamie started looking for his yacht. He found *Possibilities* for sale in Brisbane Waters near Gosford. She is a Mark I Top Hat, built in 1971. *Caprice*, the Top Hat Ian and I had sailed around the world, was built in 1969 by Geoff Baker, of *Fibreglass Yachts* at Mona Vale. *Possibilities* was probably one of the last Top Hat yachts built under Geoff Baker's supervision.

Jamie had saved enough money to buy his boat for cash and he moved on board to live, sailing her to Sydney Harbour and after a while, he decided to make Balls Head Bay at Wollstonecraft his 'home port'. As there was nowhere he could safely keep his little motorbike (it didn't fit on *Possibilities*), he sold it and for transport, used his bicycle which he could padlock to the park fence or take on board.

While he attended Macquarie University, Jamie perfected a low cost lifestyle.

*Jamie in cockpit of* Possibilities
*Photo by Laura Tyllila*

No need to clutter up *Possibilities* with a whole lot of text books! It's easier to use the ones in the university library,' he said.

Cycling home from university, Jamie would stop at the Buttercup Bakery factory where, at day's end, staff put outside crates of bread and other unsold bakery items.

'They just throw it out. If I get there at the right time, it's still in good condition,' he said. I only take stuff in plastic bags, otherwise the birds will have pecked it.'

Once a week, Jamie worked in a Wahroonga garden for the day, then rode a couple of kilometres home for a big dinner with meat. He would return to *Possibilities* with a kilo bag of home-made muesli for his breakfasts. Having no refrigeration, his dinners on board were usually vegetarian – often beans and rice, unless it was shopping day, when he bought fresh meat.

He had all he needed. The university provided showers in the gym. A fresh water tap in the park at Berry's Island supplied his water on board, and he could dry his hand-washed laundry on the boat rails.

David continued living at home. Having successfully completed his HSC, he enrolled at Meadowbank TAFE to study for the Advanced Diploma in Mechanical Technologies.

When David topped the graduating class, we were very proud to attend a ceremony at the TAFE College and hear him give a small speech in front of the teachers, students and assembled parents.

David also bought his first multihull at the end of that year.

*David with his first multihull*

A year after Ian's diagnosis with Chronic Fatigue Syndrome, we were managing his illness to the point where we could visit the boat again, although we weren't able to sail far. Often it was merely a day out on board at the mooring or a short motor to another bay. Frequently, he needed to lie down to rest, but just being on the water was therapeutic.

With our children now adults and becoming independent, Ian and I needed to concentrate on adapting to our illnesses and to make a new life for ourselves – one we hoped would include cruising again. But first, we had to ensure we could live together in close quarters again for an extended period – just the two of us.

# 16  South in Company with Jamie

Life had been steadily improving for all of us since Ian retired and in 1998, it was a time for new beginnings. My mother's death in 1997 had laid me low with grief and depression, but a year later, I was beginning to cope better again with my natural therapies teachings, and was making some money in my aromatherapy massage business.

By 1998, Jamie was in the final year of his Bachelor of Science degree in Geomorphology and Environmental Science at Macquarie University. David also went to University, enrolling in 1998 to study Mechanical Engineering at Newcastle University.

David's self-confidence had improved enormously with his success at TAFE – he topped the class in his Mechanical Technologies course. In Newcastle, he found living quarters in a share house at Birmingham Gardens, a suburb near the university and there, he developed enduring friendships with a couple of his housemates.

With Ian's health slowly improving, we began to think of voyaging under sail again. Ian and I started using *Realitas* for daysailing, and occasionally for a weekend with the Coastal Cruising Club. Ian's mental outlook improved hugely, just by having the energy to muck about with boats again, and to attend the CCC monthly meetings at Cremorne. As for me, I wanted to travel again; my feet were itchy.

We spent a few days of the Easter holidays at Broken Bay that year, in company with Richard and his wife, Dagmar, on *Mistress*. Jamie joined us too and he went ashore at Jerusalem Bay to Cowan station, where he met up with his new friend, Laura Tyllila, who had travelled by train from Newcastle. Jamie had become friends with her when he took *Possibilities* to Newcastle in February 1998 and studied there for his Coxswain's Certificate before the start of the university year.

Laura, a Finnish medical student, was living on the YWAM ship (Youth with a Mission) for six months while she studied evangelical Christianity both by book and in practice. I watched

Laura, an energetic young woman with an engaging personality, and soon came to the opinion that she was smitten with Jamie. I mentioned this quietly to Ian.

'Rubbish,' snorted Ian. 'You see romance everywhere!'

That afternoon, the two young people set off to climb to the cliff top over Jerusalem Bay. Richard, Dagmar, Ian and I watched as Jamie and Laura prepared to jump off the cliff into the deep water below. Jamie had done this jump many times before, but Laura was hesitant. They were holding hands. Jamie jumped. Laura paused momentarily, then followed. She pulled Jamie off balance and he landed awkwardly in the water. Her concern was immediate. After all, she was a second year medical student from Helsinki – almost a doctor in her estimation. They swam slowly back to *Realitas*.

'Jamie coughed up a few specks of bright red blood,' said Laura.

In no time, she had him lying down and was checking his chest for injury. He was more concerned about his nether regions, which were also hurting.

'You make sure you see a doctor to get a chest x-ray when you get back to Sydney,' insisted Laura.

I glanced at Ian meaningfully.

'That's very new, bright red blood,' I said when he coughed again. 'You've probably just broken a few bronchial capillaries.'

'You still need to get a chest x-ray. Promise me you'll see a doctor,' insisted budding Doctor Laura, before Richard took her and Dagmar to the Hawkesbury River railway station. Jamie did see a GP and had a chest X-ray. The result was clear.

'I was right about the broken capillaries and also about their relationship,' I said to Ian.

On Queen's Birthday weekend in June, we were attending a sailaway far up Middle Harbour, at Bantry Bay next to Davidson National Park. We sailed in and anchored *Realitas* close to the landing on Saturday afternoon.

Early on Sunday afternoon, Jamie arrived with his friends. Laura had come down from Newcastle with Joanna, an English optometrist, and Roland from Denmark, who were both studying on the YWAM ship too. They were all staying on *Possibilities* for the weekend.

I gazed in amazement as, under sail, Jamie manoeuvred *Possibilities* alongside *Realitas,* leaning his body and moving his feet to encourage his boat to turn. His movements reminded me of the time he had sailed his sailboard into Fame Cove at Port Stephens when he was sixteen, he and his craft moving as one. This was a skill Jamie, at age four, had begun to master when Ian took him shopping one Thursday evening and they had bought Jamie's first skateboard. He had ridden it home the few blocks from the shops and then Jamie had given me a demonstration of his new skill. Was it from his first two years on *Caprice* that he developed such wonderful balance?

That evening, we sat around a campfire on shore, telling stories. There was no question that Jamie and Laura were in love. My heart warmed towards this vivacious, fun-loving and adventurous Finn, but was she the right partner for our Jamie? She planned to return to medical school in Helsinki when her six months on the YWAM ship was over. A trans-world relationship would bring problems as would her evangelical religious beliefs.

During the summer of 1998/99, Ian spent a lot of time helping Jamie prepare *Possibilities* for a long voyage. Jamie's university course was near completion and Laura was back from Helsinki for our summer holidays. It was her third visit to Australia and Jamie had travelled to Finland to see her too. Their relationship was serious and it seemed distance wasn't a problem.

This time, Laura flew into Brisbane and David crewed for Jamie to take *Possibilities* up the coast. Jamie and Laura wanted to sail together back to Sydney – that was the whole point of her arriving in Queensland. David came home by land.

Once they arrived back at Balls Head Bay, Laura helped Jamie in his preparations wherever she could, even painting the plastic toilet seat blue in her enthusiasm. Inside the boat, she labelled as many items as possible with their Finnish names. Although she had to return to Helsinki to continue her medical studies, the pair had been discussing where and when they would meet next. Jamie started talking of sailing to Europe. We had Christmas at home in 1998 and I even accompanied Laura to church.

*Ian and our boys, Christmas 1998*

Seeing this as the end of an era in our family life, I photographed the 'boys' together.

During January, David wanted to take a leaf from Jamie's experience and live on board a boat during his second year at university. Much later, he told me the real reason was not to save money.

'I hoped I would appear more romantic to the female students. I wanted a girl to move on board with me,' said David.

David had been impressed with *Possiblities'* performance and he began searching for his own Top Hat yacht. We drove him to the yard at Brooklyn to look at an advertised yacht, but while we were waiting for the broker, David fell into conversation with the owner of another boat in a cradle on the hardstand. It was a Mark II Top Hat and it transpired that the owner, who was preparing his boat to advertise for sale, lived near us in Normanhurst. David ended up buying *Ratu V* from this neighbour, a third Top Hat in the family.

Before Jamie set off on his long voyage, he helped David sail her north to Lake Macquarie. It was gratifying for Ian and me to see our boys becoming good friends.

David took his boat to the far northern end of Lake Macquarie and anchored her near the art gallery at Booragul.

From there, he rode his motorcycle the fourteen kilometres to university. Unfortunately, during that year no girls whom David met found the idea of sharing a twenty five foot yacht with him an attractive prospect. However, he did have a number of female visitors and enjoyed sailing the boat with his friends at the weekends.

'After living in the share house with my mates, life on board was a bit lonely,' David told us. He moved back with his friends for third year and soon sold *Ratu V* for a small profit.

⚓

Jamie and his mate, Marcus, were ready to leave Sydney Harbour in *Possibilities* towards the end of January. Ian and I were keen to go sailing again and we decided to follow *Possibilities* south for the first two legs of her voyage down the coast. We thought we might sail as far as Eden in Twofold Bay.

After we had waved goodbye to *Possibilities* in Sydney Harbour, we took Laura to the airport and waved goodbye to her too. She was returning to university in Helsinki.

With the young people gone sailing or back to their studies, we had to prepare for our own ocean voyage. The previous year, the mechanic had reconditioned our diesel *Bukh* engine, which Ian had reinstalled. We had recently purchased and installed a headsail furler - a *Reefurl* design. Of those available, it was the simplest, the cheapest and made in Australia. Jamie's boat already had one installed, and when Ian examined it, he was impressed with the simplicity of the design and ease in using it.

'It's an agricultural design,' said Ian.

From Ian, that was high praise. He saw it as a practical, no-frills design with little chance of failure. The furler was attached to the forestay, and when rolled in by a line led back to the cockpit, the headsail could be made as small as the skipper wished or rolled up completely.

We bought a large second-hand head sail (genoa), which we took to Keith Brown's sail making loft to have adjusted for use on the furler. Having a furler took away the arduous business of changing headsails at sea, making life much easier for Ian.

It also meant I could shorten sail by myself using those lines which led back to the cockpit. Being able to shorten sail without leaving the cockpit meant we were both much safer at sea if we ever had to single-hand our yacht.

The same applied to Jamie on *Possibilities,* with his *Reefurl.* He had a GPS too, which meant the navigator didn't have to hold on precariously while taking a sextant sight. Although he took a sextant and navigation tables as back-up, at that stage Jamie had not perfected how to use them; GPS was the modern way to navigate.

We also bought our own GPS. That and the furler made a world of difference to how we sailed *Realitas,* and meant that even if Ian was tired and lying down, I could reef the headsail on my own and mark our position on the chart.

This was short-handed sailing with Chronic Fatigue Syndrome.

We spent a couple of days provisioning *Realitas* before following the boys to Jervis Bay where Jamie was to change crew. He dropped Marcus off to join his girlfriend, another Laura, who was working for the summer vacation as a diving assistant in a research project there. Laura Anthony, from Hornsby, was an honours student at Macquarie University in 1999. We came to know her and Marcus much better in the future.

Whilst in Jervis Bay, we happened to see Graeme Solomon, a member of our yacht club. He had just returned from a visit to Gabo Island. We invited him on board for a meal.

'Gabo's a wonderful island,' said Graeme. 'You'd be mad not to visit there when you're so close. Do you have to rush home for anything?'

'No, we don't.'

'Why don't you give it a go?' he said. 'I'll draw you a mud map of the entrance to the anchorage.'

Graeme's tales of Gabo Island inspired us. We had passed this island a few times, but never stopped. We resolved to visit there before turning for home.

After Jamie picked up his friend, Dave Connolly, at Huskisson (a small town on the western shore of Jervis Bay), together we sailed the two yachts south to Batemans Bay. It was a different and not unpleasant experience to be sailing in company with our son.

To our surprise, *Possibilities,* with her outboard motor raised, averaged five knots, the same as *Realitas* which is eight feet longer. On *Caprice*, also a Top Hat, we had averaged only four knots, although *Caprice* had been more heavily laden and fitted with an inboard motor – that made the chief difference. *Caprice's* propeller could not be lifted out of the water.

We took only a day to reach Batemans Bay. Although not the easiest port to enter, the bar is more sheltered than some on the NSW coast. Boats can be lost on these bars, which need to be taken seriously. The one at Batemans Bay has an entrance with a dog-leg around the end of the frequently shifting sand bar.

Once securely inside the river, we anchored the boats fairly close to each other off the nearest landing to the supermarket. We needed to top up on groceries for both boats.

The shopping done, we contacted some friends who lived a short distance from the town. They drove us to their house on the cliffs for a lovely leisurely outdoor lunch followed by a walk on the beach below.

Possibilities *at anchor in Batemans Bay*

Another day-sail brought both yachts to Eden.

'This is as far as we're coming with you, Jamie. We part company with you and *Possibilities* tomorrow,' said Ian.

'I'll cook a farewell dinner for you both tonight,' I said to the boys. 'Come over by six o'clock.'

'How come you and Jamie know each other,' I asked Dave over dinner.

'I was in some of the same classes as Jamie at Macquarie Uni,' Dave told us. 'My degree is also in Applied Science (Environmental Studies).'

'Sadly,' he said, 'I can only afford to sail with Jamie for four weeks. I need to look for a job when I get back to Sydney.'

Jamie planned to continue his environmental studies on the ocean. They set off early the next morning, February 4th, 1999. Jamie was twenty-three years old and embarking on his own version of what we, his parents had done. His departure date was exactly twenty-five years from the day we had sailed out of Pittwater on our epic voyage around the world. (See *Two in a Top Hat*.)

Possibilities *departs Eden*

'Bye Jamie. Safe trip!'

Jamie waved back and then turned to look across his bow and concentrate on sailing his boat.

The newly painted blue hull of *Possibilities* slowly merged with the blue of the ocean as our elder son and his boat glided away from Twofold Bay in the early morning light. Soon the white sail disappeared too.

Ian and I were still standing in the cockpit of *Realitas*, holding hands, our eyes misty.

'I wonder when we'll see Jamie again.' I said, tearfully.

'All we can do is hope he returns safely.'

'Hmmm. I did give him that "key to the world" for his eighteenth birthday,' I said as I wiped my eyes.

'You did', said Ian. 'We've done our best for him. It's up to him now.'

'He's always been a survivor.'

A few hours later Ian had made some adjustments to our new furler and we set sail for Gabo Island. We too, were ready to explore new horizons.

The extraordinarily good weather continued and following Graeme's map, we anchored in Santa Barbara Bay, Gabo Island at six-thirty the same day.

'Now we're awake, let's get breakfast over, so we can go ashore and explore,' I said.

'Give me a hand to take the dinghy off the deck and then I'm ready when you are,' said Ian.

I love rambling over islands and we were alone on this one except for the lighthouse keeper. Deserted and almost deserted islands reminded me especially of Cocos Island in the eastern Pacific. That island was the basis for Robert Louis Stevenson's novel, *Treasure Island,* and we had spent a glorious week alone there in March 1977. This island was a treasure too, full of surprises.

The blackberries were ripe, and I was gorging myself on the sweet fruit when a cow walked round the bend in the track, startling me. I hadn't expected to find domestic animals on the island, which is a state owned park, but of course, it was the only source of milk for the lighthouse keeper and those who rented the spare cottages from Parks Victoria.

As we explored further, we found a small graveyard where we spent an hour or so reading the headstones and trying to reconstruct something of the stories of those long gone people. It is so sad when you read of the deaths of so many young children and wonder at the sorrow of their parents.

'What do you think? Did they drown in a boating accident coming to or from the island? Or maybe it was diphtheria or whooping cough that carried them away?'

'Probably the latter,' said Ian.

Having exhausted our ruminations about earlier days on the island, we went on, searching for the lighthouse, its adjacent buildings and the keeper.

'I'll unlock one of the cottages so you can have a look through,' said the lighthouse keeper, showing us the old keepers' cottages, which are available for rent from Parks Victoria. 'When you've had a look here, just pull the door shut. You can follow me up to the lighthouse if you like.'

The climb to the top of a lighthouse is always worth the effort. The sea looks so different from up there – all the waves and swells appear smoother and the horizon is so far away, a container ship looks like a child's toy boat, but for the tiny puff of smoke from its funnel. We admired the polished lens and glass that reflected the light so many miles across the water. The lighthouse keeper took us out onto the balcony. Pointing down at the rocks below, he told us a story. '

'Do you see the gap between those rocks? It's not very wide. One night a yacht was sailing by. The owner decided he didn't want to stop at the island. Perhaps he thought it too difficult to enter the harbour in the dark. His boat had other ideas. The current drove his hull right between those rocks and it was stuck fast in the gap.'

'Why would the yacht sail so close to the island in the first place if they weren't planning to stop?' *What would it be like to find yourself in that situation?* Right then, a colony of seals was basking in the sunshine on those same rocks.

'Those seals must have been unhappy to have a yacht smash into their haven,' I said.

Having seen all we wanted to see, we returned to *Realitas*, happy that Ian's energy levels were so much better at last. Being on the boat agreed with him so much that it was beginning to seem we might be able to do some serious cruising again before too long.

The next day's forecast indicated that a south-west change was due late that day – a favourable wind for sailing north. While we waited for the wind to change, Ian installed a handhold at the companionway (entrance to the main cabin) for me, and made a holder for the GPS above the chart table.

'I'm going to have a sleep now. Why don't you have one too? Remember, we haven't sailed overnight for a long time,' said Ian.

'I think I will join you,' I said.

Near the time of our departure from Gabo, Ian called Penta Comstat, the private yacht monitoring service run by Derek and Jeanine Barnard from their home near Gosford.

'Penta Comstat, Penta Comstat, Penta Comstat, this is *Realitas, Realitas, Realitas.*'

'*Realitas,* this is Penta Comstat,' responded Derek.

'Penta Comstat, this is *Realitas*. We are departing Gabo Island in half an hour. Two POB. Destination, Jervis Bay.'

'*Realitas,* this is Penta Comstat. You are departing Gabo for Jervis Bay with two POB. What's your weather?'

'Penta Comstat, this is *Realitas*. The forecast south-westerly change hasn't arrived yet. Currently, we have a westerly with a slight amount of rain.'

'Penta Comstat to *Realitas*. Romeo. I'll look for you on the sked tomorrow morning. Penta Comstat standing by.'

'Thanks Penta Comstat. *Realitas* out.'

We hadn't bothered logging on with Derek and Jeanine on our way down the coast because we were keeping in touch with *Possibilities*. These days, we feel it is good practice to keep someone aware of our whereabouts when we are on the ocean.

The long distance HF (High Frequency) radio wasn't our only means of communication though. We used the VHF radio for local communications and we had been tuning in to

Mallacoota, the closest Victorian Volunteer Coastguard station, for weather updates.

We had also brought along our new mobile phone. They were becoming commonplace by 1999. I nearly jumped off the settee the first time it rang out at sea, it was so unexpected.

Two days later, we arrived back in Batemans Bay. After spending a day with our friends, Ruth and Hugh, we stayed on board at anchor for the next two days. The weather had turned damp and depressing, with drizzle and a north-easterly breeze. We needed a westerly at least to be able to make comfortable progress up the coast.

Early the next morning the first large roll of cloud was visible, signalling the approach of the cold front. Within half an hour, the second roll came over with the wind change. Soon after that the sun came out, and the wind came in from the south-west – not strong but consistent – blowing the sky back to clear blue.

In the middle of the day, Ian was sleeping and I was on watch, enjoying the sunshine and reading a book in the cockpit.

There was a fishing boat about with its trawling nets down. I glanced at it occasionally, but didn't think I needed to change course for it. I became engrossed in my book and when Ian came into the cockpit, he saw that I had allowed *Realitas* to cut right across the bows of the fishing boat. Oooops! I deserved the earful he gave me.

'We don't have right of way over a working vessel, Jan. They can only slow down, not change course easily when they have their booms and nets down. That was very careless of you.'

We went into Jervis Bay, stopping at Honeymoon Bay on the northern side. It being a beautifully warm day, we decided to leave the dinghy on the deck and swam ashore to the beach. We underestimated the distance and when we stepped ashore, we weren't happy with the swarms of bloodthirsty mosquitoes at the beach. After a brief encounter with those vampires, we plunged back into the water. It was a long swim and we were both fairly tired by the time we climbed back on board *Realitas*. Moreover, the water was full of stingers from jelly fish smashed up during the rough weather.

'I wonder whose honeymoon they named this bay after,' said Ian.

'Must have been someone who wasn't allergic to mozzie bites or stingers,' I replied.

The next morning, we motored over to Huskisson on the Western shore, picking up a mooring there. We probably could have gone right into the river mouth at high tide, but with our keel depth, there was not much clearance.

Ian checked the tide tables and high tide depths were falling. Just as on our previous visit, he opted to motor the dinghy in to the village for fuel rather than risk being grounded for days or weeks until the next higher tide.

The wind turned light and we motor-sailed north over the next few days. With those light conditions, we needed our *Autohelm* electronic steering, but unfortunately it failed. A part had become loose inside and Ian was reluctant to open the plastic case of the unit because it was still under warranty. Whenever the wind became very light and there was insufficient wind to work the *Aires* vane, we had to hand-steer.

At Wollongong, we needed fuel again. The port there is very small and is used mainly by fishing boats. To gain any shelter, we needed to manoeuvre our way around to the inside of the wharf. Even so, we still experienced considerable movement because the swell swirls around the point and into the tiny harbour.

Early on Sunday morning, a couple walked down the wharf. When they observed Ian getting fuel cans out of the cockpit locker, they spoke up.

'Do you need fuel?'

'Yes,' said Ian. 'How far is it to the nearest garage?'

'Too far to walk carrying cans of fuel,' said the lady. 'We'll drive you to our Shell garage where we have diesel, and bring you back again,' said her thoughtful husband.

This couple actually ran the garage and their steel 34 foot S&S yacht was on a cradle alongside their business. Such kindness is frequently found in the boating community, more so in country areas than in the big cities.

Our fuel tanks full again thanks to this friendly couple, we pulled out of the harbour and set off for home. There was still no favourable breeze and unfortunately, the engine stopped halfway up the coast. Upon investigation, Ian discovered that our fuel pump had failed. However before long, an easterly breeze came up and we were able to continue sailing while Ian removed and dismantled the non-functioning part.

'Look Jan. See, this is where the problem lies. I can't fix it out here. We'll just have to hope this breeze holds and sail home.'

By mid-afternoon, the breeze had increased sufficiently for us to set the *Aires,* reducing our tiller duty considerably.

After rounding South Head into Sydney Harbour, the breeze died yet again. Ian pressurised the fuel pump by mouth and managed to start the engine. We motored up the harbour to Balls Head Bay and anchored there for the remainder of the night.

We had completed our first cruise since Ian had become ill in August 1995. That was cause for celebration and a great deal of satisfaction. Voyaging was possible again, it seemed, but could we sustain a lengthy, congenial on-board relationship after so many years?

# 17   Queensland – Mecca of Winter Cruising

Ian and I needed to reassure ourselves we were still compatible for long-term cruising, so we hired a HiAce campervan, driving through five states over six weeks during the winter of 1999. We passed through NSW, Victoria, South Australia, part of the Northern Territory and Queensland. Apart from seeing areas of this magnificent country that we hadn't before visited, we needed to see how Ian, with chronic fatigue syndrome, fared on such a long journey.

It was a fabulous trip. I loved it and Ian did too. Having the campervan meant we could stop for him to lie down whenever necessary, just as he could most of the time in the boat, and we could cook and eat the food we knew wouldn't upset both of us. It appeared that so many years after our circumnavigation, we could live together in close confinement for an extended period.

Our plan now became to make an extended voyage to Far North Queensland in *Realitas* the following winter. We spent many days on the boat during the late summer and early autumn of 2000, preparing the yacht for our voyage.

'One of the things we need to do before we go north is fix that water tank,' said Ian.

'I agree. It's a damned nuisance having to change the jerry cans all the time.'

'My concern is that we might be caught in rough weather at sea without water,' said Ian.

'I don't want to fibreglass the tanks though. Neither of us needs that chemical onslaught,' I said.

After we had returned from the voyage to New Zealand, I had found I didn't have the heart to work on those water tanks again. All we did was remove the *O and T* paint. Initially, we kept several jerry cans in the main water tank, with the hose leading to the sink pump from the can currently in use.

For safety, all other cans were securely sealed. The lid of the tank, a sheet of three quarter inch plywood, was screwed down with ten heavy screws.

Whenever we emptied one jerry can and needed to change the hose to the next, all ten screws had to be removed to access the tank, which was located under the starboard settee. The situation remained like this for several years.

'I think we should install two more flexible water tanks.'

'Do you mean *Plastimo* fifty litre tanks like we installed under the vee berth for the bathroom?' Ian nodded. 'Okay. And could we put in a deck-filler too?'

'No. I don't want to do that. Those deck openings are too easily a source of seawater contamination of the main fresh water supply,' said Ian.

I thought the modern deck-filler fittings probably didn't leak nowadays. Everyone else used them, but it was better to go along with Ian on this matter. His agreement to install two *Plastimo* tanks was a huge step forward. Maybe I'd get a deck-filler one day if I was patient enough, and then we wouldn't need to remove the tank lid at all during a cruise.

We bought the tanks and fittings. After we had installed them, we needed to undo the lid only when the tanks required filling. We still needed to bring a hose inside to fill all three tanks, but at least we'd got rid of the jerry cans, except for two stored in the aft cockpit locker with thirty litres of spare water. We kept extra cans of fuel there too. Ian had never got around to connecting up the thirty litre day-tank we'd had made in New Zealand. All this extra water and fuel in the aft cockpit made *Realitas* a little heavy in the stern and probably affected her quality of sailing.

Two thousand was the year of the Olympics in Sydney. The government advised people that if convenient, they should leave the city to reduce crowding and demand on services, and we did.

Eventually, in mid-May, we were ready to set off north. While Ian was on deck getting ready to leave the mooring, I placed a *Scop* patch on my upper thigh, in preparation for leaving the harbour. Seasickness for the first three days of a voyage was still my scourge. *Scopolamine* patches deliver anti-nausea medication through the skin. If I didn't need to swallow a medication I couldn't bring it up again. My previous experience with *Scop* was that it needed a minimum of two hours to be effective.

I set about tidying the cabin and washing up our break-fast dishes. However, after just ten minutes, I found my vision blurring, I yawned and felt queasy. Suddenly I heaved.

'Ian, you won't believe this. I'm seasick now.'

'Why? What's happened?'

'I put my *Scop* on just ten minutes ago. It's the new one my brother, Greg, sent over for me from New Zealand.'

'I wonder what's different about it.'

'I think they must have made it much stronger, especially when you first put it on.'

'You're probably right. Racing sailors wouldn't think to use it until just before the race. Especially if they are in something like the Sydney to Hobart, they need it to be effective immediately the boat hits the swell at Sydney Heads.'

The *Scop* my brother had sent was the new formulation never approved in Australia. I stripped off the patch and wrapped it up for later use.

Every time I needed medication, I would unwrap the patch, apply it for about five minutes, then remove it again. Goodness knows how bad the side effects would have been had I followed the maker's instructions and placed the patch behind my ear, close to my brain.

'If you're feeling okay now, I'll drop the mooring,' Ian said a while later.

'Yeah, I'll be all right. The wooziness is easing. Let's get on our way.'

We motored out of Five Dock Bay and turned to starboard, heading down river towards the Gladesville Bridge. With the sails up and drawing, I went below to turn off the engine controls. Suddenly, I was very concerned.

'Ian,' I called to him out in the cockpit, 'there's water trickling out from under our double bunk.'

'Come out and take the helm, while I have a look.'

Ian returned to the cockpit.

'I don't think it can be serious. The leak is very slow and it only started when the boat heeled.'

'What do you think we should do?'

'We'll pull into the yacht club mooring at Bottle and Glass Bay to investigate the source of the leak.'

When we'd picked up our club mooring, I unpacked the lockers under the vee berth.

'I can't see any leak Ian. As far as I can see, the pipe joins look secure,' I said. 'Why don't you come down here in my place and look to see what you might find?'

Using a torch for extra light, Ian checked all the pipe connections between the water tank and the bathroom. The flexible tank lay against the forward hull, below the lockers.

Fortunately, there was no leak. Apparently water had spilled when we filled the tank. We guessed that it had sat against a stringer until the boat began moving, when the movement allowed the water to trickle out. Reassured, we moved off the mooring.

When heading north, usually we stop at Port Stephens to give me time to become accustomed to the boat motion. Ian also needed to rest after the effort of stowing stores before departure.

'Without heating on the boat, Jan, it's too cold once the sun's gone down. I think we should move on as quickly as we can,' said Ian.

'You're right. Winter's fast approaching.'

We ought to have given ourselves a full rest day, but with a southerly wind blowing, we pushed on north the next day.

It was several years since we had last been long distance cruising and it seemed strange at first that there were just the two of us on board. David was at the University of Newcastle, studying third year Mechanical Engineering. Jamie had already crossed the Indian Ocean in *Possibilities* and was in Kenya where Laura had joined him from Finland.

Before long, we settled into our old rhythm of sailing together, Ian taking over when I was seasick, vice versa when his fatigue levels became too high. Both of us would work on deck when a sail change was needed.

Seven days after we'd left Sydney we were sailing past Byron Bay. We sat in the cockpit eating breakfast and looking at the lighthouse up on its promontory.

'Remember when we saw Byron Lighthouse in *Caprice*?' Ian asked. 'We were trying to find our way home from Lord Howe Island twenty eight years ago!'

'Of course I remember. That's when we finally knew our position on the coast. What a nightmare that trip was!'

Our progress north was slow, but steady. The wind came around to the south-south-east and we poled out the full main. We were keeping close into the coast where the counter-current gave us a small lift.

Further out, on the one hundred fathom line, the south-going Australian East Coast current runs. We would use that current coming home again. At times, it can flow at several knots.

Later in the day, we passed the Tweed River mouth. 'Hey,' I said to Ian, 'do you realise it's only a week since we left home and here we are already at the Queensland border.'

The wind was still chilly from the previous cool change, but the air was crisp and the sky blue, giving good visibility. In the distance, we could see many high rise buildings.

'That's the Gold Coast,' said Ian, pointing. 'All those towers of units are built right alongside the beach. In recent years Gold Coast City has become the fastest growing urban area in all of Australia.'

When we became closer, Ian called the Gold Coast Seaway tower on the VHF radio.

'Gold Coast Seaway, Gold Coast Seaway, this is *Realitas, Realitas, Realitas*.'

'*Realitas,* this is Gold Coast Seaway. Change up to channel 22 please.'

'*Realitas* going up. Gold Coast Seaway, this is *Realitas* on channel 22.'

'Go ahead *Realitas*.'

'What are conditions like for entry at the seaway?'

'This is Seaway Tower. Conditions are good. It's safe to enter.'

Soon, we were turning to port and sweeping in with the tide through the channel under the watchful eye of the officers in the Seaway Tower. Turning to port again, we entered the south channel leading to Bums Bay, as it is known to cruising yachties. There we anchored adjacent to SeaWorld. I have no idea what is the real name of this anchorage. Maybe it was labelled 'Bums Bay' because of the number of unemployed people living there on their boats.

The next morning, an easy dinghy ride across the wide channel took us to Australia Fair, a large, newish shopping mall, where we stocked up on fresh food and checked our email. We also phoned Max and Shirley Van der Bent, people we wanted to see again, inviting them to *Realitas* for lunch.

Back in 1974, we'd become friends with the Van der Bents in Western Australia when, prior to setting off across the Indian Ocean, we stayed in Rockingham on *Caprice* for three months. We had been present in 1974 when they launched their beautiful forty foot yacht, *Shikama*, which Max had designed and built with Shirley's help.

They named *Shikama* after the members of their family, taking the first two or three letters of each name – Shi from Shirley, Ka from Karen, their daughter and Ma from Max. I found the name as beautiful as their boat.

Soon after we had returned from the supermarket, Max and Shirley drove up and Ian brought them aboard in the dinghy.

'I think we told you on the phone that we saw *Shikama* in Sydney Harbour,' I said.

'The new owners are friends of ours. They told us you'd met,' said Max.

'Yes, we pulled alongside and spoke to them. They said you were long-term friends, and that they were also from Holland.'

'We've known them for many years,' said Shirley.

Our lunch together passed quickly with chat about cruising life and common acquaintances. Their visit came to an end all too quickly, but they invited us to visit them on our return voyage.

From our anchorage, it was a moderate walk past Sea World to the chandlery where, next morning, we purchased the tide charts and the Queensland Department of Transport charts which are necessary for transiting the protected waterways of the Broadwater, Moreton Bay and further north, the Great Sandy Straits.

The Broadwater lies north of the Gold Coast and bordered by South Stradbroke Island, it consists of many channels wending between exposed sandy bars. Moreton Bay, a wide area to the east of greater Brisbane, is bordered by North Stradbroke and further north, Moreton Island. All three of these coastal islands are formed from sand. The channels in Moreton Bay are deeper, and the sand banks are mostly covered by water except at very low tide. The whole area is just sand and water.

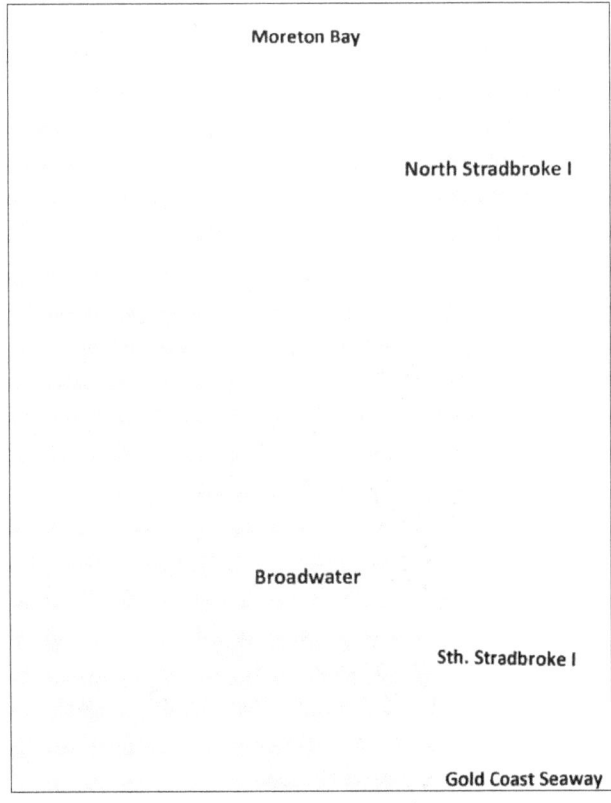

*Figure 8. The Broadwater*

Despite having up-to-date charts, we went aground twice before reaching Runaway Bay Marina. Signage in Queensland is not the same as in NSW, and Ian's brain fatigue caused him to make an occasional error. I didn't have that excuse. The Broadwater is very shallow and there is little room for mistakes.

Ian gunned the engine while I stood on the bow, bouncing my body weight. Sand swirled up from the revving propeller and gradually, we managed to back off into deeper water again.

'Phew, no need to call up the VMR this time (Volunteer Marine Rescue) or wait for the tide to rise,' I said.

In these waters, where progress is via marked channels, it is too difficult to travel at night. Even though there are lights on the markers, it's too hard to distinguish one from another in the dark and the visual clue of water depth by colour is not available.

Sometimes, marinas are the only option for overnight, but often safe anchorages are available. We chose according to our need for showers, laundry and filling up the water tanks.

Cruising during the summer allows more freedom to swim, or to strip off for an all over wash, but in winter, I prefer a hot shower every couple of days. We needed to choose our anchorages carefully and calculate the tidal depths overnight; otherwise we could be left stranded on the sandy bottom, the boat heeling over at an uncomfortable angle.

'For my birthday, I would like to stay overnight in a marina, please. I'd like to have a hot shower and hair wash.'

'I'll try. We'll see what we can find,' said Ian.

On the eve of my fifty-fifth birthday, we did find a half built marina which accepted us for the night. However, the facilities left much to be desired and I didn't manage to have that longed for hot shower and hair wash.

Despite a forecast for gusty winds and choppy seas, we continued on our way early the next morning. That day we went aground twice more, once within the channel, but apparently too close to the starboard marker. The second time, I managed to steer out of the channel, being confused by the markers for an adjoining channel. Fortunately, both times we were able to get off without having to wait for the tide to rise.

Our anchorage that night was off Cox Bank in just enough water that we didn't touch bottom at low tide during the night.

'You're very good at calculating the depths and the tides,' I told Ian. 'We had no bumps during the night.'

'Don't praise me too much. I might have a foggy brain next time and get it all wrong,' said Ian with a laugh.

When we set out to cross Moreton Bay, the winds were gusty from the west. Ian loves these sailing conditions. He stands in the cockpit, the wind blowing through his hair and the widest grin on his face. It is the only time he doesn't mind hand-steering.

By contrast, I find it really uncomfortable. I have to hang on with both hands, so moving about is difficult and cooking is a juggling puzzle, with the ever present threat of dropping a can on my toes.

If the motion is rough, I strap myself into the galley to cook, which restricts my involuntary movements, but also sometimes prevents my reaching for items I need.

Huge pylons dominate the commercial shipping channels striding across the bay and out towards the open sea.

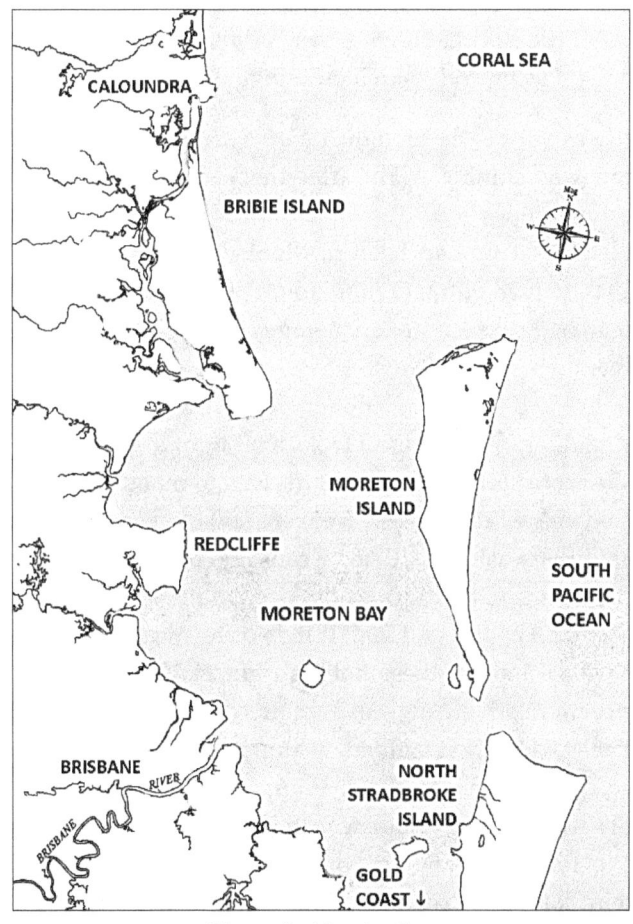

Figure. 9. Moreton Bay

'I find those pylons somehow shocking, intimidating,' I said. 'They really spook me, and they are visible for such a long way. Do they affect you?'

'They do seem odd, disappearing away into the distance.'

'I suppose it is best they are there, though. At least we know where the big ships will be,' I said.

After spending a somewhat uncomfortable night anchored in the lee of a small island, we sailed through the wide northern entrance of Moreton Bay and past Bribie Island, gusty westerlies still buffeting us.

'So that's Bribie Island,' I said. 'I've often heard the name, but I've never had any idea where it is, how big or what it might look like.'

The island looked dry and dusty – even the trees were dull. Ian took little notice. He was busy adjusting the *Aires,* persisting in having it steer *Realitas* in increasingly light conditions.

It was very early June the day we arrived in Mooloolaba and the sun was shining again after the passage of another south-westerly.

Neither of us had been to Mooloolaba before. We motored inside the river entrance and found a small sheltered marina, wharf area and a pleasant anchorage close by, around the curve in the river.

'I think there's just enough room for us to anchor in the river,' said Ian. 'That marina looks a bit tight to get in and out of.'

We were still didn't trust ourselves to manoeuvre the boat in confined space. In the river, we were still close enough to the fuel jetty to dinghy ashore with jerry cans and top up our fuel tank.

'Hey, this place looks really nice,' I said, grinning at Ian.

'Not bad at all,' said Ian. 'It'll do quite nicely.'

'Take a look at these houses right next to the river,' I said. 'They seem relatively new and architect-designed.'

Each wall was painted a different colour with tones of purple, puce, rich chocolate, orange and yellow. 'I would get heartily sick of those colour schemes if I had to live with them'

We took the time to go for a wander through the town. 'There're lots of tourists, Ian,' I said, 'but this town isn't spoiled yet. They're mostly backpackers and Australians.'

'It's quite a pleasant town, but I'll bet it will go upmarket in the next few years. You can see how it has already started.'

'Hmm. A shame how nice coastal towns succumb like that. They become just like any other tourist town anywhere in the world and lose all their individuality. I suppose some of these large blocks of units are for short term lease too – just like the ones on the Gold Coast.'

After Mooloolaba, we sailed north, around Double Island Point and into Wide Bay, where we waited for the right conditions to cross the Wide Bay bar into The Great Sandy Straits. This sand bar has a fearsome reputation, which is not to be ignored. Generally, it is quieter to cross at night, but this was our first time, so we wanted to go over the bar in daylight.

'While we wait for the tide, you'd better rest,' I told Ian.

I spent the morning in the cockpit, sometimes reading, sometimes watching the four-wheel drive vehicles zooming along the beaches and observing the changing play of light on the sand hills behind Rainbow Beach as the sun rose higher in the sky.

We crossed the Wide Bay bar at slack water just after the midday high tide. By then, the sea breeze was up and therefore the choppiness on the water also increased, so it wasn't the quietest of crossings. Despite our concerns, we managed with no drama. We didn't have a relay screen in the cockpit for the GPS so I called the position to Ian from down below.

As the first waypoint showed on the screen, I called up to him, 'Now.'

Ian made a port-hand turn to follow the best water over the bar and into the shallow channel. There was breaking water not far away, but by following the leads and GPS points, we stayed safe. The next turn to starboard brought us into waters protected from seaward by Fraser Island. Inside the bay, there is a large area for anchoring and across the channel lie the marina entrance and the village of Tin Can Bay.

'Phew, we've done it,' I said to Ian, as we finished anchoring. 'We've successfully negotiated the dreaded Wide Bay bar. What now?'

'If you put the dinghy into the water while I have a rest for twenty minutes, we can go ashore and see who we know at the marina,' he suggested.

'I'm taking my shower gear with me. We might be able to borrow a bathroom key so I can wash my hair,' I said.

'I'm fairly salty too. I wouldn't mind a shower and shave either.'

After his rest, Ian manoeuvred the outboard from the aft rail onto the dinghy. Although it was the weekend when most marinas are busy, strangely, the jetty was deserted, the office shut. We saw no Coastal Cruising Club boats, so we went in search of a shower at the nearby sprawling caravan park. That office was locked too, but when we found the unlocked amenities block, we were able to just walk in and turn on the hot water. My hair was salt encrusted from flying spray, so I relished my hair wash, staying under the hot water for longer than usual. Nevertheless, I did feel slightly guilty – after all, we were virtually 'stealing' the park's hot water.

Large sections of the Australian east coast are formed from low lying sandy dunes, estuaries and salt water 'lakes'. There were a lot of these sandy shallow areas both south and north of Brisbane and we crossed most of them by motoring. The Great Sandy Straits were the next section of the coastal way north.

Because we dislike doing a lot of hand steering, we used our yachting model electronic self-steering system when we were motoring, or sailing in very light conditions. We had bought a new *Autohelm* in 1999, before leaving Sydney to sail south, but it was not really robust enough for ocean cruising, except in very calm conditions. Now we used it mainly in sheltered waters.

The next morning, we moved on to Garry's Anchorage on the western shore of Fraser Island. This is a very large sand island – in fact the world's largest. The channels up to Garry's Anchorage had triangular channel markers both on the shore and on the sand banks, and we had to keep in line with them as we proceeded north.

At Fraser Island, we went ashore to walk, and although it wasn't possible to cover very much on foot, we did cross to the eastern shore that morning. Early next morning, Ian went for another walk, this time heading north up the four wheel drive track.

'I'm astonished,' he told me on his return. 'I was stalked by two young dingoes. They were lying on the track in front of me and I was quite close to them before they moved. They went into the bush at the side and then returned to the track behind me and followed about twenty metres behind me all the way back. Next time I go for a walk, I'll pick up one of those heavy sticks propped against the National Parks' sign on the shore.'

'That's probably what they are there for,' I said.

A few years later, we heard much more about the Fraser Island dingoes, which are as close to pure bred as any left in Australia. However, there is very little prey for them on the island and they are frequently hungry, hanging around the camping ground rubbish bins and resorting to catching fish in the surf.

A year or so later, there was a large media story when a young boy, seven years old, was attacked and killed. He had been walking on the island track with his older brother when two dingoes stalked them and attacked the younger boy, who died. Many people were calling for the dingoes to be removed from the island. As far as I know, National Parks and Wildlife have resisted this call and the dingoes are still there.

The killing of that child on Fraser Island brought attention back to the Chamberlain case and the possibility that a dingo really had taken baby Azaria at Ayers Rock (Uluru) in the mid nineteen-eighties. Back then, that case had divided Australia. In 2012, thirty-three years after Azaria died, a fourth Coronial Enquiry found that a dingo was responsible for her death and Lindy Chamberlain was exonerated.

It was at Garry's Anchorage that we first met Chris and Elaine Kleiss on *K Sera*. They later became well-known in the cruising community for their book *Three Grannies go to Sea* and later, with articles in the Australian magazine, *Cruising Helmsman*. Chris told us he had retired from a career in journalism and newspaper publishing, to design and build their thirty-five foot fibreglass boat with help from Elaine. When we went on board their boat we could see the interior was not quite finished. They were also cruising north and we were to share numerous anchorages with them.

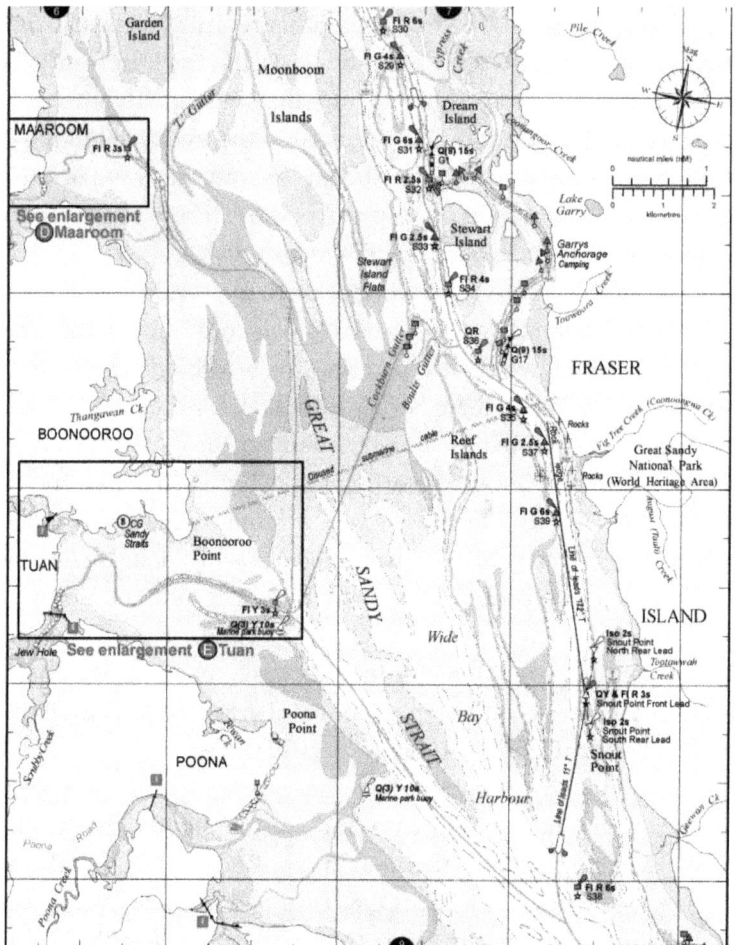

Fig. 10. *The Great Sandy Straits (Beacon to Beacon)*

'It's good that they are out enjoying their boat already,' I said to Ian. 'So many people wait for perfection before they set out.'

While travelling through the Great Sandy Straits, the *Autohelm* unit failed. We could hear the motor whirring, but the ram wasn't moving. It was no longer under warranty so Ian opened the casing.

'Hmm, the little gear wheel's no longer fixed to the motor shaft,' he said.

At Urangan, Ian rang the supplier, who suggested we send the unit back to Sydney for repairs.

'I don't want to do that. We are cruising north for the winter and we need it.'

'Well, just stick the gear wheel back onto the motor shaft with super glue. X brand is best. '

Ian sat staring at the array of delicate electronics. 'There are some pretty fragile electrical bits in here. I'd rather not risk having to dismantle this again,' he said. 'I'll make a little scotch key for it before I glue it all back together.'

'No wonder these things are temperamental. And how typical of you to want to improve on that,' I said.

Urangan, lying at the southern entrance to Hervey Bay, is a pretty place, located on the north western corner of the Great Sandy Straits. The town is a short distance inland from the marina and I rode on the bus into the main shopping mall for groceries and fresh food. In the way of country towns, the bus took a round-about route from the marina into town, so that by the time I had finished my shopping expedition, I had seen a fairly large area of the surrounding countryside.

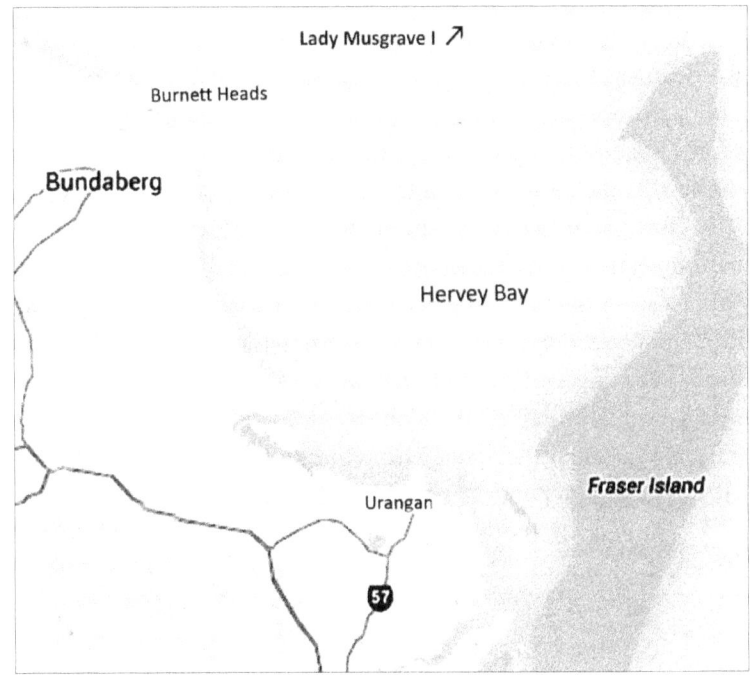

*Figure 11. Hervey Bay*

A fibreglass whale in the water at the marina emphasises the town's main attraction – whale watching.

'Did you know that Hervey Bay is an important location for humpback whales to calve and nurture their babies during early spring?' I said.

'Probably because Bunker and Capricorn Islands form a slight barrier from the fully open sea,' replied Ian. 'It's a big bay, but relatively sheltered from the north-east.'

Lady Musgrave is perhaps the best known of the Bunker Group and Fitzroy Reef and Heron Island are familiar names from the Capricorn Group to the north. The Burnett River, which empties into the north western corner of the bay, is navigable a few miles up-river to the city of Bundaberg.

Next morning, after we pulled out of the Urangan marina, we set up the automatic steering.

'Ta da! It works.' Ian grinned. 'We can be on our way again. '

'Excellent. You did a good job.'

We still had a long way to go to get to the Whitsundays, and we didn't plan to go to Bundaberg on our way north, though we did on our return voyage south. In dull, quiet conditions, we motored across Hervey Bay. Gradually, the wind picked up from the south and soon we were under sail.

'I'm going to troll a fishing line,' I said. 'I'd like to have fresh fish for dinner.'

Despite the sky being heavily overcast with occasional light rain, it was a fairly pleasant sail across the bay with the fishing line streaming out behind the boat. Visibility was sufficient to make out landmarks. We could see Burnett Heads about five nautical miles to the west. The wind and rain increased towards late afternoon, when we changed tack to steer for Bustard Head.

I pulled in the trolling line and found a small flathead attached to the squid lure – a pleasant surprise. It *was* fish for dinner that night.

I take an assortment of fishing lines and lures with me, but I actually know very little about fishing. I love it when an edible fish takes my hook. Even better, I like it when the fish is already dead when I bring it over the rail and into the cockpit. It doesn't flop about and I don't have to kill it.

We remained close to the Curtis coast, and continued sailing north overnight, by-passing all those islands on our way north to Pancake Creek. Being too early to enter the creek, we hove to under Bustard Head to await daylight and the tide. I become very tense when we heave to so close to land. We need to take turns being in the cockpit on watch because currents are the big danger. They can move the boat too close to shore, or out to sea, or too far north or south.

By the time we arrive off an entrance like this, I am usually quite tired, but my fear of the boat drifting into danger prevents me from sleeping, even when I'm off watch.

By seven o'clock, it was daylight. We started the motor and followed the dog-leg channel up the creek. Only half an hour later, we were securely at anchor inside. There were many yachts already at anchor, including *Been-a-long* and *Ambience*, both members of the CCC. *Wundstraum*, an American yacht was also there. One of our club members, David Barrett, was crewing on this yacht. David came over to welcome us into Pancake Creek. He invited us to visit *Wundstraum* later that day, and to meet her owner.

The next day, the weather worsened and most people stayed aboard their vessels. Conditions outside resulted in a lot of chatter on channel 77, the dedicated VHF radio channel for club chit-chat. Conversations are listened into by all within line of sight, so it is reminiscent of the old 'party line' telephone system from sixty years ago. We heard Warwick Wood of *Ambience*, report that his masthead instruments had measured a forty knot wind gust.

Our instruments are considerably simpler. We have a handheld gizmo with a small styrene foam ball which blows up a scale, indicating the wind strength. If we cannot stand on deck to hold this instrument up, we know that it is blowing far too hard to go sailing!

The strong winds and rain squalls eased overnight, so that on Sunday there was social activity ashore. We failed to find the track out to the lighthouse, where many of the folk walked; others, like us, just wandered about closer to the anchorage.

That afternoon, many of us gathered aboard *Ambience* for drinks and nibbles. It was our introduction to Warwick and his wife Chris, whom we would get to know a lot better during this cruise. It was also our introduction to the social side of cruising the Queensland coast in winter. In our previous cruising, except in Durban and Cape Town, we had not experienced this degree of socialising.

Gales were forecast along that part of the coast for Monday as well, so we stayed put until Tuesday morning, departing under motor on the ebb tide. Once outside the shelter of the creek, conditions were still moderately rough, making it necessary to furl the headsail to the size of a number three and triple-reef the mainsail. The sky had cleared and we enjoyed sunny conditions. As the wind dropped, we were able to gradually increase sail until we were moving under full working rig with the wind behind us.

By late morning, we had turned into the main shipping channel leading to the port of Gladstone. With the wind on the beam after we'd turned, we had to reduce sail again.

'Do you remember coming here by motorcycle in 1971?'

'Of course,' said Ian. 'That's when we flew out to visit Heron Island in a helicopter.'

'I will never forget the magnificent shades of blue and turquoise as I looked down from that helicopter onto tiny islands, cays, sand bars and reefs.'

'I remember I didn't like the harsh voice of the woman who was on the flight with us.'

'I don't remember her,' I said. 'You know, I'm really looking forward to swimming around coral again. Back then, I just used the mask like a see-through bucket.'

'A pity we can't sail *Realitas* to Heron,' said Ian. 'That's the problem with people owning whole islands; they don't make yachties welcome.'

On the way into the Gladstone Marina, *Realitas* had to wend her way through the port, past all the commercial vessels.

'Keep your eyes peeled for ships under way,' said Ian.

'It's hard to tell if they are moving when they tower over us,' I replied.

'It's our responsibility to stay out of their way. The rule that power gives way to sail doesn't apply in a commercial harbour.'

Upon entering the marina, we saw *Wundstraum* was already in a berth. The Gladstone marina became one of my favourites on the Queensland coast. It is friendly, not too big, and is tucked away so that there is no wake from passing traffic. It is also efficiently run by the town council, which means that the fees are very reasonable and the bathrooms hygienically clean. Marina standards vary greatly according to who owns or manages them, in much the same way as town swimming pools.

Another advantage of the Gladstone marina is that if you catch the bus outside the office, ten minutes later, you reach the bus-stop outside Woolworth's supermarket in the middle of town. Almost all necessities are available within walking distance of this bus stop. The bus service is cheap and regular.

Unfortunately, at that time, there was no internet service at the marina, so we went to the town library, hoping to use a computer there.

'Sorry,' said the librarian, 'both of our computers are booked up for the entire school holidays.'

When we eventually found a computer to use, there was a letter from Jamie and his Finnish girlfriend, Laura. They told us they were in Mayotte in the French Comoros Islands (Mozambique Channel on south-east coast of Africa) and they were using a French Keyboard. We had a good laugh at the consequent typos. It was good to hear from them.

From Gladstone, we could have continued up the coast on the outer side of Curtis Island.

'Instead of going outside Curtis Island, how about we follow the alternative route through the *Narrows*,' said Ian.

'I'd like that,' I said. 'Just out of curiosity, I'd like to see this "cattle crossing" people talk about.'

At the marina, we met Gay, a local live-aboard yachtswoman. We told her of our plan to take *Realitas* inside of Curtis Island where it is very tidal and quite shallow. The cattle crossing dries at low tide, allowing the local farmer access to his land on both sides of the channel.

Gay loaned us her out-of-print copy of *Sailing the Curtis Coast* and we were able to get several pages photocopied. These were the guidelines for traversing the Narrows. Gay was also very happy to tell us of her personal experiences navigating this waterway in her yacht, *Dancing Dolphin*.

'You'll be fine,' Gay reassured us, when we returned her book. 'Just follow the directions and you won't have any trouble. I've been through there several times.' She grinned at our anxious faces.

Before one reaches the narrowest part of the waterway, there are a couple of magnificent inlets suitable for overnight anchoring and crab fishing. Grahams Creek used to be a wonderful retreat, just half a day's sail from Gladstone. Unfortunately, heavy industry operates on the island now.

After lunch, donning long shirts and trousers against sandflies, we used the dinghy and outboard to go further up the creek. With the outboard off, we sat looking at mud skippers plopping about on the bank and watching a gorgeous russet-breasted kingfisher darting about the bushes. I feel so sad to know that fifty-nine percent of the wonderfully pristine area we visited fifteen years ago is now home to natural gas production.

*Jan and dinghy at Grahams Creek*

As evening approached, mosquitoes emerged. I felt like we were the only fresh blood in the area, with mine being the most delectable. Despite the bities, the brilliance of the sunset drew us outside with our cameras, but once I had my photographs, I dragged Ian below and erected the mosquito netting over the hatches and vents.

Somewhere along the coast, I was given a recipe for homemade insect deterrent that consisted of baby oil, vinegar and tea tree oil. This worked fairly well, but I still received many bites. I found it better to prevent myself from being bitten than to try to stop the itch afterwards, and the swollen welts that arose if I scratched. Consequently, I wouldn't turn off the light to sleep at night if there was a mosquito in the cabin.

A common scenario followed:

Ian: 'Turn the light off please.'

Jan: 'No, not yet. There's still a mosquito in here. I'll get it soon.'

Sometimes, this annoyed Ian intensely. Off would go the light. A mosquito would start to dive bomb me. On with the light again. Search for the pest. The mozzie would hide in the dark green carpet lining the sides of our sleeping cabin. Tired, I'd turn off the light again. The whine would start before I could fall asleep. On with the light yet again... Next morning, there remained a smear of my blood somewhere, the dead body of the insect and the itch.

Departure time from Grahams Creek is dependent on the tide, boat speed through the water and the estimated time of high water at the cattle crossing. The tide runs in opposite directions towards each end of the channel. The point of 'tidal convergence' lies a short distance south of the cattle crossing. Make a mistake in your calculations and you are likely to find yourself aground on gravel. Estimations have to be made based on tidal data for the Fitzroy River to the north and Gladstone to the south.

One travels with the tide to the point of convergence, waiting there for high tide. I watched the water flow around every marker post we passed, checking that the north-going tidal flow was still with us. We came to a wider area of the passage, where the water was almost still. This was the point of convergence and the tide was due to start going out. We continued motoring slowly north.

'Look at that,' I said, pointing to a wooden structure on the bank of the island, where the channel was very narrow. 'That looks a bit like something that might be used for cattle to cross at low tide.' The structure reminded me of a ramp for loading cattle onto a truck.

'According to the GPS, this should be it. This should be the cattle crossing,' said Ian.

He checked the depth sounder reading again.

'Nearly three metres,' he said.

I spotted the post of the next channel marker and watched the water there.

'I think the water has just starting to flow north. It looks like the tide is beginning to ebb,' I said.

My tension was lifting. We were through the really shallow patch and our keel was safe from hitting the stony bottom. We were already in five metres of water and the tide was helping us north.

I had been concerned about Ian making all these calculations with his frequently foggy brain. Since I have a permanently foggy brain when it comes to numbers, I had to rely on him. However, Ian had calculated correctly and we made a perfect passage.

I hugged him in gratitude. 'You're so clever,' I told him. 'Thank you for getting this right.'

The "Narrows" exits between the mouth of the Fitzroy River and an area on the northern tip of Curtis Island known as Yellow Patch, which is a sand blow. We missed seeing that. There is also a lighthouse on the northern end of Curtis Island. Although the water is fairly shallow, it is possible to find a safe anchorage on the inland coast of the island, from where one can go ashore and climb to the lighthouse.

'Let's make a stop here,' I said. 'I'd like to climb up to the lighthouse. Besides, we might get phone coverage up there.'

'I could do with stretching my legs ashore,' said Ian. 'It would be nice to talk to David too.'

'It's three days since we talked to him and I think his exams start soon. We should let him know we're thinking of him.'

We found a spot to land the dinghy ashore. There was a vehicle track nearby, which led us up the headland to the lighthouse. As we'd hoped, there was plenty of mobile phone coverage from a tower on the mainland. David answered when I rang.

'Hi Mum. How are you both? Is Dad okay?'

'Yes, Dad's coping really well with being on the boat. We left Gladstone yesterday and we've just come through "The Narrows". We'll cross the tropic of Capricorn and reach Great Keppel Island tomorrow.'

'Hey, you're making really good progress then. How soon do you think until you reach Airlie?'

'Not sure, love. Probably a few more days. How long until your exams begin?'

'They start in a couple of days.'

'What are you intending to do during semester break?'

'I'm not sure.'

'Would you like to fly up to the Whitsundays and join us for a few days on *Realitas*?'

'Yeah. I would like that.'

'I'm not sure when we could transfer some money for you to book your flights, but we'll do it as soon as we can – maybe from Great Keppel tomorrow.'

'Thanks Mum. That would be really great.'

'I'll pass the phone to Dad now. He's waiting to talk to you too.'

The Tropic of Capricorn passes through Rockhampton and just clips the northern tip of Curtis Island. We spent the night at anchor only a mile or two south of the line and crossed over the next morning.

It was a couple of hours sailing across a pleasant bay to reach Great Keppel Island, our first tropical island on this trip north. Crossing the tropic of Capricorn was our second milestone of the voyage. Reaching Queensland had been the first.

# 18  The Tropics at Last

Great Keppel Island, which we reached a few hours after leaving Curtis Island, marked the beginning of tropical waters - just warm enough for winter swimming. We felt we had reached the area of the Queensland coast which was part of our cruising ground for that year and we no longer had the urge to push north so quickly.

Rather than go to Rosslyn Bay, the marina on the mainland, we opted to anchor off Great Keppel Island on the southern shore.

Ian pointed to the other boat in the anchorage.

'That's *Cooee*, Jill Knight's boat,' he said.

I'd read her articles in *Cruising Helmsman* magazine. 'I'd like to meet her,' I said. 'Let's keep an eye out for when she returns to her boat.'

It wasn't to be. She didn't return to her boat while we were at that anchorage. Much of what we'd read dealt with how she had renovated her vintage classic timber yacht, and we had been keen to have a closer look at it.

We took the dinghy ashore to the beach and started exploring. There was a walkway through the scrub for a couple of kilometres, but nothing very exciting to see, so we turned back. On board again, Ian set about trying to find why our VHF radio was misbehaving. He spent the rest of the day cleaning up all the contact points and connections between the radio and the aerial. When he sent a test transmission to Yeppoon VMR, he was pleased to find the radio transmitted and received clearly again.

The next day, we sailed seawards to get to the north-eastern side of the island. Here, at Svensons Beach, we found the remains of an old homestead and garden, including pandanus trees. I had seen pandanus at Lord Howe Island, but not in fruit.

'Look at these, Ian,' I said. 'They look like pineapples on the outside.'

I pulled one apart to show him. 'The segments are very hard and have a seed. It seems they're not edible after all.'

Shortly afterwards, we met a couple of other crews who were

keen to explore too. One was CCC members, Joan and George Hibbard from the yacht, *Oasis*. Although they were CCC members, we hadn't really known them before this.

After anchoring and tidying up, Ian was tired, so I left him to have a long rest and went ashore with the others. Taking our dinghies ashore near a small creek, we set off to walk. This track took us for several kilometres.

'I don't like the look of this weather,' I said. 'I've felt a couple of raindrops.'

'It certainly looks like we're going to get rain very soon,' said one of the others.

'I vote we turn back,' I said.

Just as we turned around, the wind became colder and rain started to fall quite heavily. Back on board, I dried off, made hot drinks for both Ian and me and curled up with a good book. Reading while at anchor is a favourite pastime of mine.

Overnight, the weather cleared and it was a crisp morning when the sun rose.

'Let's go round to the main resort beach today,' suggested Ian. 'It's very shallow though. We'll probably have to anchor a long way out.'

'That won't matter,' I said. 'There's very little wind.'

Once among the islands, we had to take more notice of the tidal currents which flow north when the tide is ebbing, and south when flooding. It was the same as it had been coming through "The Narrows".

A few hours later, we motored with the tide through a narrow pass between the island and some very large rocks, to reach Great Keppel Bay in front of the resort. To have enough swing room for *Realitas*, we had to drop anchor several hundred metres from the beach.

Once ashore, we needed to pull the dinghy a long way up the shallow beach and then we set off to find out what the resort had to offer. We were able to leave our garbage and buy ice. We even had a swim in the warmer, shallow water, after which we put coins in the slot to use the showers. In the village there were a few boutique shops and a post office, but no internet café.

Early in the morning and in the evening, a string of camels

walked down the beach, taking tourists for rides. No, we didn't take camel rides. Sailing gives me enough bruises. Just three years later, in the winter of 2003, there were internet facilities at every marina and resort on the Queensland coast, but the camels at Great Keppel had gone.

Our next anchorage was at Port Clinton where there were nine yachts already at anchor. In the morning, we were surprised to find ourselves enveloped in fog. On the radio, we learned that there was almost no visibility out at the Keppel Islands. The fog had rolled in from the sea and we were unable to move on for some hours. When we did, we took a look into Pearl Bay, which we'd been told was a 'must go' place. This pretty anchorage was full, so we went on into Island Head Creek, just a short distance further north.

In search of some solitude away from the sun-seeking masses of silver sailors, we headed up the less popular branch of the creek. We soon found out why that branch was less popular. Our keel touched bottom. Unfortunately, the tide was falling and soon so were we. Unlike the sandy bottom in the Broadwater and the Great Sandy Straits, here we couldn't just back off using the engine. *Realitas* slowly settled down on her side on hard mud.

Life aboard was going to be very uncomfortable until the tide rose again six hours later, so I packed a picnic bag and we set off in the dinghy to explore our surroundings. These proved very dull. There was little bird life to be seen and the vegetation was monotonously straw-like. Eventually, dusk fell and we returned to the boat, which was still lying over on her side. We sat on the edge of the deck, our legs dangling over the side, to await the incoming tide, which would bring our little floating home upright again.

'Come on, Ian. Let's sing to pass the time.' I started singing old folk songs from the 1960s.

'Just as well there's no one around to hear you,' said Ian.

'If you sang too, I'd be able to keep tune better,' I retorted.

About two hours after dark, *Realitas* started to move into a more upright position, and I was able to begin cooking dinner. Before we were able to eat, *Realitas* floated clear of the bottom.

Ian raised the anchor, turned on the motor and we moved closer to the mouth of the creek, where Ian secured the yacht. Finally, we ate our meal and settled down for the night.

Pancake Creek, "The Narrows", Port Clinton and Island Head Creek... we'd heard all these names so often at yacht club meetings from members who'd sailed north to the Whitsundays. For me, these place names had taken on a sort of mystical aura, but now, one by one, I had real images in my mind.

'Where are we aiming for today?'

'Hexham Island,' said Ian, 'and then Thomas Island after that.

These two islands are at the southern end of the chain of Whitsunday Islands.'

'So we're almost there,' I said, pleased.

There was some more sea fog but it wasn't as thick as the previous day. We had visibility and it was therefore possible to motor clear of Island Head, raising sail by mid-morning as the breeze came in. The swell was very small in relation to the breeze, due to the increase in shelter from the Whitsunday Islands.

'Hey, Ian, take a look at the water. It looks like it's boiling,' I said.

'To me, it looks the same as it did in Cook Strait. Do you remember you thought we were about to cross some shallow rocks?' said Ian.

'So it's just the meeting of currents making the water roil.'

At Thomas Island, we discovered the savagely biting green tree ants of the tropics. I finally found out what was inside these tightly webbed pockets hanging from branches. We'd seen them the previous winter when we'd been travelling inland. I had imagined them to be full of tiny spiders, but I was soon to learn otherwise.

Ashore, we pulled the dinghy up under the only tree near the beach, and tied the painter to the trunk. The tree was low hanging and smallish, but had enough foliage to provide some shade for our *Avon* inflatable. The dinghy is manufactured from Hypalon, a very tough plastic material covering a fibre core. If the fabric becomes too hot, the air in the pontoons expands enough to distort the inflated areas.

In the tropical sun, we needed to let out some air and find shade for it. We also needed to have a place to tie the painter so that if the tide rose before we returned our dinghy wouldn't float away without us.

When I pushed in under that tree with the dinghy, I knocked against a green tree ant nest. Only as we walked away up the hill to look out north over the various islands, did I start to itch and feel something crawling on my skin.

'What's biting me? Can you look please Ian?' I said.

He pulled back my shirt and peered in. 'I can't see anything.'

'There must be something. There! Now! Under my bra strap.'

'Ah, you have an ant there,' he said.

'Just one! It feels like several at least.'

Ian removed the offending green tree ants, but the welts where they had bitten me were already starting to rise. Feeling grumpy with both the incessant itchiness and the surge of histamine, I continued walking with Ian up the hill. The view from the top made the hike worthwhile. To our north, we could see the rest of the Whitsunday Islands spreading out into the distance.

By the time we were back at the dinghy, the tide was well on its way up the beach. *Been-a-long*, owned by Joan and Trevor Long, had come in to anchor, and just before dark, *Oasis* anchored in the same bay. The Long's boat is a forty-three foot Mauritius ketch, well known for having a very difficult helm. Many owners have rebuilt the rudder, but Joan and Trevor opted to carry a very robust electric self-steering strong enough for a fishing boat.

We left the anchorage at Thomas Island early in the morning, just after *Been-a-long*. That boat was unable to keep a straight course and Trevor was at the helm. My first impression was that he was drunk, but much as Trevor likes a drink and brews his own beer on board, I've never seen him drink before the sun is over the yardarm.

When we met again in Airlie, he explained. 'The *Coursemaster* steering failed again. The boat is a real bummer to hand steer.'

'I thought those fishing boat steering systems would be much stronger than that. 'I thought it was only yachting gear that seemed to be designed to break down.'

'I suppose a *Coursemaster* is much tougher,' agreed Trevor, 'but we've been through several of those already.'

While *Been-a-long* was having steering problems, we were having difficulties with our engine gears. The gear box seemed to be locked into forward. Ian diagnosed a worn clutch cable that was sticking inside its sheath.

'I'm glad the gears are locked in forward, not reverse,' I said.

Ian looked at me oddly. My approach to mechanical things often leaves him perplexed.

'I have a spare *Morse* cable on board. I can replace it at the next anchorage.'

We sailed past the Percy Islands. The wind and tides were just not suitable for us to call there at that time.

'We'll stop there some other time,' said Ian and I believed him, but we never have found conditions suitable to visit there.

I looked at the chart to view our position.

'Is that Whitsunday Island?' I asked, indicating a large island to our right.

'Yes, it is,' said Ian.

After many weeks of sailing north, we were almost at our destination. That afternoon, we found ourselves in the channel leading to Airlie Beach in the Whitsundays, the mecca of cruising yachties in winter. With the help of the tide, *Realitas* was crossing the ground at six to seven knots. It felt like we were floating down-stream in a river. I stood in the cockpit, eagerly watching the passing scenery. Ian had the Whitsundays cruising guide open and we were mentally ticking off the landmarks.

Suddenly, the channel opened out into a large bay. We turned to follow the coast around to port and soon, there was the town of Airlie and the marina. Outside the large marina was an even larger mooring area and anchorage in Pioneer Bay. We took in the sails and under motor, found ourselves a spot to drop our anchor not too far from shore.

'Maybe you could untie the dinghy, so that we can put it into the water,' said Ian.

We lowered the dinghy from the deck and Ian lifted the outboard from its bracket on the back of the yacht, clamping it firmly to the stern of the inflatable.

Always, our first duty is to check out the domestic facilities. At the marina, I found the laundry and showers, which were not restricted to marina users only, thank goodness. We had to pay by coins in the slot machines – the normal procedure.

We found the fuel dock and checked the price of diesel – not too expensive, thank goodness.

Having sorted the important things, we set off to explore the town. In 2001, there were two small grocery stores in Airlie, but no major supermarket. This, we found, was at Cannonvale, about two kilometres away. There was a bus, but we decided to walk rather than wait, discovering on our way, that if we brought the dinghy ashore at the Volunteer Marine Rescue launching ramp near where we'd anchored, we were much closer to the supermarket.

'Over there by the fence would seem a likely place to lock the dinghy if we come ashore here to get to the shopping area,' I said.

'Mmm, I think so. Locking it there should be out of the way if Marine Rescue needs to launch their boat too,' said Ian.

Locking the dinghy is always an important consideration. On *Realitas*, we needed a dinghy where we could roll up the nose when it was stowed on deck; inflatable dinghies are expensive – about $2000 or more in 2000.

Many cruising yachts carry their dinghies on davits hanging over the stern of their boats, but we had the *Aires* self-steering gear on our stern, so the dinghy had to be pulled onto the deck.

Being reliant on walking, buses or taxis to get groceries back to the dinghy from the shops, we carried a fold-up trolley on the boat. Trolleys are available in many styles and prices, the most expensive being from West Marine in the USA. Mine is a cheap, 'made in China' variety bought for $20 at the discount shop. Onto the frame, I secure a large backpack with elastic straps. Filled with meat and groceries, I often carry up to twenty-five kilos this way. Ian has also moved a 12 volt boat battery, but that was asking a lot of the trolley.

Members of our yacht club, the Coastal Cruising Club of Australia had moved recently from Sydney to Cannonvale.

During the time of our visit, Alan and Sue were acting as 'port officers' for visiting members. Apart from *Realitas*, club boats, *Been-a-long*, *Ambience*, *Oasis*, *Reeflection* and *Marguerita*, from South Australia, had already arrived, so a gathering was organised for dinner at Alan and Sue's comfortable apartment. The visitors brought drinks and food or sent out for pizza. On this trip, we socialised more with other club members than at any other time during our years of cruising.

In the days that followed, we caught up on laundry, wrote emails, sent David money for his fare north and topped up our depleted groceries. We found that the butcher beside the supermarket was well used to yachties wanting their meat vacuum packed.

We had no refrigeration on *Realitas*, just an icebox. Here in the tropics, we needed to buy ice every third day to keep our meat cool. Having it vacuum packed served two purposes. It slowed the deterioration and it prevented blood from dripping inside the icebox, which would have made it very smelly.

For Ian, it was a priority to replace the *Morse* cable to the gearbox. In crowded waterways and bays, he needed to have the engine in good working order. Once that cable was greased and in place, we had reverse gear again.

The tourist brochures would have you believe there is eternal sunshine and gentle breezes in the Whitsunday Islands, but although the sun frequently shines, the wind also blows, especially the strong afternoon 'sea breeze' of thirty to thirty-five knots from the north-east, creating a wind chill that can induce hypothermia in the unwary. Sometimes, the wind blows strongly from other directions too.

The first strong blow from the east sent us over to Cid Harbour to shelter on the western shore of Whitsunday Island. We anchored and went ashore for a walk. Ian found the track, which led from Sawmill Bay up to Whitsunday Peak.

Off we went, at every bend in the track, expecting to find a good view. No, not this one – maybe the next. By the time we found our 'good view', we had reached the peak. As we looked about, I realised that it was nearly sunset.

'We'd better hurry to get back down, Ian,' I said, setting off again. I was almost running.

'What's your hurry?' called Ian, following me.

'I don't like walking in the dark. It's too easy to trip and fall.'

As the sun went down, darkness descended. I wasn't happy to find ourselves in this situation. I was becoming cold too. We had no jumpers with us and no food, just some water that we'd nearly finished.

'I think you've forgotten how quickly it gets dark up here,' I said. 'There's no twilight.'

I tried to keep my anxiety in check. We plodded on, no longer rushing along the track. I was tripping over sticks as we went, but I managed to remain upright. Ian held my arm. At least an hour after dark, we descended to the beach where we'd left the dinghy.

The next problem was to find our boat. We hadn't left the anchor light on and I was cold, tired, hungry and cross with Ian for leading me on such a long walk, and placing us in this predicament. While I was imagining a night out in the cold, Ian, in his usual steady, methodical way, was reconstructing the anchorage in his mind's eye and working out the best approach to find *Realitas*.

Of course, he found our boat and once inside with lights on, I felt mollified and set about cooking some dinner.

We had been asleep for a couple of hours when a man's voice woke us and we saw the beam of his torch.

'Ahoy there! Your vessel is dragging anchor.'

I was first out of bed, sticking my head out of the companionway.

'So we are,' I said. 'Thanks for waking us.'

The wind had turned more northerly and was gusting strongly. In moments, *Realitas* had dragged past our saviour's boat.

'The engine's ready to start,' I said, as Ian emerged.

'Go ahead and start her up. Where's the boat hook? Be prepared to fend us off while I get the anchor up,' he ordered.

We re-anchored without bumping any other boats.

This time, Ian asked me to rev the engine in reverse really hard, to ensure the anchor was well dug in and going to hold. When he was sure we weren't going to drag again, we headed back to our bunk.

In the morning, Ian went over to the man who had woken us, to thank him.

'No worries mate. I thought it was a charter yacht at first and I wasn't going to bother. Then I realised I'd seen you come in earlier.' Was he joking?

Until the wind eased, we holed up in Nara Inlet. There were three more days before David was due to arrive, and in that time, we were able to visit some of the other anchorages written up in the *Whitsundays Cruising Guide*. David was keen to spend a week with us exploring the Whitsunday Islands and we planned to return to the places we liked best, showing him the jewels of Whitsunday cruising.

*Jan snorkelling on the reef (Photo by Ian Mitchell)*

On our way back to Airlie, we stopped off at Moonlight Bay on South Molle Island. Behind the resort, there was a walk we wanted to take, which led to a knoll at the north-eastern end of the island. After skirting the golf course, we came upon a bat colony. Hundreds of fruit bats were hanging upside down from the fig trees, many of the adults enfolding babies under their wings.

'They are noisy and smelly, but also somehow endearing,' I remarked.

'It's that instinctive connection we have with mammals,' said Ian. 'If they're furry and have big eyes, we love them.'

We gazed for at least ten minutes before continuing on our walk. This path became my favourite walk in the Whitsundays. It was about the right length, taking an hour to reach the summit, from where we could look down into a tiny bay - a jewel-like aquamarine anchorage, barely big enough for one small yacht.

To return to Airlie from South Molle, we had to pass Middle Molle, then go through the 'Unsafe Passage' and skirt to the north of Daydream Island. Although the name 'Unsafe Passage' implies danger, it is quite safe enough for small boats, especially since leading lights were installed there many years ago.

On the appointed day, Ian travelled by bus to the airport in Proserpine to meet our son. David had influenza, so it was a strange few days we spent with him. We sailed about the islands, went swimming, snorkelling and walking, trying to show him the joys of being in the Whitsundays, but he was feverish, aching, slept a lot and later found he remembered very little of his visit.

After David flew home, we decided to continue sailing north. Ian was coping extremely well, and there were not too many days when he was unable to sail. He was healthier than he'd been since before the onset of Chronic Fatigue Syndrome. It was obvious that cruising kept him well. The air was cleaner and he was doing something he loved.

*Coral in the Whitsundays, 2000 (photo by JanMitchell)*

Since reaching Queensland, our sailing on this voyage had been completely different from anything else we'd ever done. There had been a lot of motoring and motor sailing, which seemed rather like travelling in a campervan, but on water. Ian didn't want to stay in these crowded anchorages, preferring to head away to more open water and the possibility of the freedom of a solitary anchorage. He seemed so well that further up the coast to Far North Queensland seemed the way to go.

# 19  Far North Queensland

At Woodwark Bay, just a short sail north of Airlie, we found some of the solitude Ian was seeking. There were no other yachts in the anchorage.

'This is better,' sighed Ian. 'A bay to ourselves!'

'The Whitsundays don't really live up to the advertising, do they?' I said. 'Except for Butterfly Bay, the coral is degraded. Even there, people stand on the outcrops and break bits off. And no one mentions the strong afternoon winds.'

'It is still a beautiful cruising area, but now I've seen it, I'm ready to move on,' said Ian. 'Let's go ashore for a walk this afternoon. I need to stretch my legs.'

We hiked through the grassy vegetation to the top of the island. From the knoll, we could look south down over Pioneer Bay, crammed with yachts and beyond that, the busy Airlie marina. To the east, we could see Hayman Island and to its south, we could just make out Whitsunday Island beyond Hook Island, but to the north, there were fewer boats.

'I'm convinced I can keep going north,' said Ian, when we returned to *Realitas*. 'Let's go on tomorrow to the Gloucester Passage and then on up to Bowen.'

'I'm happy to keep going north if you feel up to it,' I said. 'We can always turn around if you feel you've had enough.'

That night, on the 14th July, there was to be a lunar eclipse. The sky was clear, so we stayed up until nearly midnight to view this strange phenomenon. Neither of us remembered ever having seen the moon eclipsed before, though of course, we had observed solar eclipses. A lunar eclipse happens when the earth moves between the moon and the sun, blocking sunlight from reaching the moon.

By the following afternoon, we had anchored in the Gloucester Passage off Montes Reef Resort. At the time, the resort was rather run down and listed for sale, but the management welcomed yachties and invited us to use their facilities. I understand that under new ownership, the resort has since been considerably upgraded.

My most significant memory of this location was of watching dugong (nicknamed "sea cows") grazing on the sea grass in the passage near to our anchorage. The water was very clear and their grazing pattern did remind me of the way my parents' cows wandered slowly over the paddock, slurping their tongues around a clump of grass and pulling it free, before chewing slowly and methodically.

The other image I have retained is of a helicopter circling the anchorage and resort before landing. A bevy of Asian gentlemen, dressed in suits, descended from the copter and disappeared to talk business with the owners. I've always wondered whether they eventually bought the resort.

From Montes it wasn't far to Bowen, our next stop. We sailed away with the fishing line streaming out behind us, but caught no fish that day.

'You know how famous Bowen is for its mangoes and tomatoes. I think I'll try to go to the farmers' markets tomorrow morning,' I said. 'It's good that tomorrow is Saturday.'

At the market, I found cheap and plentiful good quality produce to stock our larder. That was such a good thing to do that I wished we were in towns on a Saturday more often to be able to take advantage of local markets.

The winds were still good for sailing north. We made a couple of overnight stops behind headlands. The one at Cape Cleveland provided a particularly uncomfortable night. *Realitas* rolled wildly and snapped the nylon snubber attached to the anchor line. This line provides shock absorbency for the anchor chain. Ian had been in the habit of attaching a hook to the end of the line, ready to catch hold of the anchor chain about four metres down from the bow. He had purchased a stainless steel hook at Bowen and that night, after the line broke, the hook followed its predecessors to the ocean floor.

'It's too expensive to keep buying hooks,' said Ian. 'From now on, I will use only a rolling hitch to attach the snubber.'

We'd stopped at the outer anchorage in Townsville. 'This is too inconvenient,' I said. 'There's nowhere safe to leave the dinghy. Let's check out the marina prices.'

Ian motored the dinghy in to the fuel dock and to our surprise, compared to the prices we had been used to in NSW and southern Queensland, the fees for a ten metre yacht were very reasonable, and there was a discount if you stayed a week. It was much more convenient at the marina with its bathroom and laundry facilities than the awkwardness of the outer anchorage. From the marina we were within easy walking distance of the waterfront park and the shopping area.

We enjoyed this small city in Far North Queensland. One of the highlights was our visit to the Maritime Museum with its exhibits of various corals, tropical fish and clams. Townsville is home to the Australian Research Council Centre of Excellence for Coral Reef Studies located within James Cook University. The University has a research outpost on the outer reef at Lizard Island.

I particularly liked the foreshore development with its colourful children's playground and water features. The park teemed with people all daylight hours, but I noticed they were nearly all white. There were certainly no Aborigines to be seen. Yet they had to be about.

At the supermarket, methylated spirit was not on the shelf. I asked where I could buy some.

'We keep it in the storeroom at the back of the shop,' said the manager. I looked puzzled.

'The Aborigines drink it otherwise.' He continued, 'One morning when I arrived to open the shop, there was an Aboriginal woman dead on the door step. She had an empty meths bottle lying beside her.' I nodded in sympathy.

It seems that the police kept the shame of the Aborigines' plight away from any area of town frequented by tourists. I thought that the Aborigines could be helped to feel pride in their culture if they were assisted in turning it into an educational and tourist attraction. In my opinion, any shame about the condition of Aborigines in this country should be felt by the non-Aboriginal society.

After a week in Townsville, we were ready to move on again. When we finally pulled away from the fuel dock, our tanks full, it took less than a couple of hours to sail across to Magnetic Island. Captain Cook gave the island its name because his compass misbehaved in that area, but there is no magnetic anomaly caused by the island and we don't know why his compass showed incorrect readings.

However, the island's beauty is magnetic. There are bush walks, walks through the sand dunes to magical beaches, glorious sunsets and a sense of freedom that no city, however small and friendly, can emulate. A public bus meanders around the island to tiny villages, bays and resorts.

At the southern end of the island, not far from the ferry terminal, a company had begun work to build a marina. The developer had spent a lot of money on earthworks to provide shelter for the, as yet, non-existent berths. Then work had stopped. There was still no progress on this facility when we saw it again in 2003. Maybe there was no call for marina berths in the south-east of the island.

Everyone preferred to anchor in Horseshoe Bay on the northern shore. Anchored in the north, we renewed acquaintance with *Ambience*, *K Sera* and a couple of other boats and their crews. I very much enjoyed the social life with our fellow yachties, especially those who ventured further north of Airlie. Several evenings, we had happy hour ashore and on at least one occasion, followed this with a barbeque.

One evening, Chris, from *Ambience* mentioned a sore neck. During the mid-1990s, soon after completing a postgraduate diploma in Nutrition, I had become a qualified Bowen Practitioner.

'Would you like me to massage it,' I asked.

I soon realised she needed a little more than massage. The other ladies present and I helped Chris onto a picnic table and I proceeded to give her a Bowen Therapy treatment. The next morning, I asked how she felt.

'Wonderful. Thank you so much. I haven't felt this relaxed for some time.'

From Horseshoe Bay there is a short walk across to the eastern shore to a beautiful beach. Normally, I don't like beaches. I hate being knocked about by the waves or having my bathers full of sand, but at this beach the sand is very firm, and there were no big waves. It was perfect for swimming, and we walked across there several times.

'All this socialising', said Ian, 'it's starting to feel like the Whitsundays all over again.'

'Time to move on then?'

Our next destination was Hinchinbrook. En route, we stopped over-night in the Palm Islands, tucking ourselves in behind Orpheus Island. I was very curious about Palm Island and the bad press it had received about police brutality towards the indigenous people there, but we didn't go ashore, preferring to get under way early to reach the Hinchinbrook channel in good light.

Lucinda, a port for the export of sugar, lies to the south of the Hinchinbrook Channel. We stopped there briefly, awed by the six kilometre long wharf for loading sugar onto ships.

About one-third the distance through the Hinchinbrook Channel, we stopped at Deluge Inlet. We had hoped to go for a bush walk, but there were no tracks for any distance and the area consisted of low-lying mangrove forest. There we found the remains of Aboriginal stone fish traps.

During 1999, we had visited a site near Portland in western Victoria where Aborigines had farmed eels, smoked and traded them far and wide, but I didn't know that some tribes had trapped fish.

'I find it interesting that such historic artifacts, which are indicative of Aboriginal ingenuity and industry, are not marked and sign posted,' I said to Ian. 'I suppose they don't fit with the national stereotype of the Aborigines being primitive itinerant hunters and gatherers.'

'Probably not,' said my Australian-born husband.

He had grown up with the typical Australian attitude and although he isn't racist himself, it doesn't upset him like it does me. To this day, I cannot understand the disdain with which the Aboriginal people are treated in this country. When I was growing up in New Zealand, Maoris were discriminated against, but never to the extent faced by the natives of Australia.

Hinchinbrook had been very much in the news because of the controversy about the developer who was building the marina and developing a resort beside the channel. Green groups had protested actively about the destruction of the sea grasses and mangroves which provide nurseries for marine species. As the marina was not yet fully operational we were offered a berth at a reduced rate.

On the VHF radio, the marina manager assured Ian that the side channel leading into the marina was dredged to two metres at high tide. *Realitas* draws 1.7m, but we dragged our keel through the mud to enter – at high tide.

'So much for the two metre depth,' muttered Ian.

The marina had operational showers, toilets and laundry facilities, so bodies and clothing clean again, we decided to continue the next afternoon past Cardwell and towards Cairns.

In the morning, after hanging out our laundry I accepted a lift into the nearby town of Cardwell to shop for supplies. From the fish shop, I bought a large crab, which was still alive, but had been in the refrigerator to keep it sedated. The shopkeeper took a long skewer and inserted it inside the shell.

'What are you doing?' I asked.

'Severing the brain stem,' he said.

'I normally drop them into a pot of boiling water and they're dead in a second.'

'This is much kinder,' he told me. I was doubtful.

I cooked the crab for lunch. The skewer had damaged the crab's stomach and intestines and the body fluids had seeped all through the flesh.

I washed it well before cooking. I don't know what else the man had severed, but we were both sick after eating the creature.

Not far north of the Hinchinbrook Channel is the beautiful gem of Dunk Island – one of my favourites in North Queensland. Previous owners of the island had lived there, but now a corporation owns it.

Glittering white coral sand adorns the shore. Every monsoon season, storms break coral off the reef and waves deposit this ashore where it is gradually ground into sand.

Although there is a resort, most of the rest of the island development is low key. There are cabins and a camping ground, a few small businesses offering snacks, souvenirs, snorkeling, diving, fishing, jet-ski hire and kite surfing. Campers are welcomed and we were able to use the free showers provided for them and the day trippers.

There are many walking tracks and we relished the chance to stretch our legs. A walk out past the airstrip and resort leads to the beautiful rainforest-clad Mt. Kootaloo, a moderate climb on well-maintained paths. The view of turquoise ocean and reef from the lookout makes the half day climb well worthwhile.

The second walk of note is to the other end of the island, where there is an artists' retreat, often with an artist in residence. The track to reach the retreat crosses a grassy expanse, where I very nearly stepped on a snake lying across the path. Typically, it resembled a stick on the ground, but fortunately, something made me step over rather than onto it. I was shocked when the "stick" slithered rapidly away. It was a close call.

'Did you see that snake?' I asked.

'No. What kind was it?'

'How would I know? I just came really close to stepping on it.' After a few seconds, I added, 'It was greenish brown, long and skinny, just like a stick.'

'Sounds harmless,' said Ian.

Less dangerous, but equally memorable, were the small tortoises in the stream where we entered the grounds of the retreat. We had passed from the grassy area back into rainforest, where a tiny bridge spanned the stream. I looked down.

'Look at this! There are tortoises here eating hibiscus flowers!'

'I've never heard of tortoises eating flowers.'

I scanned the area. 'Someone must have brought the flowers for them There are no hibiscus flowers anywhere near here.'

Like the rest of the publicly accessible areas of the island, the artists' retreat was also low key, with some trestle tables exhibiting locally made items for sale. Most of these were products made by artists during their retreat.

Once we felt we had sufficiently sampled the delight of Dunk, we moved on to Mourilyan Harbour on the mainland, about twenty miles north. This is the heart of a sugar and banana growing area. Much of the produce is exported through that long wharf that had awed us at Lucinda.

The town of Innisfail, located up the Moresby River, is the commercial hub of the area. As usual when travelling up river, one has to work the tides. In this manner, we took *Realitas* right up to the town where we anchored just off the town wharf. Two live-aboard yachts blocked the wharf, giving the impression they had been there for years.

'Look,' said Ian and pointed to the sign restricting access to the town jetty. 'These two have been here for a very long two hours.'

Innisfail was a fairly prosperous country town. I say 'was', because it was almost flattened by Cyclone Larry in 2006, and severely damaged again in February 2011, when Cyclone Yasi hit. A big surprise for me was the Innisfail Art Gallery. It exhibited the work of many local artists, and I was very impressed with the quality of the work on display.

Another hop up the coast took us to Cairns. The alternative to the big city marina there was to anchor in Trinity Inlet, but we chose not to venture up that inlet because of the mosquitoes. Yorkeys Knob, not very far north of Cairns, was a cheaper and more pleasant alternative to being in the middle of the city. We booked a berth at the Half Moon Bay Motor Yacht Club at Yorkeys Knob.

From Yorkeys, a very cheap public bus took us to the large local mall, or a somewhat longer ride of fifty minutes landed us into Cairns central shopping district. The bus ride was an adventure in itself. There were no seat belts, but I felt I needed one because of the way we were thrown about. I felt sure at least one passenger would land on the floor yet no one did.

'Look at this Ian, the city council has built its own beach in the city with imported sand, pools and shaded areas, picnic lawns and a playground for children.'

'Hmmm. They've picked a good location for it – close enough for city workers at lunch time and good for tourists and children too,' said Ian.

Cairns sits on a low-lying narrow coastal strip of land, and the gently sloping alluvial plain extends well out to sea. The local beaches are very shallow, the water being less than waist deep well off shore.

The bus route followed south along this narrow plain, where sugar cane and bananas are farmed on large properties.

Our visit to the Cairns district coincided with the Sydney 2000 Olympic Games in September. The Motor Yacht Club staff erected a huge television screen in the bar. I sat there to watch Cathy Freeman's historic win of the 800m final and the uplifting vision of her jogging around the arena dressed in her smart gold and green running suit, the Aboriginal flag draped over her shoulders. While I was busy watching, Ian was planning chores to be done.

'I want to make the floor anti-skid,' he said. 'I think I'll paint it with deck paint.'

'No you won't,' I said. 'That will look awful.'

'It's too slippery when it's wet. What do you suggest?'

'I suggest we sprinkle sand onto wet varnish.'

During our stay at the yacht club marina, we sanded back the floor of the boat and, each morning, I applied a coat of varnish and added a sprinkling of fine sand between coats to create grip on the floor. Only then did we turn ourselves into tourists and head out for the day.

During those two days, we visited several places. A point of interest nearby was the Skyrail cable car, which we rode through the rainforest canopy and over the escarpment. The cable car stopped half way up, where we all climbed out to hear the guide talk about the trees, vines and birds of the canopy – all interesting.

'Do you know why they call this the lawyer vine?' he said. 'It clings until you bleed, and it's difficult to make it let go.'

This joke about the lawyer vine was probably well worn, but we hadn't heard it before and everyone on the platform laughed.

At the top of the escarpment is the small town of Kuranda, where we visited the famous Butterfly House. We were captivated. I had never seen so many species of butterfly with such variety of colours and patterns. It was very special to see them up close, landing on our hats and clothing, even our arms and hands.

'That more than lived up to my expectations,' I said as we waited at the station for the train back down.

'I really enjoyed the butterflies flying about me,' said Ian.

'I wanted to photograph them on you, but they moved too quickly.'

For the return trip down the escarpment, we chose to travel in the scenic train on its historic line back to Cairns. There were some breath-taking engineering feats of design and construction on that railway. After a long and exhilarating day, we took the local bus from Cairns to the marina. 'For me, today was one of the highlights of our trip,' I said.

'I'd have to agree,' said Ian.

The Skyrail departed next to an Aboriginal Heritage Centre. 'Let's visit there tomorrow,' I said.

'I'll go along with that,' said Ian

We spent half the next day there, looking at exhibits of handcrafts, and listening to talks about the Aboriginal way of life before Europeans arrived. We were able to try boomerang and spear throwing, as well as learn about Aboriginal cooking and watch a concert. All the people running the centre were local Aborigines and the quality of everything in the centre was high.

'This centre is a tribute to what Aboriginal people can achieve if given the chance.'

The following day, we hired a car. That day, after applying a coat of varnish to the floor, we drove to Port Douglas and Cape Tribulation.

'I don't want to come back here,' I said after seeing Port Douglas.

'Not my scene with its expensive boutiques and cafes,' said Ian. 'I don't want to bring *Realitas* in here.'

'I don't want to return here at all.'

Cape Tribulation was another matter. We loved the walk through the rainforest to the shore, where one bursts out onto the blindingly white beach. We were both very happy in the rainforest with its vines and myriad kinds of trees. Tropical rainforest is so different from the temperate forest in New

Zealand, which has fern trees and mosses and sodden soil that squeaks as you walk over it. In the Daintree, we had to stay on the man-made path. One would need a team of people wielding machetes to go far off the track.

At a public information centre, we were introduced to micro bats and other species that are native to this part of the world. The staff was rearing an orphaned micro bat baby. It was the cutest tiny creature with great big ears. We were both entranced and didn't want to leave.

'I'm sorry, you'll have to go now,' said one of the staff. 'We're closing for the day.' She tucked the bat up for the night and locked the door behind us.

The second day trip in the hire car was over the escarpment behind Cairns, to the Atherton Tablelands. A friend of mine from Sydney was staying there with her son. As well as visiting her, we also stopped to look at the sights and the roadside craft stalls.

After two days of these activities, the boat floor was dry enough to walk on. I was very pleased I had insisted on the varnish and sand option because now there was sufficient grip on the floor while we were sailing and we didn't slip again. It meant we could roll up and store the mats we had been using, reserving them for times when we weren't at sea.

It was while we were at Cairns we decided that Ian was coping sufficiently well for us to continue further north still. He set himself the goal to revisit Cooktown, where he had ridden on a small motorcycle in 1969.

When we had departed from Sydney, we had no idea how Ian would cope, nor how far north we would manage to sail. Just to see the Whitsundays would have been enough. However, his Chronic Fatigue Syndrome continued to be manageable. Occasionally, he would have a couple of off-days when we would remain at anchor. Otherwise, he was able to run the boat and was keen to keep sailing north.

We were both enjoying the snorkeling whenever we stopped at small islands. Although it is known for crocodiles to swim extensive distances off-shore, we felt safe enough to swim and snorkel at the more isolated coral islands and reefs. Up here, the coral was almost pristine and undamaged. We continued making day-hops and anchored at the Low Isles, Pickersgill Reef and Hope Island, before arriving at Cooktown.

I loved Cooktown and its lack of pretension. What a contrast to Port Douglas. Cooktown had just a few low-key boutiques alongside the everyday shops, and people were down to earth. A supermarket, butcher and public cold-water showers met our requirements. No one needed hot showers in those tropical temperatures.

There were several fishing trawlers in the small port. Sometimes the behaviour of their crews was decidedly odd. 'Someone told me they are all high on marihuana or other drugs,' said Sue, first mate on *Yarrandoo II*. 'But I couldn't say whether or not that is so.'

All I knew was that they didn't give their call signs and against all protocol and regulations, they chatted to each other inanely on the calling and emergency channel 16 of the VHF radio as they fished. Was that the influence of drugs? Perhaps it was just that in the isolation of their locality, they were reluctant to obey rules set by the outside world.

The anchorage for Cooktown lies inside the mouth of the Cook River. When we arrived, several acquaintances were moored there already, including *K Sera* and *Yarrandoo II*. These boats were heading out to Lizard Island which lies to the northeast, right out near the outer reef.

Ian came back on board after a long chat with Mike and Sue.

'How about we go to Lizard Island too?'

'No problem,' I said. I liked the couples from the other three yachts with us in Cooktown. I thought there wouldn't be many people at Lizard. I always prefer to go where few others do.

We topped up our provisions and set off for the outer reef, but the wind came in from the east, so we meandered north, waiting for a more favourable wind direction.

Our first anchorage was just inside Cape Flattery, where *Yarrandoo II* was also at anchor. Mike was catching fish. Unfortunately, none of his advice on fishing worked for us.

The following day, Monday 4$^{th}$ September 2000, the wind turned south-easterly and both yachts sailed to Watsons Bay, Lizard Island.

I had imagined maybe a dozen yachts at most in Watsons Bay anchorage being almost full of yachts, we squeezed in. Lizard Island proved to be another magical place, where we swam and walked every day. Only occasionally was Ian not well enough to participate. The other yachties were all like-minded – adventurous and interested in walking, snorkeling or diving, watching wildlife, and reading as well as sailing.

Like most yachties, they also enjoyed their beer or wine. When we were told that the tiny plane from Cooktown would visit we were asked to put in orders for any provisions. Ian and I were astonished to find that most of the orders were alcohol. We were on the beach when the float-plane landed and watched as the pilot extricated cases of beer and wine from cubby holes in the floats and belly of the plane. I couldn't believe he could safely carry so much heavy cargo.

A short walk over a slight sand hill from Watsons Bay, we found an isolated bay where there existed some absolutely enormous giant clams. In the water, I hovered over those clams, gazing down their tubes into their very insides.

We swam and snorkeled, wandered the island and climbed the hill to Cook's Lookout where we gazed out in the direction of Cook's channel through the Great Barrier Reef.

Ian said, 'I think of the relief that Cook must have felt when he saw that dark blue break in the line of white breakers.'

'I can feel his delight when finally he sailed clear of all the coral reefs,' I said.

We found we wanted to see for ourselves the channel known as the "Cod Hole", especially when we heard tales of a giant potato cod that allowed humans to pet it.

'For the next two days, the weather forecast is for calm conditions,' said Ian. 'How about we head out to the Cod Hole?'

'An excellent idea. We should be able to anchor there overnight,' I replied.

A few other yachts were moored out on the reef already. Soon after our arrival, I went off snorkeling on my own while Ian rested. I was astonished to find myself swimming over the edge of a "cliff" at the side of the channel leading out to the Coral Sea.

If this wasn't the channel Cook sailed out, taking his ship clear of the confines of the Great Barrier Reef, it had to be nearby.

Looking down through absolutely clear water, I noticed a reef shark about eight metres below me. *Oh, there's a shark down there,* I thought to myself. *I don't think it's a danger to me,* and I kept on snorkeling. How different was this from the nervous, tension-ridden person who started snorkeling at Lord Howe Island only a few years before. That person would have turned and fled back to the safety of *Realitas*.

Far out here, no careless swimmers had damaged the reef by standing on or kicking the coral. The water from the Coral Sea was cool enough that no coral bleaching had occurred. On the outer reef was a botanical garden full of brilliant corals, populated with hordes of many coloured fish. As the tide receded, reluctantly I left this underwater wonderland and returned to the boat before I was stranded on the reef in water too shallow for swimming.

The next morning, the tide was appropriate for another excursion.

'One of the National Parks' moorings in the channel is vacant,' said Ian. 'I'm going to move the yacht there.'

After mooring, we swam together right across the channel to near the open sea. We looked down and there we could see divers feeding the famed potato cod.

'I'm going down to have a look,' said Ian, and then he duck-dived down about nine metres.

There was a rope tied into the coral. I hung onto it, to prevent the current from dragging me away, while I tried to photograph Ian with his arms around that enormous fish.

'I didn't manage to get a photo of you down there,' I said when Ian re-surfaced. 'I had to give up. It was impossible to hold the camera steady enough to focus for a good photo while the current drifted me about.'

When the current eased, we swam slowly together, exploring the enormous wall of coral and the thousands of tiny colourful fish living in its crevices. That was the most brilliant snorkeling I have ever done. I didn't want the experience to end.

But the tide turned and the rush of water out through the pass began increasing, trying to pull us seawards. It was time to go back to our boat and move from the National Parks' mooring to a secure anchorage for the rest of the day.

Although that day was very quiet, this was not a place to linger. The weather could turn quickly. In the morning, we set off back to Lizard Island, motoring much of the return voyage to Watsons Bay. We had already spent one more night on the outer reef than we had anticipated, but what a superb experience it had been – the pinnacle of our voyage north.

*Reef fish in the pass to the Coral Sea*

'Do you think we could visit the University Research Station before we leave?' I asked. It was run by Townsville University Department of Marine Science.

Ian went ashore to ask and returned with disappointing news. 'It seems it was open the day we were at the outer reef,' said Ian. 'Mid-September is already upon us, and we are a long way from home. We can't wait here another week until the next time it's open to the public.'

As always, the season and the weather, especially the wind direction, dictated our movements. It was time to head south, hopefully before the south-easterly trade winds set in.

# 20  Homeward Bound

Back in Cooktown on the ninth of September, we found the anchorage crowded with boats waiting for a weather window to head south. The situation was awkward, because with every change of tide, the boats swung around, providing ample opportunity for vessels to bump into each other and for anchor lines to catch on keels.

Fortunately for us, a power boat owner had offered us his mooring before we'd left for Lizard Island. The power boat had a teak deck and the owner was painting over it with chlorinated rubber paint in an attempt to stop leaks. Ian had entered into conversation with the owner about their common dislike of decks that are screwed down to fibreglass and thus creating leaks.

'I'm about to head off on a long trip for several weeks,' the power boat owner told Ian. 'When you come back from Lizard, you're welcome to use my mooring.'

The weather prevented us from leaving long after we were re-provisioned and ready. The wind blew a steady south-easterly at 20 to 25 knots for days on end. *Didn't anyone tell the weather gods that it was too early for the south-east trades to set in?* All the yachts were waiting for a wind change. Not only was the wind on the nose, but it was creating a short, sharp, hull-stopping chop.

After eight days, a couple of larger yachts tried to leave, but they returned the next day, saying they couldn't make headway southwards. The following day, the wind dropped from twenty knots to fifteen knots, and Ian decided we should leave, even though no one else was going.

We couldn't sail, so we motored into sea and wind to get back to Cairns. That passage was very rough so, of course, I was seasick again and I lay in my bunk, my small white bucket close to hand for twenty six hours. For the forty-six nautical miles, our progress averaged less than two knots.

I had anticipated an easier passage from Cairns to Townsville, but the winds foiled us there too. The land curves south-east from Cairns to Townsville and with the wind on the nose, there wasn't much sailing on that leg either, though the passage was not as rough.

I recalled someone at Yorkeys saying, 'Everyone motor-sails in Queensland.'

'We don't,' I had replied. Now, I had to rethink my attitude.

'I think we should travel south as quickly as we can do comfortably,' said Ian. 'The summer cyclone season is approaching fast, and we daren't risk being caught in a tropical storm.'

With Ian's dubious health and strength, I had to agree with him.

'Yes,' I said, 'and we certainly don't want to take the option of leaving *Realitas* tied in a marina berth, even if it has been certified as "cyclone safe", or up a creek and lashed to trees.'

We were back in Airlie Beach in the Whitsundays by the 10th October, 2000. Our good friends Judy and Mike had driven north from Tasmania with their camper. Mike doesn't like to go sailing in any vessel "without three rows of portholes" as he says, but we persuaded him to come out on *Realitas* to visit some of the sights and he even managed to sleep on board one night. Judy was much more in her element, and she and I enjoyed snorkeling together at Hayman Island. We had a wonderful time, as we always do on any holiday together. I had met Judy when I first moved to Australia from New Zealand in 1970 and we had remained firm friends ever since.

There was a large school of fish in one corner of the anchorage at Hayman and I swam through the middle of these hundreds of glittering, silvery fishes. They reformed and kept on going around and around, through a hole in the rock and back around yet again. What a truly awesome feeling it was to be surrounded by hundreds of fish that took almost no notice of my presence in their midst.

The strong easterlies continued to blow. In Nara Inlet, a school of manta rays was, like us, sheltering from strong easterly winds. They provided a magnificent black and white-winged display for the yachts anchored in that sheltered bay. Judy was particularly keen to watch them.

'This is the most famous beach up here,' I said to Judy and

Mike as we sailed past Whitehaven which features in all the tourist advertising. We were disappointed not to be able to go ashore, but the easterlies were too strong for us to anchor upwind of the beach. The danger was that we might drift into shallow water while we were raising the anchor to leave again. I am not disappointed now to have never stopped there. One beach is pretty much the same as another to me. You get sunburnt lying on the sand and, in the water, it's difficult to swim across the waves. Then there's the sand in your bathers.

'We can always say we've seen it even if we didn't go ashore,' said Mike. One beach was the same as another to him, provided he could read a book in the shade.

Judy and Mike stayed for six days before heading off to complete their camping adventure. By then, as people found cyclone-safe places for their boats, or turned south the number of boats in the anchorage was diminishing.

We joined those sailing back to NSW, stopping at many of the same bays, anchorages and marinas, as we had stopped at on the way north. We didn't make it to Middle Percy Island though, the conditions being unfavourable again.

We did stop at Rosslyn Bay, where the wind had brought the red scum and stink of rotting algae into the corners of the marina. We stayed two nights, travelling by bus into Yeppoon to buy groceries and use the internet during the day.

'How would you like to visit Lady Musgrave Island?' asked Ian when we were close to Hervey Bay.

'That would be excellent. We can have one last snorkeling experience before leaving coral waters.'

At Lady Musgrave, an atoll, we motored through the narrow channel into the lagoon and after checking that the boat was secure, went ashore for a late afternoon walk. The island was a typical sandy knoll, growing a few palm trees and some coarse grass. Seabirds were nesting in the scrubby trees.

Upon our return to *Realitas*, Ian turned on the High Frequency radio to listen to the weather forecast. We were shocked to find that an intense low was forming just north of Fraser Island, predicted to bring threatening weather within twenty four hours.

We were not far north of Fraser Island and the centre of that low was too close to be ignored. Not wishing to be in an exposed anchorage in strong winds, we pulled up the anchor before sunrise the next morning and negotiated the passage out – a frightening exercise because the
tide was still rushing in through the passage we were trying to exit; the wind was already building and the sun was about to rise. We were both scared for the safety of the boat and ourselves as Ian battled the tiller against the swirling tidal currents trying to swing us into the coral. Until we were clear of the rocks that guarded the passage out of the lagoon, I peered ahead trying to see them. We were very pleased to leave behind both the smell of rotting seaweed and the now exposed coral.

*Ian, wearing waterproofs, steps into cockpit*

All day we hurried *Realitas* across the large expanse of Hervey Bay. The sun had already set when we turned into the Burnett River and, eventually, in the dark, with the smell of engine fuels and that warm earthy odour redolent of land, we found our way into the marina at Port Bundaberg.

The next forecast predicted even stronger winds overnight, so we tied *Realitas* up securely in her berth with heavy lines and lashed the Avon dinghy well down to the deck. It was just as well we did because when the wind gusts topped over sixty knots (more than 120 kmh) later that evening, the dinghy was struggling to fly off the deck until Ian tied yet another line over it.

In the middle of the night, Ian got up to check again that our lines were secure.

'If the wind is this strong in the shelter of the marina, I wonder what it would have been like if we'd stayed at Lady Musgrave?' said Ian as he slipped back into bed.

The next morning, the sky was overcast but the rain had cleared. We caught the bus from outside the marina into the city of Bundaberg, and for about twenty minutes, we travelled through sugar cane fields and alongside the river, before reaching the urban area. The centre of this graceful town has wide leafy avenues lined with shops and businesses. Life seemed prosperous there, but relaxed in comparison with bigger cities.

We collected a parcel of mail from the post office, visited the internet café to check our email and sent out a newsletter to friends and family, reporting that all was well with us and *Realitas*.

It was already the end of October. We needed to be home by the end of November, so we had just one month to sail from Bundaberg to Sydney.

The Great Sandy Straits, The Wide Bay bar, Mooloolabah and Moreton Bay all slipped quickly past our keel. We stopped at Southport close to the Gold Coast Seaway, anchoring in Bums Bay again.

Ian's health had been so good during this voyage, that we had decided we should buy another cruising boat, a little larger and more comfortable than *Realitas*. At Southport Marina, we looked at a steel Ganley 39 footer. Ganley was a New Zealand boat designer, whose yacht designs impressed Ian, but we decided that the thirty-nine footer was too big for us.

When we checked our email at Australia Fair shopping centre in Southport, there was news from Jamie. He had visited Durban, South Africa, returning to the place of his birth for his twenty-fifth birthday, and now he had returned to Richards Bay, where he could anchor off as he prefers to do, It was there he received the bad news from his girlfriend, Laura Tylilla in Finland. Previously, Laura had told me that her plan was to marry Jamie by the time he turned twenty-five. She also planned to convert him to her Pentecostal version of Christianity. She had not achieved either of these goals. Obviously, she meant what she said, because now Laura phoned Jamie from Helsinki, not to give news of her return date, but to say that she had decided not to return to *Possibilities*. Jamie was heartbroken. When Laura went back to Finland, they'd both believed she would return. She had left belongings on board, and now she asked Jamie to send them to her.

'I didn't ask why she wasn't coming back and she didn't tell me. If there is someone else, I don't want to know,' Jamie told us. 'I will wait a season at Richards Bay for her to change her mind and come back.'

She didn't. We missed our contact with her. Laura's cheery emails had always filled in many more details than Jamie's.

My immediate reaction was that Jamie should come home to his family, my gut feeling being a need to hold and comfort him for his loss. He'd had a close long-term relationship with Laura for four years, and I feared that he could become very depressed, maybe even suicidal over the Christmas period he had so looked forward to spending with her. It seems that no matter how old one's children are, a mother's response is always to hold and comfort them when they are hurt.

'I think we should pay for Jamie to come home,' I said to Ian.

'I agree. He shouldn't spend Christmas alone. He should be with his family when he is in emotional pain. Write back and tell him we'll send the money for his fare home'

However, we were still in southern Queensland. Ian and I had to sail *Realitas* home first.

'The forecast looks good for sailing south over the next couple of days, Jan, said Ian. Let's not waste time. We should take this weather window and get on home as soon as possible.'

We cleared the Gold Coast Seaway mid-morning on Saturday, November 11th, and apart from a brief stop in Trial Bay, we sailed straight back to Sydney, arriving in the harbour in the early hours of Monday morning. On Tuesday morning, Ian dropped me at Balls Head Bay, from where I walked up the hill to Wollstonecraft station, to ride home by train. I collected the car and drove back to Five Dock Bay to pick up Ian, our baggage and dirty laundry.

During the few days between our arrival home and Jamie flying in, I organised a big party, having hastily asked every

school and university friend of his that I could contact. Among those present were Marcus Schnell who had crewed on *Possibilities* from Sydney to Jervis Bay, and David Connolly, who sailed with Jamie from Jervis Bay to Victoria, and his girlfriend, Lisa. Also there was Marcus's now ex-girlfriend, Laura Anthony, whom we'd met briefly in Jervis Bay. As well, I invited all our friends, who had known Jamie as he was growing up.

Jamie had been away for two years. We hadn't celebrated his birthday earlier in November and it was also our twenty-ninth wedding anniversary at the end of the month. We'd been away from home for six months, and it was almost Christmas. I thought these were all good reasons for holding a party.

Not being keen on big social events, Ian reluctantly went along with my plans. It was a "pot luck" affair, where everyone brought a contribution to the food or drink.

*Two bearded sailors: Jamie and Ian 2000*

Seeing all his friends and having emotional support from his family certainly seemed to help Jamie with his disappointment that Laura had changed her mind about returning to *Possibilities*.

The other Laura found Jamie an attractive prospect and she initiated a new relationship that evening, persisting over several months despite Jamie's reluctance at first to become involved with anyone else while he was still getting over Laura Tylilla. Eventually, they did become an item, another relationship which lasted several years.

After Christmas, Jamie flew back to South Africa and *Possibilities*, his little home, which was still safely at anchor in Richards Bay. There, he decided to accept an offer he had received to study for his honours degree at the University of Zululand. Jamie says now that, as much as anything, he might have needed to do something else for a year, rather than sail long distances alone, when he could dwell on the past relationship. At the time, he indicated to us that he was sure Laura would eventually see sense and return to him if he waited.

⚓

With Jamie's departure, we set about making plans for our own future. We'd proved that Ian could cope with cruising again, and by now, his health was very much better. If we were to live on board and go cruising, we didn't need a house.

'Why don't we rent out the house?' I said.

'I'd rather sell the house, buy a home-unit and put tenants in that,' said Ian. 'There's no yard upkeep to complicate matters with a unit.'

'I guess so. And if we sell the house, that bigger boat is also more affordable.' I was thoughtful for a moment. 'If we downsize, it's harder for the kids to move back home.'

I had gone from desperately hoping Jamie wouldn't leave home ten years back, to worrying that at twenty-one, David would not move out permanently. There comes a time when every child should leave the parental nest. But I needn't have worried. David had gone off to university in Newcastle, a happy, confident young man.

On his passage across The Great Australian Bight, when Jamie didn't have crew, he was obviously thinking back over his childhood. He wrote us a letter thanking us for taking him sailing and for giving him the opportunities afforded at Chevalier.

Despite the ups and downs of family life, it seemed that in the end, we had succeeded with both our sons. They have each grown into healthy young adults with plans for their futures. We credited all the voyages we made with them over the years as a positive influence on their development and the maintenance of our family ties, which to me, seem even closer today than they were then.

It was time to attend to our own plans. We needed to find a bigger, better designed boat for the more comfortable cruising we both desired.

I love going shopping for major items, especially with the prospect of more adventures. Ian was keen, too, to be fully involved in the search for another cruising boat but he wanted me be the one to select an estate agent, sell the house and choose a home-unit (apartment) to buy and let out.

The old dream of Cape Horn and the Chilean channels was rearing its head again. Would we ever get there?

www.ingramcontent.com/pod-product-compliance
Lightning Source LLC
Chambersburg PA
CBHW071858290426
44110CB00013B/1193